Vulkan Fundamentals: A Beginner's Guide

Vulcan Fundamentals

Kameron Hussain and Frahaan Hussain

Published by Sonar Publishing, 2023.

While every precaution has been taken in the preparation of this book, the publisher assumes no responsibility for errors or omissions, or for damages resulting from the use of the information contained herein.

VULKAN FUNDAMENTALS: A BEGINNER'S GUIDE

First edition. October 19, 2023.

ISBN: 979-8215926369

Written by Kameron Hussain and Frahaan Hussain.

Table of Contents

Chapter 1: Introduction to Vulkan

Section 1.1: What Is Vulkan?

Understanding the Need for Vulkan

Key Concepts of Vulkan

Section 1.2: Why Learn Vulkan?

1. High-Performance Graphics:

2. Cross-Platform Development:

3. Modern Graphics Features:

4. Low-Level Control:

5. Community and Resources:

6. Industry Demand:

7. Future-Proofing Your Skills:

Section 1.3: Graphics API Overview

1. Graphics APIs:

2. OpenGL:

3. DirectX:

4. Metal:

5. Vulkan:

6. Differences Between Vulkan and Other APIs:

7. When to Use Vulkan:

8. Learning Vulkan:

Section 1.4: Setting Up Your Development Environment

1. Operating System Compatibility:

2. Vulkan-Capable GPU:

3. Development Tools:

4. Graphics Drivers:

5. Code Editor and Compiler:

6. Setting Up Your Development Environment - Windows:

7. Setting Up Your Development Environment - Linux:

8. Verifying Your Setup:

Section 1.5: Your First Vulkan Program

1. Setting Up Your Project:

2. Including Vulkan Headers:

3. Creating a Vulkan Instance:

4. Enumerating Available Physical Devices:

5. Cleaning Up:

Chapter 2: Vulkan Basics

Section 2.1: Vulkan Objects and Concepts

1. Vulkan Objects:

2. Object Creation and Destruction:

3. Vulkan Layers and Extensions:

4. Validation Layers:

Section 2.2: The Vulkan Application Structure

1. Initialization:

2. Windowing System Integration:

3. Swapchain Creation:

4. Rendering Resources:

5. Pipeline Configuration:

6. Command Buffer Recording:

7. Rendering Loop:

8. Cleanup:

Section 2.3: Vulkan Layers and Extensions

1. Vulkan Layers:

2. Vulkan Extensions:

Section 2.4: Debugging Vulkan Applications

1. Validation Layers:

2. Vulkan Debug Utils Extension:

3. Vulkan Validation Layers Messages:

4. Vulkan Debugging Tools:

5. Testing on Different Hardware:

6. Memory Debugging:

Section 2.5: Vulkan Validation Layers

1. Types of Validation Layers:

2. Enabling Validation Layers:

3. Validation Layer Messages:

4. Validation Layer Configuration:

5. Disabling Validation Layers for Release Builds:

6. Validation Layer Best Practices:

Chapter 3: Creating a Vulkan Instance

Section 3.1: Initializing Vulkan

1. Application Info:

2. Enabling Validation Layers:

3. Instance Creation:

4. Validation Layer Verification:

Section 3.2: Creating a Vulkan Instance

1. Instance Creation:

2. Instance Validation:

3. Instance Extensions:

4. Instance Cleanup:

Section 3.3: Instance Layers and Extensions

1. Instance Layers:

2. Enabling Instance Layers:

3. Instance Extensions:

4. Extension Availability:

Section 3.4: Enumerating Physical Devices

1. Enumerating Physical Devices:

2. Selecting a Physical Device:

3. Device Selection Criteria:

4. Device Validation:

5. Error Handling:

Section 3.5: Selecting a Physical Device

1. Device Selection Criteria:

2. Querying Device Properties and Capabilities:

3. Device Scoring and Selection:

4. Device Validation:

5. Error Handling:

Chapter 4: Logical Devices and Queues

Section 4.1: Creating a Logical Device

1. Logical Device Creation:

2. Queue Families and Capabilities:

3. Queue Operations:

4. Queue Synchronization:

5. Multiple Queues:

Section 4.2: Working with Vulkan Queues

1. Queue Families:

2. Queue Creation:

3. Queue Operations:

4. Queue Synchronization:

5. Multiple Queues:

Section 4.3: Queue Families and Capabilities

1. What Are Queue Families?

2. Querying Queue Family Properties:

3. Queue Family Properties:

4. Queue Capabilities:

5. Selecting the Right Queue Family:

6. Multiple Queue Families:

Section 4.4: Synchronization in Vulkan

1. Semaphores:

2. Fences:

3. Pipeline Barriers:

4. Command Buffer Submission:

Section 4.5: Semaphore and Fence Objects

1. Semaphores:

2. Fences:

3. Using Semaphores and Fences Together:

Chapter 5: Swapchain and Presentation

Section 5.1: Introduction to Swapchains

1. What Is a Swapchain?

2. Why Do We Need Swapchains?

3. Swapchain Creation:

4. Swapchain Images and Presentation:

Section 5.2: Creating a Swapchain

1. Selecting a Presentation Mode:

2. Swapchain Extent and Format:

3. Creating a Swapchain:

4. Swapchain Images:

Section 5.3: Presenting Images to the Screen

1. Presentation Process:

2. Using Semaphores for Synchronization:

3. Frame Timing and Synchronization:

4. Resource Cleanup:

Section 5.4: Swapchain Configuration

1. Image Views:

2. Framebuffers:

3. Handling Window Resizing:

Section 5.5: Handling Window Resizing

1. Detecting Window Resizing:

2. Recreating the Swapchain:

3. Updating Framebuffers and Resources:

4. Handling Viewport and Scissor Changes:

Chapter 6: Rendering in Vulkan

Section 6.1: Introduction to Rendering

Section 6.2: Creating Vulkan Render Passes

Render Pass Creation:

Attachment Descriptions:

Subpasses:

Render Pass Creation:

Render Pass Dependencies:

Summary:

Section 6.3: Framebuffers and Image Views

Framebuffers:

Image Views:

Framebuffer and Image View Usage:

Summary:

Section 6.4: Pipeline Creation in Vulkan

Graphics Pipeline:

Compute Pipeline:

Pipeline Caches:

Pipeline Derivatives:

Pipeline Creation Example:

Summary:

Section 6.5: Rendering a Triangle

Vertex and Fragment Shaders:

Vertex Buffer:

Pipeline and Render Pass:

Rendering Loop:

Render Loop Example:

Summary:

Chapter 7: Shaders in Vulkan

Section 7.1: Introduction to Shaders

Types of Shaders:

Shader Languages:

Shader Modules:

Shader Compilation:

Summary:

Section 7.2: Writing Vulkan Shaders

Shader Entry Points:

Input and Output Variables:

Shader Pipeline Stages:

Uniforms and Push Constants:

Shader Compilation:

Debugging Shaders:

Summary:

Section 7.3: Shader Modules and Pipelines

Shader Modules:

Pipeline Creation:

Pipeline Layout:

Combining Shader Modules and Pipeline Creation:

Summary:

Section 7.4: Vertex Input Descriptions

Vertex Input Binding Description:

Vertex Input Attribute Descriptions:

Binding Multiple Buffers:

Vertex Input State:

Summary:

Section 7.5: Binding Shaders and Data

Binding Shaders to a Pipeline:

Shader Specialization Constants:

Binding Data to Shaders:

Summary:

Chapter 8: Buffers and Memory Management

Section 8.1: Buffer Objects in Vulkan

Buffer Types:

Buffer Creation:

Buffer Usage and Memory Properties:

Buffer Mapping:

Summary:

Section 8.2: Creating Buffers

Buffer Creation

Buffer Mapping

Buffer Destruction

Summary

Section 8.3: Memory Allocation in Vulkan

Vulkan Memory Heaps and Memory Types

Memory Allocation with Vulkan Memory Allocator

Memory Properties and Allocation Strategies

Summary

Section 8.4: Mapping Buffers

Why Map Buffers?

Mapping a Buffer

Memory Properties and CPU Access

Synchronization

Summary

Section 8.5: Managing Buffer Data

Buffer Data Lifecycle

Memory Management

Buffer Pools

Resource Management

Resource Validation

Data Streaming

Multithreading

Summary

Chapter 9: Textures and Image Views

Section 9.1: Working with Textures

What Are Textures?

Types of Textures

Texture Formats

Texture Loading

Summary

Section 9.2: Creating Vulkan Images

Image Basics

Image Views

Creating Vulkan Images

Transitioning Image Layouts

Summary

Section 9.3: Image Views and Samplers

Image Views

Samplers

Using Image Views and Samplers

Section 9.4: Loading Textures

Texture Loading Libraries

Loading Textures with STB Image

Texture Coordinates

Shader Binding

Section 9.5: Texture Mapping

Mapping Textures to Geometry

Texture Coordinates

Wrapping Modes

Filtering Modes

Anisotropic Filtering

Chapter 10: Basic Rendering Techniques

Section 10.1: Vertex Buffer and Index Buffer

Vertex Data in Vulkan

Index Buffers

Efficient Rendering with Vertex and Index Buffers

Section 10.2: Uniform Buffers and Push Constants

Uniform Buffers

Push Constants

Choosing Between Uniform Buffers and Push Constants

Section 10.3: Descriptor Sets

Descriptor Set Layouts

Descriptor Pools

Updating Descriptor Sets

Binding Descriptor Sets

Descriptor Set Layouts and Compatibility

Efficient Resource Management

Section 10.4: Basic Rendering Pipeline

Vertex Input

Vertex Shader

Input Assembly

Tesselation

Geometry Shader

Vertex Post-processing

Primitive Assembly

Rasterization

Fragment Shader

Color Blending

Depth and Stencil Testing

Output Merger

Pipeline Configuration

Section 10.5: Rendering a Textured Triangle

Vertex Data and Shaders

Loading Textures

Texture Sampler

Fragment Shader

Pipeline Configuration

Chapter 11: Depth and Stencil Testing

Section 11.1: Understanding Depth Testing

Section 11.2: Depth Buffer and Depth Testing

Depth Buffer

Depth Testing in Vulkan

Practical Considerations

Section 11.3: Stencil Buffer and Stencil Testing

Stencil Buffer

Stencil Testing in Vulkan

Practical Applications

Section 11.4: Combining Depth and Stencil Testing

Depth and Stencil Together

Conclusion

Section 11.5: Practical Depth and Stencil Operations

Clearing the Depth and Stencil Buffers

Stencil Buffer Masking

Depth Range Adjustments

Conclusion

Chapter 12: Framebuffer and Render Pass

Section 12.1: Framebuffer Attachments

Section 12.2: Creating a Render Pass

What Is a Render Pass?

Creating a Render Pass

Conclusion

Section 12.3: Subpasses in Render Passes

What Are Subpasses?

Benefits of Using Subpasses

Creating Subpasses

Subpass Dependencies

Conclusion

Section 12.4: Framebuffer Creation

What Is a Framebuffer?

Framebuffer Attachments

Framebuffer Creation

Framebuffer Compatibility

Conclusion

Section 12.5: Render Passes in Vulkan

What Is a Render Pass?

Key Components of a Render Pass

Render Pass Creation

Render Passes and Performance

Conclusion

Chapter 13: Multisampling and Anti-aliasing

Section 13.1: Introduction to Multisampling

What is Aliasing?

The Need for Multisampling

How Multisampling Works

Benefits of Multisampling

Implementing Multisampling in Vulkan

Conclusion

Section 13.2: Enabling Multisampling

Vulkan Sample Counts

Enabling Multisampling in the Render Pass

Multisampling in the Graphics Pipeline

Resolving Multisample Images

Conclusion

Section 13.3: Sample Shading and Sample Masks

Sample Shading Basics

Sample Masks

Use Cases

Conclusion

Section 13.4: Anti-aliasing Techniques

What is Aliasing?

Multisampling Anti-aliasing (MSAA)

Supersampling Anti-aliasing (SSAA)

Post-processing Anti-aliasing

Conclusion

Section 13.5: Configuring Multisampling

Multisampling Setup

Rendering with Multisampling

Chapter 14: Dynamic State and Viewports

Section 14.1: Dynamic State in Vulkan

Dynamic State Objects

Dynamic State Commands

Section 14.2: Dynamic Viewport and Scissor

Dynamic Viewport

Dynamic Scissor

Combining Dynamic Viewport and Scissor

Section 14.3: Viewport Transformations

The Viewport and Projection Matrix

Setting Up the Viewport

Using the Projection Matrix

Adapting Viewport Transformations

Section 14.4: Using Dynamic State

Understanding Dynamic State

Enabling Dynamic State

Setting Dynamic State

Use Cases for Dynamic State

Section 14.5: Multiple Viewports and Scissors

Enabling Multiple Viewports and Scissors

Configuring Multiple Viewports and Scissors

Rendering with Multiple Viewports and Scissors

Chapter 15: Command Buffers and Rendering

Section 15.1: Command Buffer Basics

Creating Command Buffers

Recording Commands

Executing Command Buffers

Conclusion

Section 15.2: Recording Command Buffers

Command Buffer Lifecycle

Recording Basic Commands

Secondary Command Buffers

Conclusion

Section 15.3: Submitting Command Buffers

Queue Families and Queues

Semaphore and Fence

Submitting Command Buffers

Presentation

Conclusion

Section 15.4: Command Buffer Pools

Command Buffer Allocation

Creating a Command Buffer Pool

Allocating Command Buffers

Resetting Command Buffers

Conclusion

Section 15.5: Rendering Multiple Objects

Object Representations

Creating and Managing Objects

Rendering Loop

Object Culling and Optimization

Chapter 16: Syncing Frames and Presentation

Section 16.1: Semaphore and Fence Usage

Semaphores

Fences

Section 16.2: Acquiring Swapchain Images

The Swapchain Image Acquisition Process

Handling Swapchain Recreation

Section 16.3: Submitting Command Buffers

Submission to the Graphics Queue

Presentation Semaphore

Frame Synchronization

Section 16.4: Presentation and Syncing

The vkQueuePresentKHR Function

Frame Synchronization

Fences for CPU-GPU Synchronization

Section 16.5: Practical Frame Synchronization

Triple Buffering

Double Buffering with V-Sync

Adaptive Sync

Dynamic Frame Rate Control

Conclusion

Chapter 17: Resource Cleanup and Validation

Section 17.1: Cleaning Up Vulkan Resources

RAII (Resource Acquisition Is Initialization)

Cleanup Order

Validation Layers

Resource Management Libraries

Section 17.2: Resource Management Best Practices

1. Resource Reuse

2. Descriptor Sets

3. Descriptor Pooling

4. Memory Allocation

5. Pipeline Caching

6. Resource Tracking

7. Multi-threading

8. Validation Layers

9. Resource Release Order

10. Testing and Profiling

Section 17.3: Vulkan Validation Layers Revisited

Importance of Validation Layers

Enabling Validation Layers

Validation Layer Messages

Disabling Validation Layers in Release Builds

Section 17.4: Debugging and Validation Tips

1. Vulkan Validation Layers

2. Vulkan Debugging Tools

3. Vulkan Memory Debugging

4. Vulkan Validation Layers Tweaks

5. Thorough Error Checking

6. Validation Callbacks

7. Vulkan Validation Reports

8. Incremental Testing

9. Version Compatibility

10. Documentation and Community Resources

Section 17.5: Finalizing Your Vulkan Application

1. Memory and Resource Cleanup

2. Error Handling and Graceful Failure

3. User Interface (UI) and User Experience (UX)

4. Performance Optimization

5. Testing and Quality Assurance

6. Documentation

7. Licensing and Legal Considerations

8. Packaging and Distribution

9. Versioning and Updates

10. User Support and Feedback

Chapter 18: Beyond the Basics

Section 18.1: Advanced Vulkan Features

1. Compute Shaders

2. Multi-threading with Vulkan

3. Vulkan Extensions

4. Exploring Vulkan Ecosystem

5. Advanced Rendering Techniques

Section 18.2: Compute Shaders in Vulkan

Understanding Compute Shaders

Key Components of a Compute Shader

Dispatching Compute Shaders

Synchronization

Use Cases

Section 18.3: Multi-threading with Vulkan

Vulkan and Multi-threading

Multi-threaded Command Buffer Recording

Thread Safety and Synchronization

Benefits of Multi-threading in Vulkan

Section 18.4: Vulkan Extensions

What Are Vulkan Extensions?

Using Vulkan Extensions

Extension Examples

Considerations When Using Extensions

Section 18.5: Exploring Vulkan Ecosystem

Vulkan SDK

Vulkan Libraries

Community Resources

Vulkan on the Web

Conclusion

Chapter 19: Real-world Vulkan Applications

Section 19.1: Vulkan in Game Development

Performance Benefits

Cross-platform Support

Efficient Multi-threading

Memory Management

Tools and Libraries

Challenges

Conclusion

Section 19.2: Vulkan in Simulation and Visualization

Simulation

Scientific Visualization

Virtual Reality (VR) and Augmented Reality (AR)

Engineering and Architecture

Data Visualization

Challenges and Considerations

Conclusion

Section 19.3: Vulkan in Scientific Computing

High-Performance Computing (HPC)

Parallelism and GPU Acceleration

Machine Learning and Deep Learning

Numerical Libraries and Frameworks

Data Visualization and Analysis

Challenges and Considerations

Conclusion

Section 19.4: Vulkan in Automotive and Aerospace

In-Vehicle Infotainment Systems

Automotive Simulations

Aerospace Simulations and Training

Embedded Systems and Compact Hardware

Cross-Platform Compatibility

Challenges and Considerations

Conclusion

Section 19.5: Vulkan in Cross-platform Development

Cross-Platform Development with Vulkan

Abstraction Layers

Performance and Efficiency

Considerations for Cross-Platform Vulkan Development

Vulkan in Cross-platform Games

Conclusion

Chapter 20: Building Your First Vulkan Project

Section 20.1: Planning Your Vulkan Project

Section 20.2: Project Setup and Organization

Development Environment

Project Structure

CMake Build System

Version Control

Section 20.3: Implementing Your Application

Vulkan Initialization

GLFW Window and Main Loop

Vulkan Rendering

Resource Management

Error Handling and Validation

Cleanup

Section 20.4: Testing and Debugging

Vulkan Validation Layers

Debugging Tools

Error Handling

Validation and Debug Callbacks

Vulkan Debugging Tips

Section 20.5: Deploying Your Vulkan Application

Platform Considerations

Packaging Your Application

Dependency Management

Vulkan Loader

User Documentation

Deployment on Multiple Platforms

Version Management

Testing on Target Platforms

Digital Distribution

Chapter 1: Introduction to Vulkan

Section 1.1: What Is Vulkan?

Vulkan is a high-performance, cross-platform graphics and compute API developed by the Khronos Group. It was first released in 2016 and has since gained popularity in the world of computer graphics due to its efficiency and flexibility. Vulkan provides low-level access to the GPU (Graphics Processing Unit), allowing developers to harness the full power of modern graphics hardware.

Understanding the Need for Vulkan

Before delving deeper into Vulkan, it's essential to understand why it exists and why learning it can be beneficial. Traditional graphics APIs like OpenGL had become somewhat outdated and had limitations in terms of performance and control. Vulkan was designed to address these shortcomings and provide a more modern and efficient alternative.

Vulkan is particularly appealing for several reasons:

1. **High Performance:** Vulkan is known for its high-performance capabilities. It allows developers to utilize the full potential of the GPU by minimizing driver overhead and providing fine-grained control over rendering operations.
2. **Cross-Platform:** Vulkan is designed to work on multiple platforms, including Windows, Linux, Android, and more. This cross-platform compatibility makes it a versatile choice for developers.
3. **Low-Level Control:** Unlike some higher-level graphics APIs, Vulkan gives developers low-level control over the

rendering pipeline. This allows for optimization and customization tailored to specific applications.

4. **Efficiency:** Vulkan is built with efficiency in mind. It reduces CPU overhead, which is crucial for achieving high frame rates in games and other real-time graphics applications.

5. **Modern Features:** Vulkan includes modern graphics features, such as support for multiple threads, explicit multi-GPU support, and improved memory management.

6. **Community Support:** Over the years, Vulkan has garnered a robust community of developers, making it easier to find resources, libraries, and tools for Vulkan development.

Key Concepts of Vulkan

To start working with Vulkan effectively, you need to understand some fundamental concepts:

• **Vulkan Instance:** The Vulkan instance is the first object you create when using Vulkan. It represents the connection between your application and the Vulkan library.

• **Physical Devices:** These are the actual GPUs present in your system. Vulkan allows you to enumerate and select the GPU you want to use for rendering.

• **Logical Device:** A logical device represents an interface to a physical device. It is created from a physical device and is used for most interactions with Vulkan.

• **Queues:** Vulkan introduces the concept of queues for different types of operations, such as graphics rendering and compute tasks. Queues allow for efficient parallel execution.

- **Pipeline:** The Vulkan pipeline defines the sequence of operations required to render or compute. It consists of multiple stages, including vertex processing, fragment processing, and more.

- **Shaders:** Shaders are small programs that run on the GPU and define how vertices and fragments are processed. Vulkan uses SPIR-V, a binary intermediate representation for shaders.

- **Buffers and Images:** These are used to store data on the GPU, such as vertex data, textures, and more.

- **Swapchain:** A swapchain manages the presentation of images to the screen. It is essential for creating a visible output in your application.

In the upcoming sections of this book, we will dive deeper into these concepts, explore how to set up a Vulkan development environment, and create your first Vulkan program. Whether you're a game developer, graphics enthusiast, or someone interested in high-performance computing, Vulkan offers a powerful toolset for unleashing the potential of modern GPUs. Let's embark on this journey into the world of Vulkan!

Section 1.2: Why Learn Vulkan?

Vulkan, as a graphics and compute API, offers several compelling reasons to invest your time and effort in learning it. Whether you're a seasoned graphics programmer or just starting in the field, understanding why Vulkan is worth learning is crucial.

1. High-Performance Graphics:

Vulkan is designed for high-performance graphics rendering. It provides low-level access to the GPU, allowing you to optimize your code for maximum efficiency. With Vulkan, you can minimize CPU overhead and fully utilize the capabilities of modern GPUs. This is particularly important for applications like games and simulations that demand smooth and responsive visuals.

2. Cross-Platform Development:

Vulkan's cross-platform support is a significant advantage. Whether you're targeting Windows, Linux, Android, or other platforms, Vulkan can be used to develop applications that run consistently across them. This cross-platform compatibility reduces the need for platform-specific code and saves development time.

3. Modern Graphics Features:

Vulkan supports modern graphics features and techniques, such as tessellation, compute shaders, and explicit multi-GPU support. These features enable you to create visually stunning and highly interactive applications. Vulkan also keeps up with the latest developments in GPU technology, ensuring your applications can leverage new hardware capabilities.

4. Low-Level Control:

One of Vulkan's key strengths is its low-level nature. Unlike higher-level APIs that abstract many details, Vulkan provides fine-grained control over the rendering pipeline. While this may initially seem more complex, it empowers developers to optimize their code for specific requirements and hardware.

5. Community and Resources:

Vulkan has a growing community of developers, and a wealth of resources are available for learning and troubleshooting. Online forums, tutorials, and open-source projects can assist you in your Vulkan journey. Additionally, Vulkan has a rich ecosystem of tools and libraries that can streamline development.

6. Industry Demand:

Many industries, including gaming, simulations, scientific computing, and automotive, have embraced Vulkan due to its performance and versatility. Learning Vulkan can open doors to various career opportunities, as there is a demand for professionals who can work with this technology.

7. Future-Proofing Your Skills:

As Vulkan continues to evolve and gain traction, it's becoming a valuable skill for graphics and compute developers. Learning Vulkan ensures that you're prepared for future advancements in GPU technology and graphics programming.

In summary, learning Vulkan is a worthwhile investment for anyone interested in graphics programming and high-performance computing. It provides the tools and capabilities needed to create cutting-edge applications, offers cross-platform compatibility, and aligns with industry trends. Whether you're developing games, simulations, or other graphics-intensive applications, Vulkan equips you with the means to achieve exceptional performance and visual quality.

Section 1.3: Graphics API Overview

Before diving deeper into Vulkan, it's essential to have an overview of graphics APIs in general. This will help you understand where Vulkan fits into the landscape of graphics programming and how it compares to other APIs.

1. Graphics APIs:

Graphics APIs, or Application Programming Interfaces, are libraries that provide a way for software applications to interact with the graphics hardware (GPU). They serve as an intermediary layer between your application code and the GPU, allowing you to issue commands for rendering and other graphical tasks.

2. OpenGL:

OpenGL is one of the most well-known and widely used graphics APIs. It has been around for a long time and is known for its cross-platform support. OpenGL provides a higher-level abstraction compared to Vulkan, making it easier for beginners to get started with graphics programming. However, it can introduce some overhead due to this abstraction.

3. DirectX:

DirectX is a collection of APIs developed by Microsoft for Windows-based systems. It includes various components, such as Direct3D for 3D graphics, Direct2D for 2D graphics, and more. DirectX is commonly used in the gaming industry and offers excellent performance on Windows platforms.

4. Metal:

Metal is Apple's graphics API for macOS and iOS devices. It provides low-level access to the GPU, similar to Vulkan. Metal is known for its efficiency and is commonly used for developing applications on Apple's platforms.

5. Vulkan:

Vulkan, as mentioned earlier, is a cross-platform, low-level graphics and compute API developed by the Khronos Group. Unlike some of the other APIs mentioned, Vulkan was designed with modern hardware and performance in mind. It offers explicit control over the GPU and minimizes driver overhead, making it highly efficient.

6. Differences Between Vulkan and Other APIs:

One of the key distinctions between Vulkan and older APIs like OpenGL is the level of control it provides. Vulkan exposes more of the hardware's capabilities to the developer, allowing for fine-tuned optimization. However, this also means that Vulkan code can be more complex and verbose compared to OpenGL.

Another notable difference is Vulkan's emphasis on multi-threading. Vulkan is designed to take full advantage of modern CPUs with multiple cores, enabling parallel execution of rendering commands for improved performance.

7. When to Use Vulkan:

Vulkan is an excellent choice when you need the highest level of performance and control over the GPU. It's particularly well-suited for game development, simulations, and other graphics-intensive applications. If you require cross-platform compatibility and want to harness the full power of modern GPUs, Vulkan is a compelling option.

8. Learning Vulkan:

Learning Vulkan may require more effort compared to higher-level APIs like OpenGL, but the benefits in terms of performance and efficiency can be substantial. Throughout this book, we will guide you through the process of learning Vulkan, starting with the basics and gradually building your knowledge and skills.

In conclusion, understanding the landscape of graphics APIs is essential for making informed decisions about which API to use for your projects. Vulkan stands out for its performance and low-level control, making it a powerful choice for developers who want to create high-performance graphics applications that run efficiently on multiple platforms.

Section 1.4: Setting Up Your Development Environment

Before you can start working with Vulkan, you need to set up your development environment. This section will guide you through the necessary steps to get your system ready for Vulkan development.

1. Operating System Compatibility:

Vulkan is designed to be cross-platform, and it supports a range of operating systems, including Windows, Linux, and Android. Ensure that your development machine is running a compatible operating system for Vulkan development.

2. Vulkan-Capable GPU:

To work with Vulkan, you'll need a GPU that supports Vulkan. Most modern GPUs from major manufacturers, such as NVIDIA, AMD, and Intel, are Vulkan-compatible. Verify that your GPU and its drivers are up to date.

3. Development Tools:

You'll need a set of development tools to work with Vulkan. Here are the essential tools to consider:

- **Vulkan SDK:** The Vulkan Software Development Kit (SDK) includes the Vulkan API, headers, libraries, and tools necessary for Vulkan development. You can download the Vulkan SDK from the official Khronos Group website.

- **IDE (Integrated Development Environment):** Choose an IDE that you're comfortable with for coding in C or C++. Common choices include Visual Studio, CLion, or Visual Studio Code.

4. Graphics Drivers:

Ensure that you have the latest graphics drivers installed for your GPU. Updated drivers are essential for optimal Vulkan performance and compatibility. Visit the GPU manufacturer's website to download and install the latest drivers.

5. Code Editor and Compiler:

You'll need a code editor (IDE or text editor) for writing and editing your Vulkan code. Additionally, make sure you have a C or C++ compiler installed on your system. Many IDEs come with integrated compilers, but you can also install standalone compilers like GCC or Clang.

6. Setting Up Your Development Environment - Windows:

If you're using Windows, you can follow these general steps to set up your Vulkan development environment:

- Install Visual Studio or another IDE of your choice.

- Download and install the Vulkan SDK for Windows from the official website.

- Ensure that you have the latest graphics drivers for your GPU.

7. Setting Up Your Development Environment - Linux:

On Linux, the process might vary depending on your distribution, but here are some general steps:

- Use your package manager to install development tools, including a C/C++ compiler and Git.

- Download and install the Vulkan SDK for Linux from the official website or through your distribution's package manager.

- Check for and install the latest GPU drivers for your Linux distribution.

8. Verifying Your Setup:

After setting up your development environment, it's a good practice to verify that everything is working correctly. You can do this by compiling and running a simple Vulkan program, such as one that creates a Vulkan instance. This will ensure that your development environment is ready for more complex Vulkan development tasks.

In conclusion, setting up your development environment for Vulkan is a crucial first step in your journey to learn and use this powerful graphics and compute API. Ensuring that you have the necessary tools, compatible hardware, and up-to-date drivers will enable you to work efficiently and take full advantage of Vulkan's capabilities.

Section 1.5: Your First Vulkan Program

In this section, you'll embark on your journey into Vulkan by creating your first Vulkan program. This program will serve as a basic introduction to Vulkan's structure and concepts. By the end of this section, you'll have a simple Vulkan application up and running.

1. Setting Up Your Project:

Before you start writing code, create a new project or directory for your Vulkan application. Organizing your project files is essential for maintaining a structured and manageable codebase.

2. Including Vulkan Headers:

To use Vulkan, you need to include the Vulkan headers in your C/C++ source code. You can typically include them using the following directive:

#include <vulkan/vulkan.h>

This header provides access to Vulkan's functions, structures, and enumerations.

3. Creating a Vulkan Instance:

The Vulkan instance is the starting point for any Vulkan application. It represents the connection between your application and the Vulkan library. Here's a basic example of creating a Vulkan instance:

```
VkInstance instance;

VkApplicationInfo appInfo = {};

appInfo.sType                                    =
VK_STRUCTURE_TYPE_APPLICATION_INFO;

appInfo.pApplicationName = "My Vulkan App";

appInfo.applicationVersion = VK_MAKE_VERSION(1, 0, 0);

appInfo.pEngineName = "No Engine";

appInfo.engineVersion = VK_MAKE_VERSION(1, 0, 0);

appInfo.apiVersion = VK_API_VERSION_1_0;

VkInstanceCreateInfo createInfo = {};

createInfo.sType                                 =
VK_STRUCTURE_TYPE_INSTANCE_CREATE_INFO;

createInfo.pApplicationInfo = &appInfo;

if (vkCreateInstance(&createInfo, nullptr, &instance) !=
VK_SUCCESS) {

// Handle instance creation failure
```

```
}
```

This code sets up an application structure (VkApplicationInfo) and an instance creation structure (VkInstanceCreateInfo). It then uses vkCreateInstance to create the Vulkan instance. Don't forget to handle error cases, as shown in the code snippet.

4. Enumerating Available Physical Devices:

Vulkan applications often need to work with a specific GPU (physical device). You can enumerate the available physical devices and select one for your application. Here's a simple example of enumerating and selecting a physical device:

```
uint32_t deviceCount = 0;

vkEnumeratePhysicalDevices(instance, &deviceCount, nullptr);

if (deviceCount == 0) {

// No available GPUs with Vulkan support

}

VkPhysicalDevice physicalDevice;

VkPhysicalDeviceProperties deviceProperties;

vkEnumeratePhysicalDevices(instance,            &deviceCount,
&physicalDevice);

vkGetPhysicalDeviceProperties(physicalDevice,
&deviceProperties);
```

This code first retrieves the number of available physical devices, checks for their presence, and then selects the first available device.

You can further refine your selection based on device properties and capabilities.

5. Cleaning Up:

Don't forget to clean up your resources when your Vulkan application is done. In this simple example, you should destroy the Vulkan instance before exiting:

```
vkDestroyInstance(instance, nullptr);
```

Proper resource management is essential to avoid memory leaks and ensure the smooth operation of your Vulkan applications.

In summary, this section provided a glimpse into creating your first Vulkan program. You learned how to set up your project, include Vulkan headers, create a Vulkan instance, and enumerate available physical devices. While this example is basic, it lays the foundation for more complex Vulkan applications you'll explore in later chapters. As you progress through this book, you'll dive deeper into Vulkan's capabilities and learn to build sophisticated graphics and compute applications.

Chapter 2: Vulkan Basics

Section 2.1: Vulkan Objects and Concepts

In the world of Vulkan, there are several fundamental objects and concepts that you need to understand. These form the building blocks for creating graphics and compute applications using the Vulkan API. Let's dive into these key concepts:

1. Vulkan Objects:

Vulkan revolves around a set of objects that represent various aspects of the graphics pipeline and resources. Some of the essential Vulkan objects include:

- **Instance:** As mentioned in the previous chapter, the Vulkan instance is the starting point for any Vulkan application. It represents the connection between your application and the Vulkan library.

- **Physical Device:** A physical device represents a GPU installed on your system. It provides information about the device's properties and capabilities.

- **Logical Device:** A logical device represents an interface to a physical device. It is used to interact with the GPU and manage resources.

- **Queue:** Queues are used to submit command buffers for execution on the GPU. Vulkan supports different types of queues, such as graphics queues, compute queues, and transfer queues.

- **Swapchain:** A swapchain manages the presentation of images to the screen. It ensures a smooth display of frames to the user.

- **Command Buffer:** Command buffers contain a sequence of commands that are executed on the GPU. These commands can include rendering, compute, and memory transfer operations.

- **Pipeline:** Vulkan pipelines define the sequence of operations required to render or compute. They consist of multiple stages, such as vertex processing, fragment processing, and more.

- **Framebuffer:** A framebuffer represents a collection of images that can be used as rendering targets. It's crucial for rendering to the screen or offscreen surfaces.

2. Object Creation and Destruction:

In Vulkan, you typically create objects by filling out structures with the necessary information and passing them to Vulkan functions. Object creation functions usually return a handle to the created object.

// Example of creating a Vulkan buffer

```
VkBufferCreateInfo bufferInfo = {};

bufferInfo.sType                                    =
VK_STRUCTURE_TYPE_BUFFER_CREATE_INFO;

bufferInfo.size = bufferSize;
```

```
bufferInfo.usage                              =
VK_BUFFER_USAGE_VERTEX_BUFFER_BIT;

bufferInfo.sharingMode                        =
VK_SHARING_MODE_EXCLUSIVE;

VkBuffer vertexBuffer;

if (vkCreateBuffer(device, &bufferInfo, nullptr, &vertexBuffer) !=
VK_SUCCESS) {

// Handle buffer creation failure

}
```

Similarly, objects need to be destroyed when they are no longer needed to free up resources:

```
// Destroying a Vulkan buffer

vkDestroyBuffer(device, vertexBuffer, nullptr);
```

Proper resource management is essential in Vulkan to prevent memory leaks and ensure efficient use of system resources.

3. Vulkan Layers and Extensions:

Vulkan allows the use of layers and extensions to extend its functionality. Layers provide additional validation, debugging, and profiling capabilities, while extensions introduce new features and capabilities. You can enable layers and extensions as needed to customize your Vulkan application.

4. Validation Layers:

Validation layers are crucial during development to catch errors and provide detailed feedback. They help you identify issues with your

Vulkan code, such as incorrect usage of Vulkan functions or objects. In production, you can disable these layers for improved performance.

// Enabling validation layers during instance creation

VkInstanceCreateInfo createInfo = {};

createInfo.sType   = VK_STRUCTURE_TYPE_INSTANCE_CREATE_INFO;

createInfo.pApplicationInfo = &appInfo;

// Enable validation layers

const   char*   validationLayers[]   =   { "VK_LAYER_KHRONOS_validation" };

createInfo.enabledLayerCount = 1;

createInfo.ppEnabledLayerNames = validationLayers;

// ...

Validation layers are an essential tool for debugging and ensuring the correctness of your Vulkan applications.

Understanding these fundamental Vulkan objects and concepts is crucial as they form the basis for more advanced Vulkan development. As you progress through this book, you'll explore these concepts in greater detail and learn how to use them to create complex graphics and compute applications.

Section 2.2: The Vulkan Application Structure

In Vulkan, understanding the structure of a Vulkan application is essential for effective development. A Vulkan application typically follows a specific structure and order of operations. Let's explore the key components of a Vulkan application structure:

1. Initialization:

The first step in any Vulkan application is initialization. This involves setting up the Vulkan instance, selecting a physical device (GPU), and creating a logical device. We discussed these steps in the previous chapters, where you learned how to create a Vulkan instance and select a physical device suitable for your application.

// Vulkan instance creation (as discussed in Chapter 1)

VkInstance instance;

// ...

// Physical device selection (as discussed in Chapter 3)

VkPhysicalDevice physicalDevice;

// ...

// Logical device creation (as discussed in Chapter 4)

VkDevice device;

// ...

2. Windowing System Integration:

If your Vulkan application is a graphical one, you'll need to integrate with a windowing system, such as GLFW, SDL, or a platform-specific library. Window integration allows you to create a rendering context and present your images to the screen.

3. Swapchain Creation:

To display images on the screen, you'll need to create a swapchain. The swapchain manages the presentation of images to the display and provides buffers for rendering. Swapchain configuration depends on the capabilities of your selected physical device and the requirements of your application.

// Swapchain creation (as discussed in Chapter 5)

VkSwapchainKHR swapchain;

// ...

4. Rendering Resources:

Vulkan applications often require various resources for rendering, such as buffers for vertex and index data, images for textures, and shaders for programmable stages of the pipeline. These resources need to be created and managed efficiently.

// Creating buffers (as discussed in Chapter 8)

VkBuffer vertexBuffer;

// ...

// Creating images (as discussed in Chapter 9)

VkImage textureImage;

```
// ...
```

```
// Loading shaders (as discussed in Chapter 7)
```

```
VkShaderModule vertexShaderModule;
```

```
// ...
```

5. Pipeline Configuration:

Vulkan pipelines define how rendering or computation is performed. Configuring pipelines involves specifying shader stages, vertex input, blending, rasterization, and more. Pipeline creation is a crucial step in preparing for rendering.

```
// Creating a graphics pipeline (as discussed in Chapter 6)
```

```
VkPipeline graphicsPipeline;
```

```
// ...
```

6. Command Buffer Recording:

Command buffers are used to record rendering commands that will be executed on the GPU. These commands include drawing, clearing, and memory transfer operations. You'll record command buffers that describe the rendering process for each frame.

```
// Recording command buffers (as discussed in Chapter 15)
```

```
VkCommandBuffer commandBuffer;
```

```
// ...
```

7. Rendering Loop:

The heart of a Vulkan application is the rendering loop. In this loop, you acquire swapchain images, record command buffers, submit them for execution, and present the images to the screen.

// Rendering loop (as discussed in Chapter 15)

```
while (!shouldExit) {
```

// Acquire swapchain image

```
vkAcquireNextImageKHR(device, swapchain, UINT64_MAX, imageAvailableSemaphore, VK_NULL_HANDLE, &imageIndex);
```

// Record rendering commands

// ...

// Submit command buffer for execution

// ...

// Present the image

// ...

```
}
```

8. Cleanup:

Proper cleanup is essential in Vulkan to release resources and prevent memory leaks. During cleanup, you destroy objects like the swapchain, pipelines, shaders, buffers, and the logical device. Cleanup ensures that your application exits gracefully.

// Cleanup (as discussed in Chapter 17)

// ...

Understanding this Vulkan application structure is crucial for building effective Vulkan applications. While this overview provides a high-level perspective, each of these components involves more detailed and specific operations, which will be covered in depth in the subsequent chapters of this book. By following this structure, you'll be well on your way to creating powerful and efficient graphics and compute applications with Vulkan.

Section 2.3: Vulkan Layers and Extensions

Vulkan's flexibility and extensibility are some of its most compelling features. Vulkan allows developers to customize and extend its functionality through layers and extensions. Understanding how to use these layers and extensions effectively can enhance your Vulkan development experience.

1. Vulkan Layers:

Vulkan layers are optional components that can be added to the Vulkan runtime to provide additional functionality. Layers can serve various purposes, including validation, debugging, profiling, and customizing Vulkan behavior.

- **Validation Layers:** These are perhaps the most commonly used layers during development. Validation layers can catch errors, validate Vulkan function calls, and provide detailed error messages. They are invaluable for debugging Vulkan applications and ensuring compliance with the Vulkan specification.

- **Standard Validation Layers:** Vulkan provides a set of standard validation layers that can be enabled during

Vulkan instance creation. These layers include "VK_LAYER_KHRONOS_validation," which checks for common errors and best practices. To enable validation layers, you specify their names in the VkInstanceCreateInfo structure during instance creation.

```
const char* validationLayers[] = { "VK_LAYER_KHRONOS_validation" };

VkInstanceCreateInfo createInfo = {};

createInfo.enabledLayerCount = sizeof(validationLayers) / sizeof(validationLayers[0]);

createInfo.ppEnabledLayerNames = validationLayers;

// Instance creation
```

- **Custom Validation Layers:** Developers can also create custom validation layers tailored to their specific application needs. Custom validation layers allow you to add application-specific checks and debugging functionality to your Vulkan code.

- **Debugging with Layers:** When validation layers are enabled, Vulkan will report errors and warnings, making it easier to identify and fix issues in your code. It's essential to resolve any validation layer errors before deploying your Vulkan application.

2. Vulkan Extensions:

Vulkan extensions are optional features and functionalities that can be added to the Vulkan API. Extensions provide a way to access features that may not be part of the core Vulkan specification but are supported by certain GPUs or vendors.

- **Device Extensions:** These extensions provide GPU-specific features or optimizations. To use device extensions, you must check if your selected physical device supports the extension and enable it when creating the logical device.

```
// Checking for extension support

VkBool32 supportsExtension = VK_FALSE;

vkGetPhysicalDeviceFeatures2(physicalDevice, &features2);

for (const auto& extension : deviceExtensions) {

if                              (extension                         ==
VK_KHR_SWAPCHAIN_EXTENSION_NAME &&

features2.features.samplerAnisotropy) {

supportsExtension = VK_TRUE;

break;

}

}

// Enabling device extensions during logical device creation

if (supportsExtension) {

deviceInfo.enabledExtensionCount = 1;

deviceInfo.ppEnabledExtensionNames = &deviceExtensions[0];
```

}

- **Instance Extensions:** Some extensions are related to the Vulkan instance rather than the device. These can be enabled when creating the Vulkan instance. For example, the VK_EXT_debug_utils extension provides debug utilities that can be enabled at the instance level.

// Enabling instance extensions during instance creation

VkInstanceCreateInfo createInfo = {};

createInfo.enabledExtensionCount = **sizeof**(instanceExtensions) / **sizeof**(instanceExtensions[0]);

createInfo.ppEnabledExtensionNames = instanceExtensions;

- **Extension Availability:** You can query whether an extension is supported by a physical device or the Vulkan instance by using the vkEnumerateDeviceExtensionProperties function for device extensions and vkEnumerateInstanceExtensionProperties for instance extensions.

Vulkan's support for layers and extensions allows developers to customize their Vulkan applications to their specific needs. Whether it's enabling validation layers for debugging or leveraging device extensions for GPU-specific optimizations, layers and extensions provide powerful tools for Vulkan development. However, it's essential to use them judiciously and ensure compatibility across different hardware and platforms when deploying Vulkan applications.

Section 2.4: Debugging Vulkan Applications

Debugging is an integral part of any software development process, and Vulkan applications are no exception. Vulkan provides various tools and techniques to help you identify and resolve issues in your applications efficiently. In this section, we'll explore some essential debugging strategies for Vulkan applications.

1. Validation Layers:

As mentioned in the previous section, validation layers are critical for debugging Vulkan applications during development. These layers can catch common errors and provide detailed error messages. It's crucial to enable validation layers when creating your Vulkan instance:

```
const      char*      validationLayers[]      =      {
"VK_LAYER_KHRONOS_validation" };

VkInstanceCreateInfo createInfo = {};

createInfo.enabledLayerCount   =   sizeof(validationLayers)   /
sizeof(validationLayers[0]);

createInfo.ppEnabledLayerNames = validationLayers;

// Instance creation
```

When validation layers are enabled, Vulkan will report issues such as incorrect API usage, memory leaks, and validation errors. It's essential to address these errors before proceeding with your Vulkan application.

2. Vulkan Debug Utils Extension:

The VK_EXT_debug_utils extension provides additional debugging tools and control over debug messages in Vulkan applications. It allows you to customize how debug messages are handled and displayed.

To enable this extension, you can set up a callback function that will be called whenever a debug message is generated:

```
// Enable the VK_EXT_debug_utils extension during instance creation
```

```
const          char*          extensions[]          =          {
VK_EXT_DEBUG_UTILS_EXTENSION_NAME };
```

```
createInfo.enabledExtensionCount    =    sizeof(extensions)    /
sizeof(extensions[0]);
```

```
createInfo.ppEnabledExtensionNames = extensions;
```

```
// Set up the debug messenger callback
```

```
VkDebugUtilsMessengerCreateInfoEXT debugCreateInfo = {};
```

```
debugCreateInfo.sType                              =
VK_STRUCTURE_TYPE_DEBUG_UTILS_MESSENGER_CRE
```

```
debugCreateInfo.messageSeverity                    =
VK_DEBUG_UTILS_MESSAGE_SEVERITY_VERBOSE_BIT_F
|
```

```
VK_DEBUG_UTILS_MESSAGE_SEVERITY_WARNING_BIT_
|
```

```
VK_DEBUG_UTILS_MESSAGE_SEVERITY_ERROR_BIT_EX
```

```
debugCreateInfo.messageType                        =
VK_DEBUG_UTILS_MESSAGE_TYPE_GENERAL_BIT_EXT
|
```

```
VK_DEBUG_UTILS_MESSAGE_TYPE_VALIDATION_BIT_EXT
|

VK_DEBUG_UTILS_MESSAGE_TYPE_PERFORMANCE_BIT_EX

debugCreateInfo.pfnUserCallback = debugCallback;

createInfo.pNext                                    =
(VkDebugUtilsMessengerCreateInfoEXT*)&debugCreateInfo;

// Instance creation
```

The debugCallback function can be customized to handle debug messages according to your requirements. For example, you can log messages, display them in the console, or even trigger breakpoints in your debugger.

3. Vulkan Validation Layers Messages:

Validation layers provide various levels of message severity, including verbose, warning, and error messages. These messages can help you identify issues in your Vulkan code and understand what caused them. Pay close attention to validation layer messages and use them as guidance for debugging.

4. Vulkan Debugging Tools:

In addition to the tools provided by Vulkan itself, there are third-party debugging tools and profilers that can be invaluable for diagnosing performance issues in Vulkan applications. Tools like RenderDoc and NVIDIA Nsight Graphics can capture frames, analyze GPU activity, and provide insights into performance bottlenecks.

5. Testing on Different Hardware:

Vulkan applications may behave differently on various GPUs and drivers. It's essential to test your application on different hardware configurations to ensure compatibility and performance consistency across platforms.

6. Memory Debugging:

Memory management issues can be challenging to debug. Vulkan offers features like memory allocation callbacks and object tagging to help you identify memory-related problems. Properly managing Vulkan memory allocations and checking for memory leaks is critical.

Debugging Vulkan applications can be a complex but rewarding process. The combination of validation layers, debug extensions, and external tools can help you identify and resolve issues efficiently. It's essential to incorporate debugging as an integral part of your Vulkan development workflow to ensure that your applications are robust, reliable, and performant.

Section 2.5: Vulkan Validation Layers

Validation layers play a crucial role in Vulkan development, helping developers identify and fix errors in their applications. In this section, we will delve deeper into Vulkan validation layers, discussing their types, usage, and best practices.

1. Types of Validation Layers:

Vulkan validation layers can be categorized into three main types based on their functionality:

- **Core Validation Layers:** These layers focus on enforcing Vulkan's core specification rules. They catch errors related to the correct usage of Vulkan objects and functions. The "VK_LAYER_KHRONOS_validation" layer is an example of a core validation layer.

- **Standard Validation Layers:** Standard validation layers provide a set of common checks that help ensure Vulkan applications follow best practices. These checks include ensuring that objects are correctly destroyed, memory is properly allocated and freed, and objects are not used after being destroyed.

- **Custom Validation Layers:** Developers can create custom validation layers to perform application-specific checks. Custom layers are useful for enforcing project-specific coding standards, detecting application-specific issues, or providing additional debugging information.

2. Enabling Validation Layers:

To enable validation layers in your Vulkan application, you must specify their names when creating the Vulkan instance. You can use the VkInstanceCreateInfo structure to enable the desired layers:

```
const       char*       validationLayers[]       =       {
"VK_LAYER_KHRONOS_validation" };

VkInstanceCreateInfo createInfo = {};

createInfo.enabledLayerCount   =   sizeof(validationLayers)   /
sizeof(validationLayers[0]);

createInfo.ppEnabledLayerNames = validationLayers;
```

// *Instance creation*

Enabling validation layers during development is crucial to catch errors early in the development process.

3. Validation Layer Messages:

Validation layers generate messages of various types, including information, warnings, and errors. These messages can be retrieved and handled by your application. For example, you can create a callback function to process validation layer messages:

VKAPI_ATTR VkBool32 VKAPI_CALL debugCallback(

VkDebugUtilsMessageSeverityFlagBitsEXT messageSeverity,

VkDebugUtilsMessageTypeFlagsEXT messageType,

const VkDebugUtilsMessengerCallbackDataEXT* pCallbackData,

void* pUserData) {

if (messageSeverity >= VK_DEBUG_UTILS_MESSAGE_SEVERITY_WARNING_BIT_ {

// *Handle warnings and errors*

}

// *You can log or display messages here*

return VK_FALSE;

}

Don't forget to set up the callback when creating the Vulkan instance, as explained in Section 2.4.

4. Validation Layer Configuration:

Validation layers provide a high level of configurability. You can customize which messages you want to receive and how you want to handle them. The VkDebugUtilsMessengerCreateInfoEXT structure allows you to specify the message severity, message types, and callback function.

5. Disabling Validation Layers for Release Builds:

While validation layers are essential during development, they can impact the performance of your application. In release builds, you should disable validation layers to ensure optimal performance. You can achieve this by not specifying any validation layers when creating the Vulkan instance.

```
// Disable validation layers in release builds

createInfo.enabledLayerCount = 0;

createInfo.ppEnabledLayerNames = nullptr;

// Instance creation
```

6. Validation Layer Best Practices:

- **Enable validation layers during development:** As previously emphasized, enabling validation layers in development helps catch and fix errors early.

- **Handle validation layer messages:** Implement a callback function to process validation layer messages. Depending on your application, you can choose to log, display, or handle messages differently.

- **Disable validation layers in release builds:** Ensure that validation layers are disabled in release builds to avoid unnecessary performance overhead.

- **Use standard and custom validation layers:** While core validation layers cover essential checks, consider creating custom layers for application-specific checks and adherence to coding standards.

Validation layers are a valuable tool for ensuring the correctness and reliability of Vulkan applications. When used effectively, they help developers identify and rectify issues, resulting in more stable and robust Vulkan applications.

Chapter 3: Creating a Vulkan Instance

Section 3.1: Initializing Vulkan

Creating a Vulkan instance is the first step in setting up a Vulkan application. In this section, we'll explore the process of initializing Vulkan, which includes setting up the application info, enabling validation layers, and creating the Vulkan instance.

1. Application Info:

To create a Vulkan instance, you need to provide information about your application. This information includes the application's name, version, and the Vulkan version it targets. You can set up the VkApplicationInfo structure as follows:

VkApplicationInfo appInfo = {};

appInfo.sType = VK_STRUCTURE_TYPE_APPLICATION_INFO;

appInfo.pApplicationName = "My Vulkan App";

appInfo.applicationVersion = VK_MAKE_VERSION(1, 0, 0);

appInfo.pEngineName = "No Engine";

appInfo.engineVersion = VK_MAKE_VERSION(1, 0, 0);

appInfo.apiVersion = VK_API_VERSION_1_0;

Here, we've specified the application and engine names, their versions, and the Vulkan API version.

2. Enabling Validation Layers:

During development, it's essential to enable Vulkan validation layers to catch errors and ensure your code adheres to Vulkan's rules. We discussed validation layers in detail in Chapter 2, Section 2.5. Enabling them during instance creation involves specifying their names in the VkInstanceCreateInfo structure:

```
const char* validationLayers[] = { "VK_LAYER_KHRONOS_validation" };

VkInstanceCreateInfo createInfo = {};

createInfo.enabledLayerCount = sizeof(validationLayers) / sizeof(validationLayers[0]);

createInfo.ppEnabledLayerNames = validationLayers;
```

Ensure that you have the necessary Vulkan SDK installed, as validation layers are part of the SDK.

3. Instance Creation:

After setting up the application info and enabling validation layers, you can proceed to create the Vulkan instance. The vkCreateInstance function is responsible for this task:

```
VkInstance instance;

VkInstanceCreateInfo createInfo = {};

createInfo.sType = VK_STRUCTURE_TYPE_INSTANCE_CREATE_INFO;

createInfo.pApplicationInfo = &appInfo;
```

```
createInfo.enabledLayerCount = sizeof(validationLayers) / sizeof(validationLayers[0]);

createInfo.ppEnabledLayerNames = validationLayers;

if (vkCreateInstance(&createInfo, nullptr, &instance) != VK_SUCCESS) {

// Handle instance creation failure

}
```

The code above initializes the Vulkan instance using the provided application info and enables validation layers. It checks for successful instance creation and handles any failures.

4. Validation Layer Verification:

After creating the instance, it's a good practice to verify that the requested validation layers are available. You can do this by checking the number of available layers and comparing them with the layers you requested:

```
uint32_t layerCount;

vkEnumerateInstanceLayerProperties(&layerCount, nullptr);

VkLayerProperties availableLayers[layerCount];

vkEnumerateInstanceLayerProperties(&layerCount, availableLayers);

bool layersFound = true;

for (const char* layerName : validationLayers) {

bool layerFound = false;
```

```cpp
for (const auto& layerProperties : availableLayers) {
if (strcmp(layerName, layerProperties.layerName) == 0) {
layerFound = true;
break;
}
}
if (!layerFound) {
layersFound = false;
break;
}
}
if (!layersFound) {
// Handle missing validation layers
}
```

This code enumerates available layers and checks if all the requested validation layers are available. If any layer is missing, you can handle the situation accordingly.

Initializing Vulkan and creating the Vulkan instance is the foundational step for building Vulkan applications. Properly setting up the application info, enabling validation layers, and checking for their availability are essential for a robust development process. Once you have a valid Vulkan instance, you can proceed to explore more Vulkan features and functionalities in subsequent chapters.

Section 3.2: Creating a Vulkan Instance

In the previous section, we discussed initializing Vulkan and setting up the application info. Now, let's dive into the process of creating a Vulkan instance, a fundamental step in any Vulkan application.

1. Instance Creation:

The Vulkan instance represents the connection between your application and the Vulkan API. To create an instance, you use the vkCreateInstance function, which requires a VkInstanceCreateInfo structure that specifies the application and engine information, as well as any enabled validation layers.

VkInstance instance;

VkInstanceCreateInfo createInfo = {};

createInfo.sType   =
VK_STRUCTURE_TYPE_INSTANCE_CREATE_INFO;

createInfo.pApplicationInfo = &appInfo; // *Application info set up in the previous section*

createInfo.enabledLayerCount   =   **sizeof**(validationLayers)   /
sizeof(validationLayers[0]);

createInfo.ppEnabledLayerNames = validationLayers;

if   (vkCreateInstance(&createInfo,   nullptr,   &instance)   !=
VK_SUCCESS) {

// *Handle instance creation failure*

}

The code above initializes the Vulkan instance based on the provided information. If the instance creation is successful, you can proceed with your Vulkan application.

2. Instance Validation:

It's important to note that instance creation itself doesn't perform validation layer checks. Validation layers are applied at the instance level, but the actual validation occurs when you create Vulkan objects, such as logical devices, swapchains, and pipelines. Validation layers help ensure that your Vulkan usage adheres to the Vulkan specification and best practices.

3. Instance Extensions:

While creating the Vulkan instance, you may also need to enable specific extensions. Extensions provide additional functionalities beyond the core Vulkan API. Enabling extensions is achieved by specifying them in the VkInstanceCreateInfo structure. For example, to enable the VK_KHR_surface extension for surface support, you would add it to the ppEnabledExtensionNames array:

```
const          char*          extensions[]          =          {
VK_KHR_SURFACE_EXTENSION_NAME };
```

```
VkInstanceCreateInfo createInfo = {};
```

```
// ...
```

```
createInfo.enabledExtensionCount = sizeof(extensions) / sizeof(extensions[0]);
```

```
createInfo.ppEnabledExtensionNames = extensions;
```

The exact extensions you need depend on your application's requirements, such as windowing system integration or platform-specific functionality.

4. Instance Cleanup:

Properly cleaning up the Vulkan instance is essential to prevent resource leaks. When you're done using Vulkan, you should destroy the instance using vkDestroyInstance:

vkDestroyInstance(instance, nullptr);

It's good practice to perform instance cleanup before your application exits.

Creating a Vulkan instance is a critical step in Vulkan application development. It establishes the connection between your application and the Vulkan API, enabling you to interact with the GPU. Understanding the instance creation process and configuring it with the necessary application info, validation layers, and extensions is foundational for building Vulkan applications.

Section 3.3: Instance Layers and Extensions

In Vulkan, instance layers and extensions provide additional functionality and customization options for the Vulkan instance. In this section, we'll explore instance layers and extensions, how to use them, and their significance in Vulkan application development.

1. Instance Layers:

Instance layers are optional components that can be added to the Vulkan runtime to provide additional functionality and validation checks. Unlike validation layers, which are focused on debugging and error checking, instance layers serve various purposes, including customizing Vulkan behavior and integrating with external libraries.

- **Standard Instance Layers:** Vulkan includes a few standard instance layers that can be useful in different scenarios. For example, the VK_LAYER_KHRONOS_validation layer provides basic validation checks, while the VK_LAYER_LUNARG_api_dump layer can log Vulkan API calls for debugging purposes.

- **Custom Instance Layers:** Developers can create custom instance layers to tailor Vulkan's behavior to their specific needs. Custom layers can be used to implement custom validation checks, modify Vulkan's behavior, or integrate with third-party libraries.

2. Enabling Instance Layers:

To enable instance layers in your Vulkan application, you need to specify their names when creating the Vulkan instance. You can use the VkInstanceCreateInfo structure to enable the desired instance layers:

```
const char* instanceLayers[] = { "VK_LAYER_KHRONOS_validation", "VK_LAYER_LUNARG_api_dump" };

VkInstanceCreateInfo createInfo = {};

createInfo.enabledLayerCount = sizeof(instanceLayers) / sizeof(instanceLayers[0]);

createInfo.ppEnabledLayerNames = instanceLayers;
```

Here, we've specified two instance layers, VK_LAYER_KHRONOS_validation and VK_LAYER_LUNARG_api_dump. You can enable the layers that are relevant to your application's development and debugging needs.

3. Instance Extensions:

Instance extensions provide additional functionality beyond the core Vulkan API. They are often used for integration with the windowing system, platform-specific features, or other external libraries. Enabling instance extensions involves specifying their names in the VkInstanceCreateInfo structure:

```
const char* instanceExtensions[] = {
VK_KHR_SURFACE_EXTENSION_NAME,
VK_KHR_WIN32_SURFACE_EXTENSION_NAME };
```

```
VkInstanceCreateInfo createInfo = {};
```

```
createInfo.enabledExtensionCount = sizeof(instanceExtensions) /
sizeof(instanceExtensions[0]);
```

```
createInfo.ppEnabledExtensionNames = instanceExtensions;
```

In this example, we've enabled the VK_KHR_SURFACE_EXTENSION_NAME extension for surface support and the VK_KHR_WIN32_SURFACE_EXTENSION_NAME extension for Windows platform integration. The required extensions depend on your target platform and application requirements.

4. Extension Availability:

Before enabling instance extensions, it's essential to check whether they are supported by the Vulkan implementation. You can query the available instance extensions using the vkEnumerateInstanceExtensionProperties function:

```
uint32_t extensionCount;

vkEnumerateInstanceExtensionProperties(nullptr,
&extensionCount, nullptr);

VkExtensionProperties availableExtensions[extensionCount];

vkEnumerateInstanceExtensionProperties(nullptr,
&extensionCount, availableExtensions);
```

After obtaining the list of available extensions, you can check if the required extensions are present in the list.

Instance layers and extensions provide a powerful mechanism for customizing Vulkan's behavior and integrating with external components. When developing Vulkan applications, it's crucial to understand how to enable and use instance layers and extensions effectively to meet your application's requirements. Whether you need to enable validation layers for debugging or specific extensions for platform integration, Vulkan offers the flexibility to tailor your application's behavior to your needs.

Section 3.4: Enumerating Physical Devices

After creating a Vulkan instance, the next step in setting up your Vulkan application is to enumerate the available physical devices (GPUs) on the system. Enumerating physical devices allows you to select the GPU that best suits your application's requirements and capabilities.

1. Enumerating Physical Devices:

To enumerate the physical devices, you can use the vkEnumeratePhysicalDevices function. This function provides you with an array of VkPhysicalDevice handles that represent the available GPUs:

uint32_t deviceCount = 0;

vkEnumeratePhysicalDevices(instance, &deviceCount, nullptr);

if (deviceCount == 0) {

// *No available physical devices*

} **else** {

VkPhysicalDevice physicalDevices[deviceCount];

vkEnumeratePhysicalDevices(instance,   &deviceCount, physicalDevices);

// *Now you have an array of physical device handles*

}

The deviceCount variable is first queried to determine the number of available physical devices. If no devices are available, you can handle this case appropriately for your application.

2. Selecting a Physical Device:

Once you have enumerated the physical devices, you may need to select a specific device based on your application's requirements. To do this, you can evaluate the capabilities and features of each device to determine which one best suits your needs.

- **Device Properties and Capabilities:** You can retrieve information about a physical device's properties and capabilities using functions like vkGetPhysicalDeviceProperties and vkGetPhysicalDeviceFeatures. These functions provide details such as the device's name, type, supported Vulkan version, and various hardware features.

- **Device Extensions:** You can also check which device extensions are supported by each physical device. This is crucial if your application requires specific extensions for functionality or optimization.

- **Queue Families:** Physical devices consist of multiple queue families, each of which can handle different types of operations, such as graphics rendering or compute tasks. You can query the available queue families and their capabilities using vkGetPhysicalDeviceQueueFamilyProperties.

3. Device Selection Criteria:

The choice of a physical device depends on your application's requirements. Consider the following criteria when selecting a device:

- **Compatibility:** Ensure that the selected device supports the Vulkan version required by your application and the extensions it needs.

- **Performance:** Evaluate the device's performance characteristics, such as GPU capabilities, memory, and supported features, to meet your application's performance goals.

- **Queue Families:** If your application requires specialized operations like graphics rendering or compute tasks, choose a device with queue families that support these operations.

4. Device Validation:

It's essential to validate the selected physical device's capabilities and features against your application's requirements. This validation ensures that the device can handle the tasks your application intends to perform.

5. Error Handling:

While enumerating and selecting physical devices, it's crucial to handle any errors or exceptional cases gracefully. For example, if no physical devices are available, you should provide a meaningful error message to the user or take appropriate action.

Enumerating and selecting the right physical device is a critical step in setting up a Vulkan application. The choice of device can significantly impact your application's performance and capabilities. By evaluating the properties, capabilities, and features of available devices, you can make an informed decision and configure your Vulkan application to work optimally with the selected hardware.

Section 3.5: Selecting a Physical Device

Selecting the right physical device (GPU) is a crucial step in setting up your Vulkan application. In this section, we'll explore the process of selecting a physical device based on your application's requirements and the available hardware.

1. Device Selection Criteria:

Choosing the most suitable physical device for your Vulkan application involves considering several criteria:

- **Vulkan Version Compatibility:** Ensure that the selected physical device supports the Vulkan version required by your application. Different devices may support different Vulkan versions, so it's essential to verify compatibility.

- **Required Extensions:** If your application relies on specific Vulkan extensions, confirm that the selected device supports these extensions. Extensions provide additional functionality beyond the core Vulkan API.

- **Performance Requirements:** Evaluate the performance characteristics of each physical device. Factors like GPU capabilities, memory capacity, and supported features can significantly impact your application's performance.

- **Queue Families:** Physical devices consist of multiple queue families, each optimized for different types of operations (e.g., graphics rendering, compute tasks). Choose a device with queue families that align with your application's workload.

2. Querying Device Properties and Capabilities:

To assess a physical device's suitability, you can use Vulkan functions to query its properties and capabilities:

- **Device Properties:** Retrieve information about the device, such as its name, type, vendor, and driver version, using vkGetPhysicalDeviceProperties.

- **Device Features:** Check the supported features of the device, including optional features like geometry shaders or tessellation, with vkGetPhysicalDeviceFeatures.

- **Device Memory:** Assess the available memory on the device using vkGetPhysicalDeviceMemoryProperties. Understanding the device's memory layout can help you manage resources efficiently.

- **Device Extensions:** Determine which extensions are supported by the physical device by querying the list of available extensions with vkEnumerateDeviceExtensionProperties.

Ensure that the device's properties and capabilities align with your application's requirements before making a selection.

3. Device Scoring and Selection:

It's common to implement a scoring system to rank available physical devices based on their suitability for your application. You can assign scores to devices based on criteria such as Vulkan version support, extension compatibility, and performance metrics. This scoring helps you make an informed choice.

Here's a simplified example of how you might score and select a physical device:

```
int highestScore = -1;

VkPhysicalDevice selectedDevice = VK_NULL_HANDLE;

for (VkPhysicalDevice device : physicalDevices) {

int score = rateDeviceSuitability(device);

if (score > highestScore) {

highestScore = score;

selectedDevice = device;

}

}
```

The rateDeviceSuitability function assigns a score to each device based on your criteria, and the device with the highest score is selected.

4. Device Validation:

After selecting a physical device, validate its capabilities and features against your application's needs. Ensure that it can efficiently handle the tasks your application intends to perform. If any validation fails, consider selecting an alternative device or adjusting your application's requirements.

5. Error Handling:

While selecting a physical device, be prepared to handle exceptional cases or errors gracefully. For example, if no suitable devices are found, provide a clear error message to the user or take appropriate action, such as falling back to software rendering if available.

Selecting the right physical device is a critical decision that impacts your Vulkan application's performance and functionality. By carefully evaluating device properties, capabilities, and features, you can ensure that your application runs optimally on the chosen hardware. Additionally, implementing a scoring system can help automate the device selection process and make it easier to adapt your application to different hardware configurations.

Chapter 4: Logical Devices and Queues

Section 4.1: Creating a Logical Device

A logical device in Vulkan represents a connection to a physical device (GPU) and serves as the primary interface for interacting with that GPU. In this section, we'll explore the process of creating a logical device and working with queues, which are essential for submitting commands to the GPU.

1. Logical Device Creation:

To create a logical device, you need to specify its configuration, including the desired queues and their properties. Here's an example of creating a logical device with a single graphics queue:

VkDevice logicalDevice;

VkDeviceQueueCreateInfo queueCreateInfo = {};

queueCreateInfo.sType = VK_STRUCTURE_TYPE_DEVICE_QUEUE_CREATE_INFO;

queueCreateInfo.queueFamilyIndex = queueFamilyIndex; // *Index of the graphics queue family*

queueCreateInfo.queueCount = 1; // *We want 1 queue from this family*

float queuePriority = 1.0f; // *Priority of the queue, usually 0.0f to 1.0f*

queueCreateInfo.pQueuePriorities = &queuePriority;

VkDeviceCreateInfo deviceCreateInfo = {};

```
deviceCreateInfo.sType                                      =
VK_STRUCTURE_TYPE_DEVICE_CREATE_INFO;

deviceCreateInfo.queueCreateInfoCount = 1; // Number of queue
create infos

deviceCreateInfo.pQueueCreateInfos = &queueCreateInfo;

if  (vkCreateDevice(selectedPhysicalDevice,    &deviceCreateInfo,
nullptr, &logicalDevice) != VK_SUCCESS) {

// Handle device creation failure

}
```

In this code, we specify that we want a single queue from the graphics queue family. You can create additional queues for different queue families if your application requires them.

2. Queue Families and Capabilities:

Before creating a logical device, you must have identified the appropriate queue family for your intended operations, such as graphics rendering or compute tasks. Each queue family has specific capabilities, and you should choose the one that best suits your needs.

You can query queue family properties and capabilities using functions like vkGetPhysicalDeviceQueueFamilyProperties and vkGetPhysicalDeviceSurfaceSupportKHR. These functions help you identify the queue family that supports your intended operations and can present images to the screen if necessary.

3. Queue Operations:

Queues are used to submit command buffers, which contain instructions for the GPU. Different types of queues can perform various operations, and they are typically associated with different queue families. For example, a graphics queue is responsible for graphics rendering commands, while a compute queue handles compute shader workloads.

To submit a command buffer to a queue, you'll use the vkQueueSubmit function. It allows you to specify the command buffers to be executed and synchronization information to control the order of execution.

4. Queue Synchronization:

Vulkan provides powerful synchronization mechanisms to ensure that command buffers are executed in the correct order and do not access the same resources simultaneously. You can use synchronization primitives like semaphores and fences to coordinate work between queues and manage resource access.

Synchronization is a crucial aspect of Vulkan programming and requires careful consideration to avoid issues like data hazards and race conditions.

5. Multiple Queues:

Modern GPUs often have multiple queues of the same type, allowing for parallel execution of commands. To take advantage of this parallelism, you can create multiple queues from the same queue family with different priorities.

For example, if you have a graphics-intensive application, you might create two graphics queues with different priorities and submit command buffers to both for parallel execution.

Creating a logical device and working with queues is a fundamental part of Vulkan application development. Logical devices allow you to interact with the GPU and submit commands for execution, while queues enable parallelism and efficient resource utilization. Properly configuring the logical device and managing queues is essential for achieving optimal performance and responsiveness in your Vulkan application.

Section 4.2: Working with Vulkan Queues

In Vulkan, queues are crucial for submitting command buffers and managing parallelism in your application. In this section, we'll delve into working with Vulkan queues, including their types, families, and synchronization.

1. Queue Families:

Vulkan classifies queues into different families, each designed for specific types of operations, such as graphics rendering, compute tasks, and memory transfers. To work effectively with queues, you must identify the appropriate queue family for your intended operations.

You can query queue family properties using vkGetPhysicalDeviceQueueFamilyProperties. This function provides information about the available queue families, their capabilities, and the number of queues that can be created from each family.

2. Queue Creation:

To use a queue, you first need to create a logical device and specify which queue families and how many queues you want from each family. For example, to create a logical device with a graphics queue, you can use the following code:

```
VkDevice logicalDevice;

VkDeviceQueueCreateInfo queueCreateInfo = {};

queueCreateInfo.sType                              =
VK_STRUCTURE_TYPE_DEVICE_QUEUE_CREATE_INFO;

queueCreateInfo.queueFamilyIndex = graphicsQueueFamilyIndex;
// Index of the graphics queue family

queueCreateInfo.queueCount = 1; // Number of queues to create

float queuePriority = 1.0f; // Priority of the queue, usually 0.0f to 1.0f

queueCreateInfo.pQueuePriorities = &queuePriority;

VkDeviceCreateInfo deviceCreateInfo = {};

deviceCreateInfo.sType                             =
VK_STRUCTURE_TYPE_DEVICE_CREATE_INFO;

deviceCreateInfo.queueCreateInfoCount = 1; // Number of queue
create infos

deviceCreateInfo.pQueueCreateInfos = &queueCreateInfo;

if (vkCreateDevice(selectedPhysicalDevice, &deviceCreateInfo,
nullptr, &logicalDevice) != VK_SUCCESS) {

// Handle device creation failure
```

```
}
```

In this code, we specify that we want one queue from the graphics queue family with a priority of 1.0f (the highest). You can create multiple queues from different families if your application requires it.

3. Queue Operations:

Queues are responsible for executing command buffers, which contain instructions for the GPU. To submit a command buffer to a queue, you use the vkQueueSubmit function. This function allows you to specify the command buffers to be executed, synchronization information, and other parameters.

Here's a simplified example of submitting a command buffer to a queue:

VkQueue graphicsQueue; *// Assume you have a graphics queue from the logical device creation*

VkSubmitInfo submitInfo = {};

submitInfo.sType   = VK_STRUCTURE_TYPE_SUBMIT_INFO;

submitInfo.commandBufferCount = 1; *// Number of command buffers to submit*

submitInfo.pCommandBuffers = &commandBuffer; *// Array of command buffers to submit*

if (vkQueueSubmit(graphicsQueue,   1,   &submitInfo, VK_NULL_HANDLE) != VK_SUCCESS) {

// Handle submission failure

```
}
```

In this code, we submit a single command buffer to a graphics queue. The command buffer will be executed asynchronously by the GPU.

4. Queue Synchronization:

Synchronization between queues is crucial to ensure that command buffers are executed in the correct order and do not access the same resources simultaneously. Vulkan provides synchronization primitives like semaphores and fences for this purpose.

Semaphores can be used to synchronize operations between different queues, ensuring that one queue doesn't start executing until another queue has completed its work. Fences are used to synchronize CPU and GPU operations, allowing the CPU to wait for the GPU to finish its tasks.

Proper synchronization is vital to avoid data hazards and race conditions in your Vulkan application.

5. Multiple Queues:

Many GPUs offer multiple queues of the same type, allowing for parallel execution of commands. To take advantage of this parallelism, you can create multiple queues from the same queue family with different priorities.

For example, if you have a graphics-intensive application, you might create two graphics queues with different priorities and submit command buffers to both for parallel execution.

Working with Vulkan queues is essential for achieving efficient parallelism and optimal resource utilization in your application. Identifying the right queue families, creating queues with appropriate priorities, and managing synchronization between queues are key aspects of Vulkan programming. Properly utilizing queues can lead to improved performance and responsiveness in your Vulkan application.

Section 4.3: Queue Families and Capabilities

Understanding queue families and their capabilities is essential when working with Vulkan. In this section, we'll explore queue families in more detail and discuss how to query their properties to make informed decisions in Vulkan application development.

1. What Are Queue Families?

In Vulkan, a queue family is a group of queues with similar capabilities and intended purposes. Queue families are a way to categorize the available queues on a physical device (GPU). Each queue family may be optimized for specific types of operations, such as graphics rendering, compute tasks, or memory transfers.

2. Querying Queue Family Properties:

To work effectively with queues, you need to query the properties and capabilities of the available queue families on the selected physical device. This information allows you to determine which queue families are suitable for your intended operations.

You can retrieve queue family properties using the vkGetPhysicalDeviceQueueFamilyProperties function. Here's an example of how to use it:

```
uint32_t queueFamilyCount = 0;

vkGetPhysicalDeviceQueueFamilyProperties(selectedPhysicalDevice,
&queueFamilyCount, nullptr);
```

VkQueueFamilyProperties queueFamilies[queueFamilyCount];

vkGetPhysicalDeviceQueueFamilyProperties(selectedPhysicalDevice, &queueFamilyCount, queueFamilies);

After calling these functions, the queueFamilies array will contain information about each queue family available on the selected physical device.

3. Queue Family Properties:

Queue family properties provide crucial details about each queue family, including:

- **Queue Count:** The number of queues that can be created from this family.

- **Queue Flags:** Flags indicating the supported operations and capabilities of the queues in the family.

- **Timestamp Valid Bits:** The number of significant bits in the timestamp values.

- **Min Image Transfer Granularity:** The granularity of the image transfer operations.

By examining these properties, you can identify which queue families are suitable for your application's specific needs.

4. Queue Capabilities:

Besides queue properties, you should also consider the capabilities of each queue family. For example, if your application requires presenting images to the screen, you need to check if a queue family supports presentation.

To check if a queue family supports presentation, you can use the vkGetPhysicalDeviceSurfaceSupportKHR function, which checks if a queue family can present images to a surface. This is especially important for applications with a graphical user interface (GUI) that need to display images on the screen.

5. Selecting the Right Queue Family:

When selecting a queue family for your operations, consider factors like the type of tasks you'll perform and the capabilities of each queue family. For instance:

- **Graphics Rendering:** For rendering graphics, you should choose a queue family optimized for graphics operations.

- **Compute Workloads:** If you have compute-intensive tasks, a queue family suitable for compute operations is preferred.

- **Memory Transfers:** Queue families optimized for memory transfer operations are ideal for tasks like loading textures or buffering data.

Additionally, ensure that the selected queue family supports the extensions you require for your application.

6. Multiple Queue Families:

Some applications may benefit from utilizing multiple queue families in parallel, allowing for efficient multitasking. Vulkan's flexible design allows you to create multiple queues from different families and submit command buffers to them concurrently.

Understanding queue families and their capabilities is crucial for optimizing the performance of your Vulkan application. By querying and selecting the right queue families based on your application's requirements, you can harness the full potential of the GPU and achieve efficient parallelism in your graphics, compute, and memory transfer operations.

Section 4.4: Synchronization in Vulkan

Synchronization is a fundamental aspect of Vulkan programming, ensuring that multiple operations, especially those involving different queues or stages of the graphics pipeline, occur in a controlled and predictable order. In this section, we'll explore synchronization techniques in Vulkan, including semaphores and fences.

1. Semaphores:

Semaphores are synchronization primitives used to coordinate operations between queues. They are often employed to ensure that one queue doesn't start executing until another queue has completed its work.

In Vulkan, you can create semaphores using the vkCreateSemaphore function. Here's a simplified example of using semaphores for synchronization:

```
VkSemaphore imageAvailableSemaphore;

VkSemaphore renderFinishedSemaphore;

VkSemaphoreCreateInfo semaphoreInfo = {};

semaphoreInfo.sType                              =
VK_STRUCTURE_TYPE_SEMAPHORE_CREATE_INFO;
```

```
if (vkCreateSemaphore(logicalDevice, &semaphoreInfo, nullptr,
&imageAvailableSemaphore) != VK_SUCCESS ||

vkCreateSemaphore(logicalDevice, &semaphoreInfo, nullptr,
&renderFinishedSemaphore) != VK_SUCCESS) {
```

// Handle semaphore creation failure

```
}
```

In this example, two semaphores, imageAvailableSemaphore and renderFinishedSemaphore, are created. The former is typically used to signal when an image is available for rendering, while the latter signals when rendering has completed.

2. Fences:

Fences are synchronization objects used for CPU-GPU synchronization. They allow the CPU to wait for the GPU to complete certain tasks before proceeding. Fences are particularly useful when you need to ensure that the CPU doesn't start processing the results of GPU operations prematurely.

You can create fences using the vkCreateFence function:

```
VkFence myFence;

VkFenceCreateInfo fenceInfo = {};

fenceInfo.sType                                    =
VK_STRUCTURE_TYPE_FENCE_CREATE_INFO;
```

fenceInfo.flags = 0; *// Optional flags*

```
if (vkCreateFence(logicalDevice, &fenceInfo, nullptr, &myFence)
!= VK_SUCCESS) {
```

// Handle fence creation failure

```
}
```

Once created, you can use a fence to wait for the GPU to complete a specific operation. For example:

vkWaitForFences(logicalDevice, 1, &myFence, VK_TRUE, UINT64_MAX);

This call will block the CPU until the fence myFence is signaled by the GPU.

3. Pipeline Barriers:

Vulkan provides pipeline barriers to explicitly control the order of execution for certain operations. A pipeline barrier is a synchronization primitive that defines memory and execution dependencies between commands.

Pipeline barriers are used to transition resources between different pipeline stages, ensuring that the previous stage's work is completed before the next stage begins. This is crucial when transitioning image layouts or managing access to resources.

4. Command Buffer Submission:

When submitting command buffers to queues, you can specify semaphores and fences to control synchronization. For example, you can specify which semaphore(s) must be signaled before the execution of a command buffer begins or which fence should be signaled upon completion.

VkSubmitInfo submitInfo = {};

```
submitInfo.sType                                  =
VK_STRUCTURE_TYPE_SUBMIT_INFO;

submitInfo.waitSemaphoreCount = 1;

submitInfo.pWaitSemaphores = &imageAvailableSemaphore;

submitInfo.pWaitDstStageMask = &waitStage;

submitInfo.commandBufferCount = 1;

submitInfo.pCommandBuffers = &commandBuffer;

submitInfo.signalSemaphoreCount = 1;

submitInfo.pSignalSemaphores = &renderFinishedSemaphore;

if (vkQueueSubmit(graphicsQueue, 1, &submitInfo, myFence) !=
VK_SUCCESS) {

// Handle submission failure

}
```

In this code, waitSemaphoreCount and pWaitSemaphores specify which semaphore(s) the queue must wait for before executing the command buffer. signalSemaphoreCount and pSignalSemaphores indicate which semaphore(s) should be signaled when the command buffer execution is finished.

Synchronization in Vulkan is a complex but vital aspect of creating efficient and reliable graphics applications. Semaphores and fences enable you to coordinate work between queues and ensure that the CPU and GPU perform operations in a synchronized manner. Properly managing synchronization helps prevent data hazards, race conditions, and other synchronization-related issues in your Vulkan application.

Section 4.5: Semaphore and Fence Objects

Semaphore and fence objects play a crucial role in synchronizing operations in Vulkan applications. In this section, we'll dive deeper into the concepts of semaphores and fences, how to create and use them, and their significance in coordinating GPU and CPU activities.

1. Semaphores:

Semaphores are synchronization primitives used to coordinate operations between queues in Vulkan. They are lightweight and designed to signal the availability or completion of specific tasks. Semaphores help ensure that certain operations do not begin until others have completed.

In Vulkan, you create semaphores using the vkCreateSemaphore function. Here's a basic example:

```
VkSemaphore semaphore;

VkSemaphoreCreateInfo semaphoreInfo = {};

semaphoreInfo.sType                                 =
VK_STRUCTURE_TYPE_SEMAPHORE_CREATE_INFO;

if (vkCreateSemaphore(logicalDevice, &semaphoreInfo, nullptr,
&semaphore) != VK_SUCCESS) {

// Handle semaphore creation failure

}
```

Once created, you can use semaphores in various ways, such as:

• **Synchronization Between Queues:** You can use semaphores to ensure that one queue doesn't start executing until another queue has completed its work. For example, you might use a semaphore to synchronize the presentation of an image with its rendering.

• **Multiple Swapchain Images:** When working with swapchains (used for presenting images to the screen), you can use semaphores to signal when it's safe to start rendering the next frame while the previous one is still in the process of being presented.

2. Fences:

Fences are synchronization objects used for CPU-GPU synchronization in Vulkan. They are especially useful when you want the CPU to wait for GPU operations to complete before proceeding. Fences are essential for ensuring that the CPU doesn't start processing the results of GPU operations prematurely.

You create fences using the vkCreateFence function:

VkFence fence;

VkFenceCreateInfo fenceInfo = {};

fenceInfo.sType   = VK_STRUCTURE_TYPE_FENCE_CREATE_INFO;

fenceInfo.flags = 0; // *Optional flags*

if (vkCreateFence(logicalDevice, &fenceInfo, nullptr, &fence) != VK_SUCCESS) {

// *Handle fence creation failure*

}

Fences are typically used in the following scenarios:

- **Command Buffer Execution Control:** You can use a fence to wait for a specific command buffer to finish execution on the GPU. This is particularly useful when you want to ensure that a series of commands are executed in order.

- **CPU-GPU Synchronization:** If your application depends on the results of GPU operations, you can use fences to block the CPU until the GPU has completed the required tasks. This is often necessary for tasks like reading back GPU-generated data or handling resource transitions.

3. Using Semaphores and Fences Together:

Semaphores and fences are often used in combination to synchronize complex Vulkan operations effectively. For example, when rendering frames for a swapchain, you might use a semaphore to signal when an image is available for rendering and a fence to ensure the GPU has completed rendering the previous frame before starting the next one.

Here's a simplified example of how semaphores and fences can be used together:

```
// Semaphore for synchronization between image acquisition and rendering

VkSemaphore imageAvailableSemaphore;

// Fence for CPU-GPU synchronization after rendering

VkFence renderFence;
```

```
// ...
```

// In the main rendering loop

```
vkAcquireNextImageKHR(device, swapchain, UINT64_MAX,
imageAvailableSemaphore, VK_NULL_HANDLE);
```

// Wait for the fence to signal that rendering is complete

```
vkWaitForFences(device, 1, &renderFence, VK_TRUE,
UINT64_MAX);
```

// Reset the fence for the next frame

```
vkResetFences(device, 1, &renderFence);
```

```
// ...
```

In this example, the semaphore is used to coordinate the presentation and rendering stages, while the fence ensures that the CPU waits for the GPU to complete rendering before continuing.

Semaphores and fences are essential synchronization primitives in Vulkan, helping you ensure that operations occur in a controlled and predictable order. Properly managing semaphores and fences is critical for creating efficient and reliable Vulkan applications, especially when dealing with tasks that require CPU-GPU synchronization or synchronization between different queues.

Chapter 5: Swapchain and Presentation

Section 5.1: Introduction to Swapchains

In Vulkan, a swapchain is a critical component of rendering graphics to the screen, allowing your application to present images to the user. Understanding swapchains is crucial for creating interactive and visually appealing graphics applications. In this section, we'll introduce the concept of swapchains and discuss their importance in Vulkan.

1. What Is a Swapchain?

A swapchain is an object that represents a series of images that can be presented to the screen. In simple terms, it is a queue of images that your application renders to, and these images are then displayed on the user's screen. Swapchains are used to achieve smooth frame rendering in graphical applications.

In Vulkan, you typically create a swapchain for each window or surface where you want to render graphics. The swapchain is closely tied to the presentation of images to the screen, making it an integral part of any graphics application.

2. Why Do We Need Swapchains?

Swapchains are essential for several reasons:

- **Double Buffering:** One of the primary purposes of a swapchain is to implement double buffering. In double buffering, your application renders graphics to one image (the "back buffer") while another image (the "front buffer") is displayed on the screen. Once rendering is complete, the roles of the front and back buffers are swapped. This technique eliminates flickering and screen tearing that can occur if you directly draw to the screen.

• **Synchronization:** Swapchains provide synchronization between your rendering code and the display refresh rate. This synchronization ensures that you present a complete and coherent frame to the user without visible artifacts. Swapchains allow you to control when and how images are presented.

• **Adaptability to Display:** Swapchains are adaptable to the properties of the target display or window. They can handle varying refresh rates, resolutions, and other display-specific characteristics. This adaptability is vital for creating cross-platform applications that work well on different devices.

3. Swapchain Creation:

Creating a swapchain involves several steps, including:

• Selecting the appropriate surface (typically associated with a windowing system or platform).

• Choosing the desired format for the images in the swapchain (e.g., RGBA8 color format).

• Specifying the extent (width and height) of the images.

• Determining the number of images in the swapchain (usually two or three for double or triple buffering).

- Handling presentation modes (e.g., mailbox mode, FIFO mode) to control how images are queued for presentation.

Swapchain creation can be complex, and you must consider the capabilities and requirements of the physical device, surface, and the desired presentation mode.

4. Swapchain Images and Presentation:

Once the swapchain is created, you can obtain a series of images from it. These images are used as rendering targets. Your application renders graphics to one image while the others are presented to the screen in sequence.

To present an image, you typically use a semaphore to ensure synchronization between the rendering process and the presentation process. You signal the semaphore when rendering is complete and wait for it to be signaled before presenting the image.

// Acquire the next image from the swapchain

vkAcquireNextImageKHR(device, swapchain, UINT64_MAX, imageAvailableSemaphore, VK_NULL_HANDLE);

// Wait for the semaphore to be signaled

vkWaitForFences(device, 1, &renderFence, VK_TRUE, UINT64_MAX);

// Reset the fence for the next frame

vkResetFences(device, 1, &renderFence);

// Present the acquired image

vkQueuePresentKHR(presentQueue, &presentInfo);

This process ensures that images are presented to the screen at the appropriate time and in the correct order.

Understanding swapchains is essential for developing Vulkan applications that deliver smooth and visually pleasing graphics. Swapchains enable you to manage the presentation of images to the screen, synchronize rendering with display refresh rates, and adapt to different display characteristics. Properly configuring and using swapchains is a key aspect of Vulkan graphics programming.

Section 5.2: Creating a Swapchain

Creating a swapchain in Vulkan is a crucial step in rendering graphics to the screen. In this section, we'll dive into the process of creating a swapchain, covering the necessary steps and considerations.

1. Selecting a Presentation Mode:

Before creating a swapchain, you must choose a presentation mode. Vulkan offers several presentation modes, including:

- **VK_PRESENT_MODE_IMMEDIATE_KHR:** Images are presented immediately, which can lead to screen tearing but offers the lowest latency.

- **VK_PRESENT_MODE_FIFO_KHR:** Images are presented in a first-in, first-out (FIFO) manner, synchronized with the display's vertical refresh rate. This mode typically eliminates tearing and is suitable for most applications.

- **VK_PRESENT_MODE_MAILBOX_KHR:** Similar to FIFO, but allows you to discard pending frames when the swapchain is full. This mode is useful for minimizing latency but may lead to dropped frames.

The choice of presentation mode depends on your application's requirements, and you should select the mode that provides the best balance between smoothness and latency.

2. Swapchain Extent and Format:

The extent of the swapchain represents the width and height of the images in the swapchain. It should match the resolution of your rendering surface or window. You can query the available surface capabilities to determine the supported swapchain extents.

Additionally, you must choose the format of the images in the swapchain, which includes color format and color space. The selected format should be compatible with your rendering pipeline and the capabilities of the graphics hardware.

3. Creating a Swapchain:

Creating a swapchain in Vulkan involves several steps:

- Query the surface's capabilities, which include supported image formats, presentation modes, and extent range.

- Select the desired extent, format, and presentation mode based on your application's requirements.

- Determine the number of images in the swapchain, typically 2 or 3 for double or triple buffering.

- Specify how images are used, such as for rendering or sampling.

- Handle sharing modes if you intend to use the swapchain images across multiple queue families or even across different Vulkan instances.

- Create the swapchain object using the vkCreateSwapchainKHR function.

Here's a simplified example of creating a swapchain:

VkSwapchainKHR swapchain;

VkSwapchainCreateInfoKHR createInfo = {};

createInfo.sType   =
VK_STRUCTURE_TYPE_SWAPCHAIN_CREATE_INFO_KHR;

createInfo.surface = surface;

// Set the desired extent, format, and presentation mode

createInfo.imageExtent = extent;

createInfo.imageFormat = format;

createInfo.presentMode = presentationMode;

// Set the number of images in the swapchain

createInfo.minImageCount = imageCount;

// Specify how images are used

createInfo.imageUsage   =
VK_IMAGE_USAGE_COLOR_ATTACHMENT_BIT;

// Handle sharing modes if necessary

```
createInfo.imageSharingMode                =
VK_SHARING_MODE_EXCLUSIVE;
```

if (vkCreateSwapchainKHR(device, &createInfo, nullptr, &swapchain) != VK_SUCCESS) {

// Handle swapchain creation failure

}

After creating the swapchain, you will have access to a series of images that you can render to and present to the screen.

4. Swapchain Images:

Once the swapchain is created, you can retrieve the images associated with it. These images serve as the rendering targets for your graphics operations. You typically acquire and release these images in a loop during your rendering process.

Acquiring an image from the swapchain is done using the vkAcquireNextImageKHR function. This function also helps with synchronization by allowing you to wait for an image to become available.

Here's a simplified example of acquiring an image:

```
uint32_t imageIndex;

vkAcquireNextImageKHR(device, swapchain, UINT64_MAX,
imageAvailableSemaphore,                VK_NULL_HANDLE,
&imageIndex);
```

Once you have acquired an image, you can render graphics to it. After rendering, you present the image to the screen using the vkQueuePresentKHR function, ensuring synchronization with the display's refresh rate.

Creating a swapchain in Vulkan involves configuring several parameters to match your application's requirements and the capabilities of the presentation surface. Properly creating and managing the swapchain is essential for achieving smooth and visually appealing graphics output in your Vulkan applications.

Section 5.3: Presenting Images to the Screen

In Vulkan, presenting images to the screen is a crucial part of the rendering process. Once you've rendered your graphics to a swapchain image, you need to present it to the user's screen. This section explores the presentation of images in Vulkan, including the steps involved and synchronization considerations.

1. Presentation Process:

Presenting an image in Vulkan typically involves the following steps:

- Acquire the next available image from the swapchain using the vkAcquireNextImageKHR function. This function provides you with an index to the acquired image. You can specify a semaphore to signal when the image is available.

- Render your graphics to the acquired image. This is the stage where you apply your rendering pipeline and shaders to produce the final image.

- Once rendering is complete, you need to signal a semaphore to indicate that the rendering process has finished. This semaphore is often referred to as the "rendering finished semaphore."

- Finally, use the vkQueuePresentKHR function to present the acquired image to the screen. You specify the semaphore to wait for before presenting the image.

2. Using Semaphores for Synchronization:

Semaphores play a vital role in synchronizing the presentation process. They ensure that the rendering of an image and its presentation to the screen occur in the correct order. Semaphores are also used to prevent resource conflicts between the CPU and GPU.

Here's a simplified example of how semaphores are used for presentation synchronization:

// Acquire the next image from the swapchain

uint32_t imageIndex;

vkAcquireNextImageKHR(device, swapchain, UINT64_MAX, imageAvailableSemaphore, VK_NULL_HANDLE, &imageIndex);

// ... Render graphics to the acquired image ...

// Signal the rendering finished semaphore

VkSubmitInfo submitInfo = {};

submitInfo.sType   =
VK_STRUCTURE_TYPE_SUBMIT_INFO;

submitInfo.waitSemaphoreCount = 1;

submitInfo.pWaitSemaphores = &imageAvailableSemaphore;

```
submitInfo.commandBufferCount = 1;

submitInfo.pCommandBuffers = &commandBuffer;

submitInfo.signalSemaphoreCount = 1;

submitInfo.pSignalSemaphores = &renderFinishedSemaphore;

if    (vkQueueSubmit(graphicsQueue,    1,    &submitInfo,
VK_NULL_HANDLE) != VK_SUCCESS) {

// Handle submission failure

}

// Present the acquired image, waiting for the rendering finished
semaphore

VkPresentInfoKHR presentInfo = {};

presentInfo.sType                                        =
VK_STRUCTURE_TYPE_PRESENT_INFO_KHR;

presentInfo.waitSemaphoreCount = 1;

presentInfo.pWaitSemaphores = &renderFinishedSemaphore;

presentInfo.swapchainCount = 1;

presentInfo.pSwapchains = &swapchain;

presentInfo.pImageIndices = &imageIndex;

vkQueuePresentKHR(presentQueue, &presentInfo);
```

In this code, imageAvailableSemaphore signals when an image is available for rendering, and renderFinishedSemaphore signals when rendering is complete. These semaphores ensure that the rendering and presentation stages are synchronized.

3. Frame Timing and Synchronization:

To achieve smooth frame rates and prevent tearing, it's crucial to consider frame timing. Vulkan allows you to specify the presentation mode when creating the swapchain, which can affect the synchronization behavior. Modes like FIFO and mailbox mode ensure that frames are presented at the appropriate times.

Additionally, fences can be used to synchronize the CPU with the GPU. After rendering, you can wait for a fence to be signaled before proceeding with the next frame's rendering.

4. Resource Cleanup:

After the presentation of an image, it's essential to properly manage and release resources associated with that image, such as framebuffers, image views, and command buffers. Failing to clean up resources can lead to resource leaks and memory waste.

Presenting images in Vulkan involves careful synchronization and resource management to ensure that frames are displayed accurately and smoothly. Semaphores are used to signal and wait for various stages of the presentation process, ensuring that rendering and presentation occur in the correct order. Understanding and properly implementing these synchronization mechanisms is crucial for creating high-performance Vulkan applications.

Section 5.4: Swapchain Configuration

Configuring the Vulkan swapchain is a critical step in the rendering pipeline, as it directly affects how images are presented to the screen.

In this section, we will explore the various aspects of swapchain configuration, including image views, framebuffers, and handling window resizing.

1. Image Views:

Swapchain images in Vulkan are typically represented as VkImage objects. To use these images for rendering, you need to create image views (VkImageView) that provide a way to interpret the image's data.

Image views specify how the image data should be interpreted in terms of format, aspect ratio (color, depth, or stencil), and other parameters. Creating image views for each swapchain image is essential for rendering, as it allows you to bind them to your graphics pipeline.

Here's a simplified example of creating an image view for a swapchain image:

```
VkImageViewCreateInfo viewInfo = {};

viewInfo.sType                                    =
VK_STRUCTURE_TYPE_IMAGE_VIEW_CREATE_INFO;

viewInfo.image = swapchainImages[i];

viewInfo.viewType = VK_IMAGE_VIEW_TYPE_2D;

viewInfo.format = surfaceFormat.format;

viewInfo.components.r                             =
VK_COMPONENT_SWIZZLE_IDENTITY;

viewInfo.components.g                             =
VK_COMPONENT_SWIZZLE_IDENTITY;
```

```
viewInfo.components.b                                    =
VK_COMPONENT_SWIZZLE_IDENTITY;

viewInfo.components.a                                    =
VK_COMPONENT_SWIZZLE_IDENTITY;

viewInfo.subresourceRange.aspectMask                     =
VK_IMAGE_ASPECT_COLOR_BIT;

viewInfo.subresourceRange.baseMipLevel = 0;

viewInfo.subresourceRange.levelCount = 1;

viewInfo.subresourceRange.baseArrayLayer = 0;

viewInfo.subresourceRange.layerCount = 1;

if      (vkCreateImageView(device,        &viewInfo,        nullptr,
&swapchainImageViews[i]) != VK_SUCCESS) {

// Handle image view creation failure

}
```

In this code, an image view is created for each swapchain image, specifying the format, aspect, and other relevant parameters.

2. Framebuffers:

Framebuffers in Vulkan are objects that represent a collection of image views and attachments that can be used as rendering targets. You typically create one framebuffer for each swapchain image, allowing you to render to multiple images simultaneously, which is essential for double or triple buffering.

Creating framebuffers involves specifying the attachments (including image views), render pass, and dimensions. Framebuffers are crucial for binding rendering targets during command buffer recording.

Here's a simplified example of creating a framebuffer for a swapchain image:

```
VkFramebufferCreateInfo framebufferInfo = {};

framebufferInfo.sType = VK_STRUCTURE_TYPE_FRAMEBUFFER_CREATE_INFO;

framebufferInfo.renderPass = renderPass;

framebufferInfo.attachmentCount = 1;

framebufferInfo.pAttachments = &swapchainImageViews[i];

framebufferInfo.width = swapchainExtent.width;

framebufferInfo.height = swapchainExtent.height;

framebufferInfo.layers = 1;

if (vkCreateFramebuffer(device, &framebufferInfo, nullptr, &swapchainFramebuffers[i]) != VK_SUCCESS) {
// Handle framebuffer creation failure
}
```

This code creates a framebuffer for a specific swapchain image, specifying the associated render pass, image view, and dimensions.

3. Handling Window Resizing:

When the window or surface is resized, the swapchain needs to be recreated to match the new dimensions. Properly handling window resizing is essential to ensure your Vulkan application remains responsive and visually appealing.

To handle resizing:

- Detect window resizing events (e.g., in a platform-specific manner).

- Destroy the existing swapchain, including framebuffers and image views.

- Recreate the swapchain with updated dimensions and configurations.

Remember to properly manage resources during this process to avoid resource leaks.

Configuring the Vulkan swapchain involves creating image views and framebuffers for each swapchain image, which are crucial for rendering. Additionally, handling window resizing events is essential to adapt the swapchain to changing dimensions. Proper configuration and resource management are key aspects of building robust Vulkan applications.

Section 5.5: Handling Window Resizing

Handling window resizing is a common challenge in graphics programming, and it's crucial for ensuring that your Vulkan application can adapt to changes in the window's dimensions while maintaining a smooth user experience. In this section, we'll explore how to handle window resizing in a Vulkan application.

1. Detecting Window Resizing:

The first step in handling window resizing is detecting when it occurs. The method for detecting window resizing events depends on the platform or windowing system you are using in your application. Common methods include listening for window events provided by the windowing system or platform-specific APIs.

For example, if you're developing a desktop application using a library like GLFW, you can register a callback function to receive window size change events:

```
void framebufferSizeCallback(GLFWwindow* window, int width, int height) {
```

// Handle window resizing here

```
}
```

// Register the callback

```
glfwSetFramebufferSizeCallback(window,
framebufferSizeCallback);
```

When a user resizes the window, the framebufferSizeCallback function will be called with the new width and height.

2. Recreating the Swapchain:

When a window resizing event is detected, you need to recreate the Vulkan swapchain to match the new dimensions. Recreating the swapchain involves the following steps:

- Destroy the existing swapchain, including framebuffers and image views.

- Query the new size of the window or surface.

- Recreate the swapchain with updated dimensions and configurations.

Here's a simplified example of how to recreate the swapchain:

// Destroy the existing swapchain

cleanupSwapchain();

// Query the new size of the window or surface

int newWidth, newHeight;

glfwGetFramebufferSize(window, &newWidth, &newHeight);

// Recreate the swapchain with updated dimensions

createSwapchain(newWidth, newHeight);

The createSwapchain function would contain the code for creating a new swapchain with the updated dimensions, which may involve selecting a suitable extent, presentation mode, and image format.

3. Updating Framebuffers and Resources:

After recreating the swapchain, you must also update any resources that depend on the swapchain, such as framebuffers and image views. These resources need to be created again to match the new swapchain images.

// Destroy and recreate framebuffers and image views

recreateFramebuffers();

Properly managing resources during resizing is crucial to avoid resource leaks.

4. Handling Viewport and Scissor Changes:

Besides recreating the swapchain and related resources, you may also need to update the viewport and scissor settings in your rendering pipeline to match the new window dimensions. The viewport and scissor settings determine the portion of the rendering surface that is actually rendered to.

```
// Update viewport and scissor settings

VkViewport viewport = {};

viewport.x = 0;

viewport.y = 0;

viewport.width = static_cast<float>(newWidth);

viewport.height = static_cast<float>(newHeight);

viewport.minDepth = 0.0f;

viewport.maxDepth = 1.0f;

VkRect2D scissor = {};

scissor.offset = {0, 0};

scissor.extent        = {static_cast<uint32_t>(newWidth),
static_cast<uint32_t>(newHeight)};

// Update viewport and scissor in your rendering pipeline

vkCmdSetViewport(commandBuffer, 0, 1, &viewport);

vkCmdSetScissor(commandBuffer, 0, 1, &scissor);
```

These settings ensure that your graphics are rendered correctly within the new window dimensions.

Handling window resizing in Vulkan involves detecting resizing events, recreating the swapchain, updating dependent resources, and adjusting viewport and scissor settings. Properly managing these aspects is essential to provide a responsive and visually appealing user experience in your Vulkan application, especially when dealing with dynamic window sizes.

Chapter 6: Rendering in Vulkan

Section 6.1: Introduction to Rendering

In Chapter 5, you learned about swapchains and how to present images to the screen. Now, it's time to dive into the heart of graphics programming: rendering. Rendering involves the process of taking the data you've prepared—vertices, shaders, textures, and more—and turning it into the final image that the user sees on the screen. In this section, we'll explore the fundamentals of rendering in Vulkan.

The Rendering Process:

Rendering in Vulkan is a complex but highly customizable process. Here's a simplified overview of how rendering works:

1. **Data Preparation:** Before rendering, you need to prepare the data that describes what should be drawn. This includes vertex data (positions, normals, texture coordinates), shaders, textures, and other resources.
2. **Pipeline Setup:** Vulkan uses a graphics pipeline that defines the stages of rendering. You'll set up the pipeline

with shaders, vertex input descriptions, and various configuration options.

3. **Render Pass:** A render pass defines how the rendering process interacts with framebuffers and attachments. It specifies the sequence of operations, such as color and depth attachments.

4. **Framebuffer and Attachments:** A framebuffer is a collection of attachments (images) that represent the rendering targets. Each attachment can store color, depth, or stencil information.

5. **Drawing Commands:** You record drawing commands into a command buffer. These commands include specifying the vertices to render, setting uniform values, and more.

6. **Submit and Present:** Finally, you submit the command buffer for execution and present the result on the screen using the swapchain.

Vertex and Fragment Shaders:

Two key components of the rendering process are vertex shaders and fragment shaders:

• **Vertex Shader:** This shader processes each vertex in the input data. It typically transforms the vertex's position, computes lighting, and prepares data for the fragment shader.

• **Fragment Shader:** Also known as the pixel shader, this shader processes fragments (pixels) generated by rasterizing the vertices. It calculates the final color for each pixel and can apply texture mapping, lighting, and other effects.

Rasterization:

Rasterization is the process of converting vector graphics (represented by vertices and lines) into a raster image composed of pixels. During rasterization, the GPU determines which pixels are covered by the primitive (e.g., triangle) being drawn.

Render Passes and Subpasses:

Render passes in Vulkan define a series of rendering operations and how they interact with attachments. A render pass can consist of multiple subpasses, allowing for complex rendering techniques like deferred rendering.

Multithreading in Rendering:

Vulkan offers the advantage of multithreaded rendering, where you can record command buffers and perform other rendering tasks in parallel. This can lead to significant performance improvements on multicore CPUs.

Summary:

Rendering in Vulkan is a multi-step process that involves preparing data, configuring pipelines, setting up render passes and framebuffers, executing drawing commands, and presenting the result. Understanding the roles of vertex and fragment shaders, rasterization, render passes, and multithreading is crucial for efficient and flexible rendering in Vulkan. In the following sections, we'll explore each of these aspects in more detail, starting with the creation of Vulkan render passes.

Section 6.2: Creating Vulkan Render Passes

In Vulkan, a render pass is a crucial concept that defines a series of rendering operations and how they interact with framebuffer attachments. Render passes are used to specify the sequence of color, depth, and stencil operations during rendering. Understanding render passes is essential for efficiently managing rendering tasks and optimizing performance.

Render Pass Creation:

To create a render pass in Vulkan, you need to specify various aspects, including the format and number of attachments, the load and store operations, and subpasses. Here's an overview of the steps involved:

1. **Attachment Descriptions:**

   – Define attachment descriptions for each attachment in the render pass.

   – Specify the format, sample count, and load/store operations for color and depth attachments.

1. **Subpasses:**

   – Create subpasses within the render pass.

   – Specify the color and depth/stencil attachments that the subpass uses.

   – Define dependencies between subpasses for synchronization.

1. **Render Pass Creation:**

– Combine the attachment descriptions and subpasses to create the render pass.

– Specify the dependencies between subpasses.

Attachment Descriptions:

Attachment descriptions define the properties of each attachment used in the render pass. These properties include the format, sample count, load and store operations, and initial/final layout. For example, a color attachment description might look like this:

VkAttachmentDescription colorAttachment = {};

colorAttachment.format = swapchainImageFormat;

colorAttachment.samples = VK_SAMPLE_COUNT_1_BIT;

colorAttachment.loadOp = VK_ATTACHMENT_LOAD_OP_CLEAR;

colorAttachment.storeOp = VK_ATTACHMENT_STORE_OP_STORE;

colorAttachment.stencilLoadOp = VK_ATTACHMENT_LOAD_OP_DONT_CARE;

colorAttachment.stencilStoreOp = VK_ATTACHMENT_STORE_OP_DONT_CARE;

colorAttachment.initialLayout = VK_IMAGE_LAYOUT_UNDEFINED;

colorAttachment.finalLayout = VK_IMAGE_LAYOUT_PRESENT_SRC_KHR;

In this example, colorAttachment describes a color attachment with a clear operation at the beginning of the subpass and a store operation at the end. It transitions from VK_IMAGE_LAYOUT_UNDEFINED to VK_IMAGE_LAYOUT_PRESENT_SRC_KHR.

Subpasses:

Subpasses define the individual rendering stages within the render pass. Each subpass specifies which attachments it reads from and writes to. For example, a subpass for rendering might look like this:

```
VkSubpassDescription subpass = {};

subpass.pipelineBindPoint = VK_PIPELINE_BIND_POINT_GRAPHICS;

subpass.colorAttachmentCount = 1;

subpass.pColorAttachments = &colorAttachmentRef;

subpass.pDepthStencilAttachment = &depthAttachmentRef;
```

In this subpass, it is specified that there is one color attachment (colorAttachmentRef) and a depth/stencil attachment (depthAttachmentRef). These references connect the subpass to the attachment descriptions.

Render Pass Creation:

Finally, you create the render pass by combining the attachment descriptions and subpasses. Here's how you create a render pass in Vulkan:

```
VkRenderPassCreateInfo renderPassInfo = {};
```

renderPassInfo.sType   =
VK_STRUCTURE_TYPE_RENDER_PASS_CREATE_INFO;

renderPassInfo.attachmentCount = 2; // *Number of attachments*

renderPassInfo.pAttachments = attachments; // *Array of attachment descriptions*

renderPassInfo.subpassCount = 1; // *Number of subpasses*

renderPassInfo.pSubpasses = &subpass; // *Array of subpasses*

Render Pass Dependencies:

Render passes can have dependencies between subpasses to ensure proper synchronization. Dependencies specify memory and execution dependencies between subpasses. For example, you can specify that a subpass should wait for a previous subpass to finish executing before it starts.

VkSubpassDependency dependency = {};

dependency.srcSubpass = VK_SUBPASS_EXTERNAL; // *Implicit subpass before or after render pass*

dependency.dstSubpass = 0; // *Index of the subpass in this render pass*

dependency.srcStageMask   =
VK_PIPELINE_STAGE_COLOR_ATTACHMENT_OUTPUT_

dependency.srcAccessMask = 0;

dependency.dstStageMask   =
VK_PIPELINE_STAGE_COLOR_ATTACHMENT_OUTPUT_

dependency.dstAccessMask   =
VK_ACCESS_COLOR_ATTACHMENT_WRITE_BIT;

In this example, srcSubpass is set to VK_SUBPASS_EXTERNAL to indicate an implicit subpass before or after the render pass. dstSubpass specifies the subpass that waits for the color attachment stage to complete.

Summary:

Creating Vulkan render passes involves defining attachment descriptions, specifying subpasses, and setting up dependencies for synchronization. Render passes play a critical role in controlling the sequence of rendering operations and managing framebuffer attachments efficiently. Understanding render passes is essential for developing Vulkan applications that make the most of the GPU's capabilities.

Section 6.3: Framebuffers and Image Views

In Vulkan, framebuffers and image views are essential components of the rendering process. They work in conjunction with render passes and provide the necessary connections between attachments and the rendering pipeline. Understanding how to create and manage framebuffers and image views is crucial for effective Vulkan rendering.

Framebuffers:

A framebuffer in Vulkan is a collection of attachments (images) that represent the rendering targets for a specific subpass within a render pass. Framebuffers are created based on the render pass and define which attachments are used during rendering. Each attachment can serve as a color buffer, depth buffer, or stencil buffer, depending on its role within the render pass.

To create a framebuffer in Vulkan, you need to specify the following:

- The render pass that the framebuffer is associated with.

- The attachments (images) that the framebuffer will use, including their formats and dimensions.

Here's an example of how to create a framebuffer:

```
VkFramebufferCreateInfo framebufferInfo = {};

framebufferInfo.sType = VK_STRUCTURE_TYPE_FRAMEBUFFER_CREATE_INFO;

framebufferInfo.renderPass = renderPass; // The render pass associated with this framebuffer

framebufferInfo.attachmentCount = 2; // Number of attachments

framebufferInfo.pAttachments = attachments; // Array of attachments (image views)

framebufferInfo.width = swapchainExtent.width; // Width of the framebuffer

framebufferInfo.height = swapchainExtent.height; // Height of the framebuffer

framebufferInfo.layers = 1; // Number of layers in the framebuffer

VkFramebuffer framebuffer;

if (vkCreateFramebuffer(device, &framebufferInfo, nullptr, &framebuffer) != VK_SUCCESS) {

throw std::runtime_error("Failed to create framebuffer!");

}
```

In this code, renderPass is the Vulkan render pass associated with the framebuffer, attachments is an array of image views representing the attachments, and swapchainExtent specifies the dimensions of the framebuffer.

Image Views:

Image views in Vulkan provide a way to interpret an image's data in a specific format and for a particular purpose. They are used to define how an attachment is accessed during rendering. Each image view corresponds to an image and specifies how it is used within a render pass.

To create an image view in Vulkan, you need to specify the following:

- The image that the view is associated with.

- The format of the view, which may differ from the image's format.

- The aspect of the image to be viewed (e.g., color, depth, stencil).

- The subresource range, which defines the mipmap levels and array layers to be accessed.

Here's an example of how to create an image view:

```
VkImageViewCreateInfo viewInfo = {};

viewInfo.sType                                        =
VK_STRUCTURE_TYPE_IMAGE_VIEW_CREATE_INFO;

viewInfo.image = image; // The image associated with the view
```

```
viewInfo.viewType = VK_IMAGE_VIEW_TYPE_2D;

viewInfo.format = format; // Format of the view

viewInfo.subresourceRange.aspectMask          =
VK_IMAGE_ASPECT_COLOR_BIT; // Aspect of the image

viewInfo.subresourceRange.baseMipLevel = 0; // Starting mip level

viewInfo.subresourceRange.levelCount = 1; // Number of mip levels

viewInfo.subresourceRange.baseArrayLayer = 0; // Starting array
layer

viewInfo.subresourceRange.layerCount = 1; // Number of array
layers

VkImageView imageView;

if (vkCreateImageView(device, &viewInfo, nullptr, &imageView) !=
VK_SUCCESS) {

throw std::runtime_error("Failed to create image view!");

}
```

In this code, image is the Vulkan image associated with the view, format specifies the format of the view (which should match the attachment's format), and subresourceRange defines the aspect, mip levels, and array layers of the view.

Framebuffer and Image View Usage:

Once you have created a framebuffer and image views, you can use them in the rendering process. Framebuffers are attached to the graphics pipeline and define the rendering targets for a specific subpass within a render pass. Image views provide a way to access the attachments and interpret their data within shaders.

Summary:

Framebuffers and image views are crucial components of Vulkan rendering. Framebuffers define the rendering targets for specific subpasses within a render pass, while image views provide a way to access and interpret attachment data. Understanding how to create and use framebuffers and image views is essential for building Vulkan applications that perform efficient and flexible rendering.

Section 6.4: Pipeline Creation in Vulkan

In Vulkan, pipeline creation is a crucial step in setting up the rendering process. Pipelines define how rendering operations are executed, and they include both graphics and compute pipelines. Understanding how to create and manage pipelines is essential for achieving efficient and customizable rendering in Vulkan.

Graphics Pipeline:

The graphics pipeline in Vulkan is responsible for processing vertex data, fragment data, and everything in between. It encompasses the entire rendering process and consists of multiple stages, each with its own functionality. To create a graphics pipeline, you need to specify the following:

1. **Shader Modules:** Vertex and fragment shaders define how data is processed at the vertex and fragment levels, respectively. These shaders are loaded into shader modules and attached to the pipeline.
2. **Vertex Input Descriptions:** You specify how vertex data is organized and how it maps to shader inputs using vertex

input descriptions. This includes attributes like position, color, and texture coordinates.

3. **Input Assembly:** This stage defines how vertex data is assembled into primitives like points, lines, or triangles.

4. **Viewport and Scissor:** Viewport and scissor configurations determine the portion of the framebuffer that rendering affects and how it's transformed.

5. **Rasterization:** This stage converts primitives into fragments, which represent individual pixels.

6. **Multisampling:** If enabled, multisampling helps reduce aliasing by taking multiple samples per pixel.

7. **Depth and Stencil Testing:** The depth and stencil stages determine whether a fragment passes depth and stencil tests.

8. **Color Blending:** Color blending combines the fragment's color with the existing color in the framebuffer.

9. **Pipeline Layout:** This defines the uniform values and descriptor sets that can be used with the pipeline.

10. **Render Pass:** The graphics pipeline is associated with a specific render pass, specifying which attachments are read from and written to.

To create a graphics pipeline, you'll need to specify all these stages and configurations and then compile them into a pipeline object.

Compute Pipeline:

In addition to graphics pipelines, Vulkan supports compute pipelines for general-purpose GPU computation. Compute pipelines are relatively simpler and do not involve vertex and fragment shaders. Instead, they rely on a single compute shader to perform computations on data.

To create a compute pipeline, you'll need to specify the compute shader module, pipeline layout, and other configurations. Compute pipelines are used for tasks like image processing, physics simulations, and more.

Pipeline Caches:

Pipeline creation in Vulkan can be an expensive operation. To improve performance, Vulkan provides pipeline caches. Pipeline caches store compiled pipeline data, allowing you to reuse pipelines across multiple frames or application runs. This can significantly reduce pipeline creation times.

Pipeline Derivatives:

Vulkan allows you to create pipelines based on existing ones, known as pipeline derivatives. This is useful for creating similar pipelines with minor variations, optimizing resource usage, and simplifying pipeline management.

Pipeline Creation Example:

Creating pipelines in Vulkan involves a series of configuration steps and requires careful attention to detail. Below is a simplified example of how to create a graphics pipeline in Vulkan:

```
// Define pipeline stages, shader modules, and other configurations

VkGraphicsPipelineCreateInfo pipelineInfo = {};

// ... (configure pipeline stages, shaders, vertex input, etc.)

// Create the graphics pipeline

VkPipeline pipeline;
```

if (vkCreateGraphicsPipelines(device, VK_NULL_HANDLE, 1, &pipelineInfo, nullptr, &pipeline) != VK_SUCCESS) {

throw std::runtime_error("Failed to create graphics pipeline!");

}

In practice, configuring all the stages and dependencies of a graphics pipeline requires careful consideration of your rendering requirements.

Summary:

Pipeline creation in Vulkan is a fundamental part of setting up the rendering process. Graphics pipelines handle vertex and fragment processing, while compute pipelines are used for general-purpose GPU computation. Pipeline caches, derivatives, and careful configuration are essential for optimizing pipeline creation and management. Understanding how to create and manage pipelines is crucial for efficient and customizable rendering in Vulkan.

Section 6.5: Rendering a Triangle

Rendering a triangle is often one of the first tasks in graphics programming, and in Vulkan, it's an excellent way to understand the basics of rendering. To render a triangle, you'll need to set up the necessary Vulkan components, including the vertex and fragment shaders, pipeline, and vertex buffer.

Vertex and Fragment Shaders:

The vertex shader processes vertex data and typically performs transformations on vertex positions. In Vulkan, shaders are written in languages like GLSL or SPIR-V. Below is a simplified example of a vertex shader in GLSL:

```
#version 450

layout(location = 0) in vec2 inPosition;

void main() {

gl_Position = vec4(inPosition, 0.0, 1.0);

}
```

This simple shader takes vertex positions as input and sets the output gl_Position after applying a transformation.

The fragment shader, responsible for color generation, can be equally straightforward:

```
#version 450

out vec4 fragColor;

void main() {

fragColor = vec4(1.0, 0.0, 0.0, 1.0); // Red color

}
```

Here, the fragment shader outputs a solid red color.

Vertex Buffer:

To provide vertex data to the pipeline, you'll need to create a vertex buffer. This buffer holds the vertices of the triangle in memory accessible to the GPU. Below is a simplified example of creating a vertex buffer in Vulkan:

```
// Define vertex data

std::vector<Vertex> vertices = {
```

```
{{0.0f, -0.5f}},

{{0.5f, 0.5f}},

{{-0.5f, 0.5f}},

};
```

// Create a vertex buffer

VkBuffer vertexBuffer;

VkDeviceMemory vertexBufferMemory;

createVertexBuffer(vertices, vertexBuffer, vertexBufferMemory);

The createVertexBuffer function allocates and binds the vertex buffer memory.

Pipeline and Render Pass:

You'll need to set up the graphics pipeline and render pass as discussed in previous sections. Ensure that the pipeline includes the vertex and fragment shaders, vertex input descriptions, and other necessary configurations.

Rendering Loop:

The rendering loop involves a series of steps:

1. **Acquiring an Image:** Obtain an image from the swapchain for rendering.
2. **Record Commands:** Begin recording command buffers for rendering. In these command buffers, you specify the rendering operations, including setting the pipeline and binding the vertex buffer.
3. **Submit Command Buffer:** Submit the recorded

command buffer for execution.

4. **Present Image:** Present the rendered image to the screen.

Render Loop Example:

Here's a simplified example of the rendering loop:

while (!glfwWindowShouldClose(window)) {

// Acquire an image from the swapchain

// Start recording command buffer

// Set pipeline, bind vertex buffer, and specify rendering commands

// End command buffer recording

// Submit command buffer

// Present image

}

This loop repeats for each frame, rendering the triangle.

Summary:

Rendering a triangle in Vulkan involves setting up shaders, a vertex buffer, pipeline, and render pass. The rendering loop acquires images, records rendering commands, and presents the final result. While this example is simplified, it serves as a foundation for more complex rendering tasks in Vulkan.

Chapter 7: Shaders in Vulkan

Section 7.1: Introduction to Shaders

Shaders are fundamental in modern graphics programming and play a central role in Vulkan-based rendering. Shaders are small programs executed on the GPU, responsible for various aspects of rendering, including vertex processing, fragment shading, and more. In Vulkan, shaders are essential components for creating stunning graphics and visual effects.

Types of Shaders:

In Vulkan, you typically work with the following types of shaders:

- **Vertex Shader:** The vertex shader processes each vertex of a 3D model, applying transformations, lighting calculations, and more. It outputs the transformed vertices to the next stage of the pipeline.

- **Fragment Shader (Pixel Shader):** The fragment shader computes the final color of each fragment (pixel) that makes up a primitive (e.g., triangle). It's responsible for applying textures, lighting, and other effects.

- **Geometry Shader (optional):** The geometry shader can create, modify, or discard geometry. It's an optional stage in the pipeline, used for tasks like tessellation, shadow volume generation, or particle systems.

- **Compute Shader:** Compute shaders are used for general-purpose GPU computation. They allow you to perform parallel processing tasks, such as physics simulations, image processing, and more.

Shader Languages:

Shaders in Vulkan are typically written in specialized shader languages, such as GLSL (OpenGL Shading Language) or SPIR-V (Standard Portable Intermediate Representation - Vulkan's binary format). GLSL is a high-level, C-like language that's easy to write and debug. SPIR-V, on the other hand, is a binary format that offers better performance and cross-platform compatibility.

Here's a simple example of a vertex shader in GLSL:

```
#version 450

layout(location = 0) in vec3 inPosition;

layout(location = 1) in vec3 inColor;

out vec3 fragColor;

void main() {

gl_Position = vec4(inPosition, 1.0);

fragColor = inColor;

}
```

This shader takes vertex positions and colors as inputs and outputs the transformed position and color for the fragment shader.

Shader Modules:

In Vulkan, shaders are encapsulated in shader modules, which are loaded onto the GPU and can be used to create pipelines. Shader modules are created from shader code (either GLSL or SPIR-V) and can be attached to pipeline stages, like the vertex or fragment stage.

Shader Compilation:

Before using shaders in Vulkan, they need to be compiled into SPIR-V bytecode, a format that Vulkan understands. This compilation step can be performed offline or at runtime, depending on your workflow and requirements.

Summary:

Shaders are the heart of Vulkan-based rendering, responsible for transforming vertices, shading fragments, and creating stunning visual effects. Understanding shader types, languages, shader modules, and the compilation process is crucial for harnessing the power of shaders in Vulkan-based applications.

Section 7.2: Writing Vulkan Shaders

Writing Vulkan shaders is a fundamental part of creating visually appealing and efficient graphics applications. In this section, we'll explore the key aspects of writing Vulkan shaders, including shader entry points, input and output variables, and the shader pipeline stages.

Shader Entry Points:

Every Vulkan shader begins with defining an entry point. In GLSL, the entry points are typically main functions for each shader stage, such as main for the vertex shader, main for the fragment shader, and so on. These functions serve as the starting point for execution when the shader is invoked.

```
void main() {

// Shader code

}
```

Input and Output Variables:

Shaders communicate with each other and the rendering pipeline through input and output variables. For example, the vertex shader might receive vertex positions and colors as input and output transformed positions and colors for the fragment shader.

```
// Vertex Shader Input

layout(location = 0) in vec3 inPosition;

layout(location = 1) in vec3 inColor;

// Vertex Shader Output

out vec3 fragColor;

void main() {

// Transform vertex position

gl_Position = vec4(inPosition, 1.0);

// Pass color to fragment shader

fragColor = inColor;

}
```

The layout(location = ...) syntax specifies the location of input variables, ensuring they match the data provided in the vertex buffer.

Shader Pipeline Stages:

Vulkan shaders are organized into different pipeline stages. The primary stages are:

- **Vertex Shader:** Processes vertex data and performs transformations.

- **Tessellation Control Shader (optional):** Used for tessellation (if enabled).

- **Tessellation Evaluation Shader (optional):** Used for tessellation (if enabled).

- **Geometry Shader (optional):** Processes and possibly modifies geometry.

- **Fragment Shader:** Computes the final color of each fragment.

The pipeline stages are linked together to form a complete graphics or compute pipeline, with data flowing from one stage to another.

Uniforms and Push Constants:

Shaders often require data that remains constant during the rendering process. Vulkan provides mechanisms for passing such data to shaders:

- **Uniform Buffers:** These are buffers allocated in GPU memory that hold constant data accessible by shaders. They are typically used for materials, camera matrices, and other data shared across multiple objects.

- **Push Constants:** Push constants allow you to send small amounts of data directly to shaders within a pipeline object. They are typically used for per-object or per-draw data that doesn't change frequently.

Shader Compilation:

Shader compilation is the process of translating GLSL or other shader languages into SPIR-V bytecode. This bytecode can be loaded into Vulkan and used in shader modules.

// Example shader compilation using glslangValidator

glslangValidator -V shader.vert -o shader.vert.spv

Debugging Shaders:

Debugging shaders can be challenging due to the limited debugging tools available on the GPU. Common debugging techniques include adding print statements to the shader code or using specialized debugging tools provided by GPU vendors.

Summary:

Writing Vulkan shaders is a crucial skill for graphics programming. Shaders define how vertices are transformed, how fragments are shaded, and how visual effects are achieved. Understanding shader entry points, input and output variables, shader pipeline stages, and mechanisms for passing data to shaders is essential for creating visually appealing and efficient Vulkan applications.

Section 7.3: Shader Modules and Pipelines

Shader modules and pipelines are key components in Vulkan that enable efficient shader execution and rendering. In this section, we'll delve into shader modules, pipeline creation, and how shaders are integrated into the graphics pipeline.

Shader Modules:

In Vulkan, shaders are encapsulated in shader modules, which are the binary representation of your shaders in SPIR-V format. Shader modules can be created from SPIR-V bytecode generated by offline compilers like glslangValidator. Here's how you can create a shader module in Vulkan:

```
VkShaderModule createShaderModule(VkDevice device, const std::vector<uint32_t>& code) {

VkShaderModuleCreateInfo createInfo{};

createInfo.sType                                    =
VK_STRUCTURE_TYPE_SHADER_MODULE_CREATE_INF

createInfo.codeSize = code.size() * sizeof(uint32_t);

createInfo.pCode = code.data();

VkShaderModule shaderModule;

if    (vkCreateShaderModule(device,    &createInfo,    nullptr,
&shaderModule) != VK_SUCCESS) {

throw std::runtime_error("Failed to create shader module!");

}

return shaderModule;

}
```

You pass the device and the SPIR-V bytecode to this function to create a shader module.

Pipeline Creation:

Vulkan uses a fixed-function pipeline architecture, where multiple stages, including vertex processing, tessellation, and fragment shading, are linked together to form a pipeline. The shaders you create are integrated into this pipeline. Here's an overview of pipeline creation:

1. **Shader Stages:** You specify the shader modules and their entry points for each stage of the pipeline. For example, the vertex and fragment shaders are set as shader stages.
2. **Vertex Input:** You define how vertex data is structured and linked to the vertex shader inputs using VkPipelineVertexInputStateCreateInfo.
3. **Input Assembly:** Specify the primitive topology (points, lines, triangles) using VkPipelineInputAssemblyStateCreateInfo.
4. **Viewport and Scissor:** Configure the viewport and scissor rectangles using VkPipelineViewportStateCreateInfo and VkPipelineRasterizationStateCreateInfo.
5. **Rasterization:** Configure how geometry is rasterized (e.g., culling, line width) using VkPipelineRasterizationStateCreateInfo.
6. **Multisampling (optional):** Enable multisampling for anti-aliasing using VkPipelineMultisampleStateCreateInfo.
7. **Color Blending:** Define how color blending is performed using VkPipelineColorBlendStateCreateInfo.
8. **Dynamic State (optional):** Specify dynamic state settings for pipeline states that can be changed dynamically during command buffer recording.

Pipeline Layout:

Pipeline layouts define the interface between the pipeline and your shader resources like uniform buffers and push constants. They specify which descriptor sets and bindings are accessible to each shader stage. You create a pipeline layout by specifying descriptor set layouts and push constant ranges.

Combining Shader Modules and Pipeline Creation:

When creating a graphics pipeline, you specify the shader modules for each stage, like the vertex and fragment shaders. Here's a simplified example of pipeline creation:

VkPipelineShaderStageCreateInfo vertexShaderStageInfo{};

vertexShaderStageInfo.sType   =
VK_STRUCTURE_TYPE_PIPELINE_SHADER_STAGE_CREA

vertexShaderStageInfo.stage   =
VK_SHADER_STAGE_VERTEX_BIT;

vertexShaderStageInfo.module = vertShaderModule; // *Vertex shader module*

vertexShaderStageInfo.pName = "main"; // *Entry point*

VkPipelineShaderStageCreateInfo fragmentShaderStageInfo{};

fragmentShaderStageInfo.sType   =
VK_STRUCTURE_TYPE_PIPELINE_SHADER_STAGE_CREA

fragmentShaderStageInfo.stage   =
VK_SHADER_STAGE_FRAGMENT_BIT;

fragmentShaderStageInfo.module = fragShaderModule; // *Fragment shader module* fragmentShaderStageInfo.pName = "main"; // *Entry point*

// *Other pipeline creation steps...*

VkPipelineShaderStageCreateInfo   shaderStages[]   =
{vertexShaderStageInfo, fragmentShaderStageInfo};

VkPipelineCreateInfo pipelineInfo{};

pipelineInfo.stageCount = 2; // *Number of shader stages*

pipelineInfo.pStages = shaderStages;

// *Other pipeline creation settings...*

if (vkCreateGraphicsPipelines(device, VK_NULL_HANDLE, 1, &pipelineInfo, nullptr, &graphicsPipeline) != VK_SUCCESS) {

throw std::runtime_error("Failed to create graphics pipeline!");

}

In this example, we create shader stage info structs for the vertex and fragment shaders, specifying their respective modules and entry points. These stages are then included in the pipeline creation process.

Summary:

Shader modules and pipelines are essential in Vulkan for defining how graphics and compute operations are executed on the GPU. Shader modules encapsulate your shaders in SPIR-V format, while pipelines bring shaders together with other pipeline stages and configuration settings to define how rendering occurs. Understanding how to create and integrate shaders into pipelines is crucial for Vulkan-based graphics programming.

Section 7.4: Vertex Input Descriptions

In Vulkan, to correctly interpret vertex data in the vertex shader, you need to specify how this data is structured and how it maps to the shader's inputs. This involves creating a vertex input description, which defines the layout of your vertex data and its association with shader input variables.

Vertex Input Binding Description:

The vertex input binding description defines the rate at which data is read from the vertex buffers. You specify the stride between data entries and whether the data should be per-vertex or per-instance. This information is crucial when dealing with instanced rendering, where you want to repeat the same geometry multiple times with different attributes.

Here's how you can create a simple vertex input binding description:

VkVertexInputBindingDescription bindingDescription{};

bindingDescription.binding = 0; // *Binding index, corresponds to the layout(location = ...) in the vertex shader*

bindingDescription.stride = **sizeof**(Vertex); // *Size of a single vertex data entry*

bindingDescription.inputRate   = VK_VERTEX_INPUT_RATE_VERTEX; // *Data is read per vertex (not per instance)*

Vertex Input Attribute Descriptions:

Vertex input attribute descriptions define the format and location of each attribute within the vertex data. Attributes typically correspond to variables in the vertex shader, and you specify the binding index and offset within the data structure.

```
std::array<VkVertexInputAttributeDescription,                2>
attributeDescriptions{};

attributeDescriptions[0].binding = 0; // Binding index, must match
the one from the binding description

attributeDescriptions[0].location = 0; // Location corresponds to the
layout(location = ...) in the vertex shader

attributeDescriptions[0].format                             =
VK_FORMAT_R32G32B32_SFLOAT; // Format of the attribute
data

attributeDescriptions[0].offset = offsetof(Vertex, position); // Offset
within the data structure

attributeDescriptions[1].binding = 0;

attributeDescriptions[1].location = 1;

attributeDescriptions[1].format                             =
VK_FORMAT_R32G32B32_SFLOAT;

attributeDescriptions[1].offset = offsetof(Vertex, color);
```

In this example, we define two attributes: one for the position and one for the color of each vertex. The offsetof macro helps you specify the offset of these attributes within the Vertex data structure.

Binding Multiple Buffers:

If your vertex data comes from multiple vertex buffers, you need to define multiple binding and attribute descriptions, each associated with the corresponding buffer.

Vertex Input State:

To use the vertex input description in a graphics pipeline, you include it in the VkPipelineVertexInputStateCreateInfo structure when creating the pipeline. This structure also includes references to the binding and attribute descriptions.

VkPipelineVertexInputStateCreateInfo vertexInputInfo{};

vertexInputInfo.sType   =
VK_STRUCTURE_TYPE_PIPELINE_VERTEX_INPUT_STAT

vertexInputInfo.vertexBindingDescriptionCount = 1;

vertexInputInfo.pVertexBindingDescriptions   =
&bindingDescription;

vertexInputInfo.vertexAttributeDescriptionCount   =
static_cast<uint32_t>(attributeDescriptions.size());

vertexInputInfo.pVertexAttributeDescriptions   =
attributeDescriptions.data();

This code specifies that we have one binding description and multiple attribute descriptions. The pVertexBindingDescriptions and pVertexAttributeDescriptions fields point to the respective arrays.

Summary:

Defining a vertex input description is crucial in Vulkan to correctly interpret vertex data in your shaders. You specify how data is laid out in vertex buffers, how it maps to shader inputs, and the rate at which data is read. This information is then used to create the pipeline's vertex input state, ensuring proper data handling during rendering.

Section 7.5: Binding Shaders and Data

Binding shaders and data is a critical step in Vulkan graphics programming. In this section, we'll explore how shaders are connected to the graphics pipeline and how data is passed between shaders and the CPU.

Binding Shaders to a Pipeline:

In Vulkan, shaders are bound to a graphics pipeline using the VkPipelineShaderStageCreateInfo structure. You specify the shader module, shader stage, and entry point (function) to be used. Here's an example of how to bind shaders to a pipeline:

VkPipelineShaderStageCreateInfo shaderStages[2];

shaderStages[0].sType   = VK_STRUCTURE_TYPE_PIPELINE_SHADER_STAGE_CREATE_

shaderStages[0].stage = VK_SHADER_STAGE_VERTEX_BIT; // *Vertex shader stage*

shaderStages[0].module = vertexShaderModule; // *Shader module created earlier*

shaderStages[0].pName = "main"; // *Entry point function name*

shaderStages[1].sType   = VK_STRUCTURE_TYPE_PIPELINE_SHADER_STAGE_CREATE_

shaderStages[1].stage   = VK_SHADER_STAGE_FRAGMENT_BIT; // *Fragment shader stage*

shaderStages[1].module = fragmentShaderModule; // *Shader module created earlier* shaderStages[1].pName = "main"; // *Entry point function name*

VkPipelineCreateInfo pipelineInfo{};

pipelineInfo.stageCount = 2; // *Number of shader stages*

pipelineInfo.pStages = shaderStages;

// *Other pipeline creation settings...*

In this example, we bind a vertex shader and a fragment shader to the pipeline. The pName field specifies the entry point function in the shader module.

Shader Specialization Constants:

Vulkan allows you to specialize shaders at pipeline creation time using specialization constants. Specialization constants are compile-time constants that can be used to optimize shaders for specific cases. You define specialization constants in the shader code and set their values when creating a graphics pipeline.

Binding Data to Shaders:

Data, such as uniform buffers, textures, and push constants, must be bound to shaders for rendering. Vulkan provides the following mechanisms for binding data:

Descriptor Sets:

Descriptor sets are a way to bundle resources like uniform buffers, texture samplers, and storage buffers and make them accessible to shaders. Descriptor set layouts define the binding points and types of resources within a set.

VkDescriptorSetLayoutBinding uboLayoutBinding{};

uboLayoutBinding.binding = 0; // *Binding point in the shader*

uboLayoutBinding.descriptorType   =
VK_DESCRIPTOR_TYPE_UNIFORM_BUFFER;

uboLayoutBinding.descriptorCount = 1;

uboLayoutBinding.stageFlags   =
VK_SHADER_STAGE_VERTEX_BIT; // *Shader stage*

In this example, we define a descriptor set layout binding for a uniform buffer that is accessible to the vertex shader.

Push Constants:

Push constants are a way to pass small amounts of data directly to shaders without the need for descriptor sets. Push constants are part of the graphics pipeline state and can be updated dynamically.

VkPushConstantRange pushConstantRange{};

pushConstantRange.stageFlags   =
VK_SHADER_STAGE_VERTEX_BIT; // *Shader stage*

pushConstantRange.offset = 0;

pushConstantRange.size = **sizeof**(PushConstants); // *Size of the data*

In this example, we specify a push constant range for the vertex shader. The PushConstants structure defines the data that will be passed to the shader.

Data Binding and Pipeline Layout:

To bind data to shaders, you need to create a pipeline layout that specifies the sets of descriptor set layouts and push constant ranges used by the pipeline.

```
VkPipelineLayoutCreateInfo pipelineLayoutInfo{};

pipelineLayoutInfo.sType                                         =
VK_STRUCTURE_TYPE_PIPELINE_LAYOUT_CREATE_INF

pipelineLayoutInfo.setLayoutCount = 1; // Number of descriptor set
layouts

pipelineLayoutInfo.pSetLayouts = &descriptorSetLayout;

pipelineLayoutInfo.pushConstantRangeCount = 1; // Number of
push constant ranges

pipelineLayoutInfo.pPushConstantRanges                          =
&pushConstantRange;

if (vkCreatePipelineLayout(device, &pipelineLayoutInfo, nullptr,
&pipelineLayout) != VK_SUCCESS) {

throw std::runtime_error("Failed to create pipeline layout!");

}
```

In this code, we create a pipeline layout that specifies one descriptor set layout and one push constant range. This layout is used when creating the graphics pipeline.

Summary:

Binding shaders and data is a crucial aspect of Vulkan graphics programming. Shaders are bound to a pipeline using

VkPipelineShaderStageCreateInfo, and data is passed to shaders through descriptor sets and push constants. Understanding how to connect shaders and data to the graphics pipeline is essential for creating efficient and powerful Vulkan applications.

Chapter 8: Buffers and Memory Management

Section 8.1: Buffer Objects in Vulkan

Buffers in Vulkan are essential for managing and transferring data between the CPU and GPU. They provide a way to store various types of data, such as vertex data, uniform data, and storage data, in a structured format. In this section, we will delve into the basics of buffer objects in Vulkan and how they are used to handle data.

Buffer Types:

Vulkan defines several types of buffers, each designed for a specific purpose:

1. **Vertex Buffer**: Used to store vertex data, which includes information about the position, color, texture coordinates, and other attributes of vertices in a 3D model.
2. **Index Buffer**: Contains indices that specify the order in which vertices are used to form triangles or other primitives. Index buffers are used to reduce the amount of data transferred and stored for complex models.
3. **Uniform Buffer**: Designed for storing uniform data that is constant for a given draw call, such as transformation matrices, lighting information, or other data shared across multiple vertices or fragments.
4. **Storage Buffer**: Used for storing general-purpose data that can be read and written by shaders. Storage buffers are often used for implementing custom data structures and for efficient data sharing between multiple shader invocations.

5. **Transfer Buffer**: These are temporary buffers used for data transfer between the CPU and GPU. They are not typically used for rendering but are crucial for uploading data to GPU-accessible memory.

Buffer Creation:

Creating a buffer in Vulkan involves the following steps:

1. **Buffer Creation**: You start by creating a VkBuffer object, which represents the buffer. This object doesn't hold the actual data but serves as a handle to the buffer.

VkBufferCreateInfo bufferInfo{};

bufferInfo.sType   = VK_STRUCTURE_TYPE_BUFFER_CREATE_INFO;

bufferInfo.size = bufferSize; // *Size of the buffer in bytes*

bufferInfo.usage = usageFlags; // *How the buffer will be used (e.g., VK_BUFFER_USAGE_VERTEX_BUFFER_BIT)*

bufferInfo.sharingMode   = VK_SHARING_MODE_EXCLUSIVE;   // *Sharing   mode (exclusive or concurrent)*

1. **Allocate Memory**: After creating the buffer, you need to allocate memory for it. Vulkan separates the creation of buffers from memory allocation to give you more control over memory management.

VkMemoryRequirements memRequirements;

```
vkGetBufferMemoryRequirements(device, buffer,
&memRequirements);

VkMemoryAllocateInfo allocInfo{};

allocInfo.sType =
VK_STRUCTURE_TYPE_MEMORY_ALLOCATE_INFO;

allocInfo.allocationSize = memRequirements.size;

allocInfo.memoryTypeIndex =
findMemoryType(memRequirements.memoryTypeBits,
VK_MEMORY_PROPERTY_HOST_VISIBLE_BIT |
VK_MEMORY_PROPERTY_HOST_COHERENT_BIT);

if (vkAllocateMemory(device, &allocInfo, nullptr,
&bufferMemory) != VK_SUCCESS) {

throw std::runtime_error("Failed to allocate buffer memory!");

}

vkBindBufferMemory(device, buffer, bufferMemory, 0);
```

In the code above, findMemoryType is a function that helps you choose the appropriate memory type for the buffer, based on the memory requirements.

Buffer Usage and Memory Properties:

When creating a buffer, you need to specify how the buffer will be used through the usage parameter. Vulkan provides various buffer usage flags, such as VK_BUFFER_USAGE_VERTEX_BUFFER_BIT, VK_BUFFER_USAGE_UNIFORM_BUFFER_BIT, and

VK_BUFFER_USAGE_STORAGE_BUFFER_BIT, among others.

Additionally, you should specify the desired memory properties using the VK_MEMORY_PROPERTY_XXX_BIT flags when choosing the memory type for the buffer allocation. Memory properties define characteristics like whether the memory is host-visible, host-coherent, device-local, and more.

Buffer Mapping:

To write data to a buffer, you often need to map it into the CPU's address space. Mapping allows you to access and modify the buffer's memory directly. Mapping a buffer looks like this:

void* data;

vkMapMemory(device, bufferMemory, 0, bufferSize, 0, &data);

// Now you can memcpy or otherwise write data to 'data'

vkUnmapMemory(device, bufferMemory);

Keep in mind that mapping a buffer can be an expensive operation, so it's generally better to minimize the number of mappings and perform bulk data transfers when possible.

Summary:

Buffer objects are a fundamental concept in Vulkan, enabling efficient data management and transfer between the CPU and GPU. They come in various types, each designed for specific use cases. Buffer creation involves defining the buffer's size, usage, and memory properties, while memory allocation and mapping allow you to work with the buffer's data. Understanding how to create and manage buffers is crucial for building Vulkan applications that efficiently handle large datasets and graphics rendering.

Section 8.2: Creating Buffers

In Vulkan, creating buffers involves a multi-step process that includes specifying buffer properties, allocating memory for the buffer, and binding it to the allocated memory. This section will guide you through the process of creating buffers in Vulkan.

Buffer Creation

1. **Buffer Properties**: To create a buffer, you first define its properties using a VkBufferCreateInfo structure. This includes specifying the size of the buffer in bytes, its intended usage (e.g., vertex data, uniform data), and sharing mode.

VkBufferCreateInfo bufferInfo{};

bufferInfo.sType   = VK_STRUCTURE_TYPE_BUFFER_CREATE_INFO;

bufferInfo.size = bufferSize; // *Size of the buffer in bytes*

bufferInfo.usage = usageFlags; // *How the buffer will be used* (e.g., *VK_BUFFER_USAGE_VERTEX_BUFFER_BIT*)

bufferInfo.sharingMode   = VK_SHARING_MODE_EXCLUSIVE; // *Sharing mode (exclusive or concurrent)*

1. **Create the Buffer**: With the buffer properties defined, you

create the buffer using vkCreateBuffer.

```
VkBuffer buffer;

if (vkCreateBuffer(device, &bufferInfo, nullptr, &buffer)
!= VK_SUCCESS) {

throw std::runtime_error("Failed to create buffer!");

}
```

1. **Allocate Memory**: Buffers in Vulkan are separate from memory. You need to allocate memory for the buffer and bind it. First, determine the memory requirements for the buffer using vkGetBufferMemoryRequirements.

```
VkMemoryRequirements memRequirements;

vkGetBufferMemoryRequirements(device,        buffer,
&memRequirements);
```

1. **Choose Memory Type**: Next, choose a suitable memory type based on the memory requirements and your application's needs. This involves querying the available memory types and their properties.

```
VkMemoryAllocateInfo allocInfo{};

allocInfo.sType                                     =
VK_STRUCTURE_TYPE_MEMORY_ALLOCATE_INFO;

allocInfo.allocationSize = memRequirements.size;

allocInfo.memoryTypeIndex                           =
findMemoryType(memRequirements.memoryTypeBits,
```

VK_MEMORY_PROPERTY_HOST_VISIBLE_BIT
|
VK_MEMORY_PROPERTY_HOST_COHERENT_BIT);

Here, findMemoryType is a function that selects an appropriate memory type based on the requirements.

1. **Allocate and Bind Memory**: Finally, allocate memory and bind it to the buffer.

VkDeviceMemory bufferMemory;

if (vkAllocateMemory(device, &allocInfo, nullptr, &bufferMemory) != VK_SUCCESS) {

throw std::runtime_error("Failed to allocate buffer memory!");

}

vkBindBufferMemory(device, buffer, bufferMemory, 0);

Buffer Mapping

After creating a buffer, you may need to map it into CPU address space to read or write data. Mapping a buffer provides a pointer to the memory region of the buffer, which you can manipulate.

void* data;

vkMapMemory(device, bufferMemory, 0, bufferSize, 0, &data);

// Now you can access 'data' and perform data operations

vkUnmapMemory(device, bufferMemory);

Remember to unmap the buffer once you're done to ensure proper synchronization.

Buffer Destruction

Don't forget to destroy buffers and free associated memory when they are no longer needed to avoid resource leaks.

vkDestroyBuffer(device, buffer, nullptr);

vkFreeMemory(device, bufferMemory, nullptr);

Summary

Creating buffers in Vulkan involves defining their properties, allocating memory, and binding the buffer to the allocated memory. Buffers are fundamental for storing various types of data used in Vulkan applications, such as vertex data and uniform data. Understanding the buffer creation process is crucial for efficient data management in Vulkan graphics programming.

Section 8.3: Memory Allocation in Vulkan

In Vulkan, memory management is explicit and highly configurable, allowing developers to optimize memory allocation for their specific use cases. This section explores memory allocation in Vulkan and how to efficiently allocate memory for buffers and other resources.

Vulkan Memory Heaps and Memory Types

Vulkan-capable devices typically expose multiple memory heaps and memory types. Each memory heap represents a different pool of memory with its characteristics, such as size and allocation behavior. Memory types, on the other hand, are specific configurations of memory heaps with particular properties like host visibility, device local, and coherency.

To allocate memory efficiently, you need to choose the appropriate memory type that matches your resource's requirements. Vulkan provides a mechanism to query available memory types and their properties using vkGetPhysicalDeviceMemoryProperties.

VkPhysicalDeviceMemoryProperties memProperties;

vkGetPhysicalDeviceMemoryProperties(physicalDevice, &memProperties);

This function populates memProperties with information about the available memory types and memory heaps.

Memory Allocation with Vulkan Memory Allocator

While Vulkan offers fine-grained control over memory management, manually handling memory allocation and deallocation can be complex. Vulkan Memory Allocator (VMA) is a popular third-party library that simplifies memory management in Vulkan.

To use VMA, you'll need to integrate it into your project and follow these basic steps:

1. Initialize VMA with Vulkan device and physical device information.

VmaAllocator allocator;

VmaAllocatorCreateInfo allocatorInfo = {};

allocatorInfo.physicalDevice = physicalDevice;

```
allocatorInfo.device = device;
```

```
vmaCreateAllocator(&allocatorInfo, &allocator);
```

1. Allocate Memory Using VMA: Instead of manually allocating memory, you can use VMA functions like vmaCreateBuffer to allocate memory for buffers.

```
VkBufferCreateInfo bufferInfo = { ... };
```

```
VmaAllocationCreateInfo allocInfo = { ... };
```

```
VkBuffer buffer;
```

```
VmaAllocation allocation;
```

```
vmaCreateBuffer(allocator,    &bufferInfo,    &allocInfo,
&buffer, &allocation, nullptr);
```

1. Use the Allocated Memory: You can now use the buffer as you normally would, and VMA takes care of the memory management.
2. Free Allocated Memory: When you're done with a resource, don't forget to free the allocated memory using VMA functions.

```
vmaDestroyBuffer(allocator, buffer, allocation);
```

Memory Properties and Allocation Strategies

When allocating memory with VMA, you can specify allocation properties and strategies to optimize memory usage. These properties include:

- **Memory Usage**: You can specify whether the memory is intended for the GPU, CPU, or both.

- **Preferred Memory Type**: You can request a specific memory type or let VMA choose the most suitable one.

- **Allocation Strategy**: VMA offers different allocation strategies, such as VMA_MEMORY_USAGE_GPU_ONLY for GPU-exclusive memory and VMA_MEMORY_USAGE_CPU_ONLY for CPU-exclusive memory.

Summary

Memory allocation in Vulkan can be a complex process due to the explicit control it offers. Vulkan Memory Allocator (VMA) simplifies this process by providing an easy-to-use API for allocating and managing memory efficiently. Understanding the available memory types, memory heaps, and the specific requirements of your resources is essential for optimizing memory usage in Vulkan applications. VMA is a valuable tool to simplify memory management and reduce the complexity of Vulkan memory allocation.

Section 8.4: Mapping Buffers

In Vulkan, mapping a buffer means making its memory region accessible to the CPU so that you can read from or write to it directly. This section explores how to map buffers in Vulkan, perform data operations, and unmap them when you're finished.

Why Map Buffers?

Mapping buffers is essential when you need to transfer data between the CPU and GPU or perform CPU-side operations on buffer data. Common scenarios include:

- Updating vertex data for rendering.

- Modifying uniform buffer contents.

- Uploading texture data to the GPU.

Mapping a Buffer

To map a buffer in Vulkan, you typically use the vkMapMemory function. Here's a step-by-step guide on how to do it:

1. **Determine the Memory Range**: You should specify the range of the buffer memory you want to map. To map the entire buffer, you can set the offset to 0 and the size to the buffer's size.

VkDeviceSize bufferSize = ...; // *Size of the buffer in bytes*

VkDeviceMemory bufferMemory = ...; // *Memory associated with the buffer*

void* data;

vkMapMemory(device, bufferMemory, 0, bufferSize, 0, &data);

1. **Perform Data Operations**: Once mapped, the data pointer points to the memory region of the buffer. You can read or modify the data as needed.

// Example: Copying data to the mapped memory

memcpy(data, yourData, dataSize);

// Example: Modifying data

((uint32_t*)data)[0] = newValue;

1. **Unmap the Buffer**: After you're done with the mapped buffer, unmap it to ensure proper synchronization.

vkUnmapMemory(device, bufferMemory);

Memory Properties and CPU Access

It's important to consider the memory properties of the buffer when mapping it. Vulkan provides different memory types, some of which are suitable for CPU access, while others are optimized for GPU access. When creating a buffer, make sure to choose the appropriate memory type based on your usage.

Synchronization

Mapping and unmapping a buffer involves synchronization with the GPU. You must ensure that the GPU is not accessing the buffer while it is mapped by the CPU. Synchronization mechanisms like semaphores, fences, and pipeline barriers are used to coordinate these actions. Always follow proper synchronization practices to avoid data corruption or access conflicts.

Summary

Mapping buffers in Vulkan allows for efficient data transfer and manipulation between the CPU and GPU. It is a crucial step when working with buffers that need to be updated or read by both CPU and GPU. Understanding memory properties, synchronization, and choosing the right memory type for your use case are key aspects of effective buffer mapping in Vulkan.

Section 8.5: Managing Buffer Data

Managing buffer data efficiently is crucial in Vulkan applications to ensure optimal performance and resource utilization. In this section, we'll explore techniques and best practices for managing buffer data effectively.

Buffer Data Lifecycle

Understanding the lifecycle of buffer data is essential. It typically involves the following stages:

1. **Initialization**: Allocate memory and create buffers.
2. **Data Upload**: Populate buffers with initial data, if required.
3. **Runtime Usage**: Use the buffers for rendering or other tasks.
4. **Data Updates**: Periodically update or modify buffer data.
5. **Cleanup**: Destroy buffers and deallocate memory when no longer needed.

Memory Management

Proper memory management is essential to avoid memory leaks and ensure efficient resource utilization. Vulkan allows for explicit memory allocation and deallocation. You should allocate memory for buffers based on their usage patterns (e.g., GPU-only, CPU-visible, or both).

Using memory allocation libraries like Vulkan Memory Allocator (VMA) simplifies memory management and reduces the risk of memory-related issues. VMA provides easy-to-use functions for allocating and deallocating memory for Vulkan objects.

Buffer Pools

To improve memory allocation efficiency, consider using buffer pools. Buffer pools preallocate a set of buffers and reuse them when needed. This reduces the overhead of frequently creating and destroying buffers, which can be expensive. You can implement your custom buffer pool or use third-party libraries that offer buffer pool functionality.

Resource Management

Managing resources efficiently is crucial for Vulkan applications. Resources such as buffers should be created and destroyed as needed to minimize memory usage. Implement resource tracking and clean-up mechanisms to ensure that resources are released when they are no longer in use.

Resource Validation

Validation layers and debugging tools in Vulkan are valuable for detecting resource management issues. They can help identify memory leaks, invalid buffer operations, or other problems early in development. Regularly run your application with validation layers enabled to catch and fix issues.

Data Streaming

In scenarios where data is frequently updated, like dynamic vertex data or streaming textures, consider using techniques like double buffering or circular buffers. These techniques involve preparing data in one buffer while rendering from another, minimizing synchronization overhead and improving performance.

Multithreading

Multithreading can be beneficial for managing buffer data efficiently. You can use separate threads for loading, updating, and rendering data. Be cautious about synchronization and data access to avoid race conditions.

Summary

Managing buffer data effectively in Vulkan applications involves careful memory management, resource tracking, and validation. Properly allocate memory based on usage patterns, consider buffer pools for efficient reuse, and implement resource cleanup mechanisms. Use validation layers to catch resource-related issues early, and consider techniques like data streaming and multithreading to optimize buffer data management for performance-critical scenarios.

Chapter 9: Textures and Image Views

Section 9.1: Working with Textures

Textures play a vital role in computer graphics and are used for various purposes, including surface appearance, environment mapping, and post-processing effects. In Vulkan, textures are represented as images, and they are essential for creating realistic and visually appealing 3D graphics. This section explores the fundamentals of working with textures in Vulkan.

What Are Textures?

Textures, in the context of computer graphics, are 2D or 3D images that are applied to surfaces or used in various rendering techniques. They provide the visual details and properties of surfaces in a scene, such as color, roughness, reflectivity, and more. Textures are an integral part of creating realistic and immersive graphics in games and simulations.

In Vulkan, textures are represented as images, which are essentially 2D arrays of pixels. These images can be used as color attachments, depth-stencil attachments, or sampled in shaders to apply textures to objects. Vulkan allows you to create and manage these images efficiently.

Types of Textures

There are several types of textures commonly used in computer graphics:

1. **2D Textures**: These are standard 2D images used for various purposes, such as applying a texture to a 3D

model's surface.

2. **Cube Maps**: Cube maps are used for simulating reflections and environment mapping. They consist of six 2D textures arranged as faces of a cube.

3. **3D Textures**: These textures have a depth component and are used for volumetric effects and simulations.

4. **Array Textures**: Array textures are collections of 2D or 3D textures that can be indexed or sampled as a single texture.

5. **Mipmaps**: Mipmaps are precomputed lower-resolution versions of a texture used to improve rendering performance and reduce aliasing artifacts.

Texture Formats

Texture data can be stored in various formats, including:

• **RGBA8888**: This format stores color information using red, green, blue, and alpha channels, each with 8 bits per channel.

• **BC (Block Compression)** formats: These formats use block compression to store textures efficiently, reducing memory usage.

• **Depth and Stencil formats**: These formats are used for depth and stencil buffers and are crucial for rendering realistic scenes.

Texture Loading

To use textures in Vulkan, you typically load texture data from image files, such as PNG or JPEG, into Vulkan images. Libraries like STB Image or third-party libraries can help with image loading. Once loaded, you create Vulkan images and image views to represent the textures in your application.

Summary

Textures are essential for creating visually appealing graphics in Vulkan applications. They provide details and properties to surfaces and objects, enhancing realism and immersion. Understanding the types of textures, texture formats, and the process of loading textures into Vulkan images is crucial for building sophisticated graphics applications. In the following sections, we will delve deeper into creating Vulkan images and working with them to achieve various rendering effects.

Section 9.2: Creating Vulkan Images

In Vulkan, images represent textures and other data used in rendering. Creating Vulkan images is a fundamental step when working with textures. This section explores how to create Vulkan images efficiently and configure them for different use cases.

Image Basics

Vulkan images are 2D arrays of pixels, but they can also be used to represent 1D and 3D textures. Images can have different formats, which define how pixel data is stored, including color formats and compressed formats. They can also have usage flags, indicating how the image will be used (e.g., as a color attachment, a depth-stencil attachment, or a sampled image in shaders).

Image Views

To use Vulkan images, you often need to create image views. An image view is a specific representation of an image that provides information about how the image should be interpreted in shaders or as a framebuffer attachment. Image views allow you to use images for different purposes without modifying the underlying image data.

Creating Vulkan Images

To create a Vulkan image, you need to perform the following steps:

1. **Image Creation**: Define the image's format, usage flags, extent (width, height, depth), and other parameters using a VkImageCreateInfo structure. You also specify the number of mip levels and array layers.

```
VkImageCreateInfo imageInfo = {};

imageInfo.sType                         =
VK_STRUCTURE_TYPE_IMAGE_CREATE_INFO;

imageInfo.imageType = VK_IMAGE_TYPE_2D;

imageInfo.extent.width = ...;

imageInfo.extent.height = ...;

imageInfo.extent.depth = ...;

imageInfo.mipLevels = ...;

imageInfo.arrayLayers = ...;

imageInfo.format                        =
VK_FORMAT_R8G8B8A8_UNORM;

imageInfo.tiling = VK_IMAGE_TILING_OPTIMAL;
```

```
imageInfo.usage                              =
VK_IMAGE_USAGE_TRANSFER_SRC_BIT         |
VK_IMAGE_USAGE_TRANSFER_DST_BIT         |
VK_IMAGE_USAGE_SAMPLED_BIT;

imageInfo.samples = VK_SAMPLE_COUNT_1_BIT;

imageInfo.sharingMode                        =
VK_SHARING_MODE_EXCLUSIVE;
```

1. **Allocate Memory**: Allocate memory for the image using the Vulkan memory allocation functions (vkAllocateMemory). The memory allocation depends on the image's requirements, such as its size and usage.
2. **Bind Memory**: Bind the allocated memory to the image using vkBindImageMemory.

```
VkDeviceMemory imageMemory;

vkAllocateMemory(device,     &memoryInfo,    nullptr,
&imageMemory);

vkBindImageMemory(device, image, imageMemory, 0);
```

1. **Creating Image Views**: To use the image in shaders or as a framebuffer attachment, you need to create an image view.

```
VkImageViewCreateInfo viewInfo = {};

viewInfo.sType                               =
VK_STRUCTURE_TYPE_IMAGE_VIEW_CREATE_INFO

viewInfo.image = image;

viewInfo.viewType = VK_IMAGE_VIEW_TYPE_2D;
```

```
viewInfo.format = imageInfo.format;

viewInfo.subresourceRange.aspectMask          =
VK_IMAGE_ASPECT_COLOR_BIT;

viewInfo.subresourceRange.baseMipLevel = 0;

viewInfo.subresourceRange.levelCount          =
imageInfo.mipLevels;

viewInfo.subresourceRange.baseArrayLayer = 0;

viewInfo.subresourceRange.layerCount          =
imageInfo.arrayLayers;

VkImageView imageView;

if (vkCreateImageView(device,   &viewInfo,   nullptr,
&imageView) != VK_SUCCESS) {

// Error handling

}
```

Transitioning Image Layouts

Images in Vulkan have different layouts for different operations (e.g., transfer, shader read, shader write). Before using an image for a specific operation, you may need to transition its layout using image barriers. Image layout transitions are essential for synchronization and resource access.

Summary

Creating Vulkan images is a crucial step when working with textures and other data in Vulkan applications. Understanding image formats, usage flags, and the image creation process is essential for efficient rendering. Additionally, creating image views and managing image memory are vital for using images in shaders and as framebuffer attachments. In the following sections, we will explore working with Vulkan images in more detail, including texture mapping and sampling.

Section 9.3: Image Views and Samplers

In Vulkan, images alone are not enough to use textures in shaders or as framebuffer attachments. You also need to create image views and samplers to facilitate texture sampling and rendering. This section delves into image views and samplers, which are essential components when working with textures in Vulkan.

Image Views

An image view is a way to interpret an image in different ways without altering its data. It specifies how the image should be accessed in shaders or as a framebuffer attachment. Image views are crucial because they allow you to use the same image for different purposes within your Vulkan application.

To create an image view, you need to specify the following:

- The image to be viewed.

- The format of the image.

- The aspect of the image (color, depth, stencil, etc.).

- The mipmap level range and array layer range.

Here's an example of creating an image view in Vulkan:

```
VkImageViewCreateInfo viewInfo = {};

viewInfo.sType                                        =
VK_STRUCTURE_TYPE_IMAGE_VIEW_CREATE_INFO;

viewInfo.image = image; // The Vulkan image you want to create a
view for

viewInfo.viewType = VK_IMAGE_VIEW_TYPE_2D; // Specify
the type of view

viewInfo.format = imageFormat; // The format of the image

viewInfo.subresourceRange.aspectMask                  =
VK_IMAGE_ASPECT_COLOR_BIT; // Specify the aspect of the
image

viewInfo.subresourceRange.baseMipLevel = 0; // The base mip level

viewInfo.subresourceRange.levelCount = mipLevels; // The number
of mip levels

viewInfo.subresourceRange.baseArrayLayer = 0; // The base array
layer

viewInfo.subresourceRange.layerCount = 1; // The number of array
layers

VkImageView imageView;

if (vkCreateImageView(device, &viewInfo, nullptr, &imageView) !=
VK_SUCCESS) {
```

```
// Error handling

}
```

Samplers

A sampler is an object in Vulkan that defines how textures are sampled in shaders. It controls filtering, addressing modes, and other properties when accessing texture data. Samplers allow you to control how textures are interpolated when sampled at various points within a fragment.

Here's an example of creating a sampler in Vulkan:

```
VkSamplerCreateInfo samplerInfo = {};

samplerInfo.sType                               =
VK_STRUCTURE_TYPE_SAMPLER_CREATE_INFO;

samplerInfo.magFilter = VK_FILTER_LINEAR; // Magnification filter

samplerInfo.minFilter = VK_FILTER_LINEAR; // Minification filter

samplerInfo.addressModeU                        =
VK_SAMPLER_ADDRESS_MODE_REPEAT;    //    U-axis
wrapping mode

samplerInfo.addressModeV                        =
VK_SAMPLER_ADDRESS_MODE_REPEAT;    //    V-axis
wrapping mode

samplerInfo.addressModeW                        =
VK_SAMPLER_ADDRESS_MODE_REPEAT;    //    W-axis
wrapping mode
```

```
samplerInfo.anisotropyEnable = VK_FALSE; // Anisotropic filtering

samplerInfo.maxAnisotropy = 1.0f; // Anisotropy level (if enabled)

samplerInfo.borderColor =
VK_BORDER_COLOR_INT_OPAQUE_BLACK; // Border
color

samplerInfo.unnormalizedCoordinates = VK_FALSE; //
Coordinates are normalized

samplerInfo.compareEnable = VK_FALSE; // Depth comparison (if
enabled)

samplerInfo.compareOp = VK_COMPARE_OP_ALWAYS; //
Comparison operation (if enabled)

samplerInfo.mipmapMode =
VK_SAMPLER_MIPMAP_MODE_LINEAR; // Mipmap
interpolation mode

samplerInfo.mipLodBias = 0.0f; // Level of detail bias

samplerInfo.minLod = 0.0f; // Minimum level of detail

samplerInfo.maxLod = static_cast<float>(mipLevels); // Maximum
level of detail

VkSampler textureSampler;

if (vkCreateSampler(device, &samplerInfo, nullptr,
&textureSampler) != VK_SUCCESS) {

// Error handling

}
```

Using Image Views and Samplers

To use image views and samplers in shaders, you bind them to descriptor sets and update your shaders to sample from the specified textures using the sampler. Image views and samplers provide the necessary abstraction to work with textures efficiently in Vulkan shaders.

In summary, image views and samplers are essential components when working with textures in Vulkan. Image views define how an image is accessed, and samplers control how texture data is sampled in shaders. Understanding how to create and use image views and samplers is crucial for texture mapping and rendering in Vulkan applications.

Section 9.4: Loading Textures

Loading textures is a fundamental part of graphics programming in Vulkan. Textures can be used to add realistic details and visual richness to 3D scenes. In this section, we'll explore how to load textures in Vulkan and prepare them for use in your rendering pipeline.

Texture Loading Libraries

Before diving into the Vulkan-specific details, it's essential to mention that Vulkan doesn't provide built-in functionality for loading image files like JPEG, PNG, or BMP. You'll need to rely on external libraries to load image files and create Vulkan-compatible textures. Popular libraries for this purpose include:

1. **STB Image**: This lightweight C library is commonly used to load various image formats. It's simple to integrate and well-suited for small projects.

2. **FreeImage**: FreeImage is a more extensive library that supports a wide range of image formats. It provides a higher level of abstraction and additional features for image manipulation.

3. **DevIL (Developer's Image Library)**: DevIL is another option that offers support for various image formats. It's known for its ease of use and flexibility.

Loading Textures with STB Image

Here, we'll briefly demonstrate how to load textures using the STB Image library, assuming you have a basic image loading function. We'll focus on preparing the Vulkan texture object.

```
// Load the image using STB Image

int texWidth, texHeight, texChannels;

stbi_uc* pixels = stbi_load("texture.jpg", &texWidth, &texHeight, &texChannels, STBI_rgb_alpha);

if (!pixels) {

// Handle texture loading error

}

// Create a Vulkan image and allocate memory

VkImage textureImage;

VkDeviceMemory textureImageMemory;

createImage(texWidth,                              texHeight,
VK_FORMAT_R8G8B8A8_SRGB,
VK_IMAGE_TILING_OPTIMAL,
VK_IMAGE_USAGE_TRANSFER_DST_BIT
```

```
VK_IMAGE_USAGE_SAMPLED_BIT,
VK_MEMORY_PROPERTY_DEVICE_LOCAL_BIT,
textureImage, textureImageMemory);
```

// Copy the loaded image data to the Vulkan image

```
transitionImageLayout(textureImage,
VK_FORMAT_R8G8B8A8_SRGB,
VK_IMAGE_LAYOUT_UNDEFINED,
VK_IMAGE_LAYOUT_TRANSFER_DST_OPTIMAL);
```

```
copyBufferToImage(pixels, texWidth, texHeight, textureImage);
```

```
transitionImageLayout(textureImage,
VK_FORMAT_R8G8B8A8_SRGB,
VK_IMAGE_LAYOUT_TRANSFER_DST_OPTIMAL,
VK_IMAGE_LAYOUT_SHADER_READ_ONLY_OPTIMAL);
```

// Clean up the STB Image data

```
stbi_image_free(pixels);
```

In the code snippet above, we load an image using STB Image, create a Vulkan image, copy the image data to the Vulkan image, and transition its layout to be ready for shader access.

Texture Coordinates

Once you have loaded a texture, you'll use texture coordinates in your vertex data to map the texture onto 3D objects correctly. Texture coordinates, often referred to as UV coordinates, specify how a texture is applied to a 3D model's surface. These coordinates are typically defined in the range [0, 1] and map to the corresponding points on the texture image.

Shader Binding

To use the loaded texture in shaders, you'll need to bind the texture image view and sampler to descriptor sets and update your shaders to sample from the texture using the sampler. This process is discussed in detail in later sections of this book.

In summary, loading textures in Vulkan involves using external libraries like STB Image to load image data, creating Vulkan images to store the texture, and properly transitioning the image layout for shader access. Texture coordinates are essential for correctly mapping textures to 3D objects, and shaders need to be updated to use the loaded textures via image views and samplers.

Section 9.5: Texture Mapping

Texture mapping is a fundamental technique in computer graphics used to apply textures to 3D objects, enhancing their visual realism. In this section, we'll delve into the details of texture mapping in Vulkan and how to achieve realistic surface appearances in your rendered scenes.

Mapping Textures to Geometry

Texture mapping involves mapping a 2D image, known as a texture, onto the surface of a 3D object. To achieve this, each vertex of the 3D object is associated with a set of 2D texture coordinates, often referred to as UV coordinates. These UV coordinates define how the texture is wrapped around the 3D geometry.

In Vulkan, you'll pass UV coordinates from your vertex data to the fragment shader. Inside the fragment shader, you can sample the texture using these UV coordinates to determine the color of each fragment (pixel) on the 3D surface. The result is a textured appearance on the object.

Texture Coordinates

Texture coordinates are defined in the UV coordinate space, which ranges from $(0, 0)$ to $(1, 1)$ for the entire texture. A UV coordinate of $(0, 0)$ corresponds to the bottom-left corner of the texture, while $(1, 1)$ corresponds to the top-right corner. Intermediate values represent positions within the texture.

Here's an example of UV coordinates for a square that spans the entire texture:

- Bottom-left corner: $(0, 0)$

- Bottom-right corner: $(1, 0)$

- Top-left corner: $(0, 1)$

- Top-right corner: $(1, 1)$

Wrapping Modes

Vulkan allows you to configure how UV coordinates outside the $[0, 1]$ range are handled. There are different wrapping modes you can choose from:

1. **Repeat**: UV coordinates outside $[0, 1]$ are wrapped back into the range, effectively creating a repeating pattern.
2. **Mirrored Repeat**: Similar to "Repeat," but the pattern is flipped every time it repeats.
3. **Clamp to Edge**: UV coordinates outside $[0, 1]$ are clamped to the nearest edge of the texture.
4. **Clamp to Border**: UV coordinates outside $[0, 1]$ are

clamped to a border color you specify.

The choice of wrapping mode depends on the desired visual effect and the characteristics of the texture.

Filtering Modes

Filtering modes determine how texture samples are interpolated between pixels when the UV coordinates are not exact pixel centers. There are two common filtering modes:

1. **Nearest Neighbor**: This mode selects the nearest texel (texture pixel) to the sample point. It can produce a pixelated appearance.
2. **Linear**: Linear filtering performs weighted averaging of nearby texels, resulting in smoother transitions between pixels. It's suitable for most cases and provides a more visually appealing result.

Anisotropic Filtering

In addition to standard filtering modes, Vulkan supports anisotropic filtering, which enhances texture quality when textures are viewed at oblique angles. This technique provides better results for textures on surfaces at varying orientations.

To enable anisotropic filtering in Vulkan, you'll need to specify the desired level of anisotropy when creating your sampler.

In summary, texture mapping in Vulkan involves associating UV coordinates with vertices, passing these coordinates to the fragment shader, and using them to sample textures. You can control how UV coordinates outside [0, 1] are handled with wrapping modes and control the quality of texture sampling with filtering modes, including anisotropic filtering for improved visual quality. Texture mapping is a powerful tool for achieving realism in your Vulkan-rendered scenes.

Chapter 10: Basic Rendering Techniques

Section 10.1: Vertex Buffer and Index Buffer

In the realm of computer graphics and Vulkan, rendering complex 3D scenes involves various stages, with the most fundamental ones being the processing of vertex data and rendering the geometry. To achieve this, Vulkan uses vertex buffers and index buffers. In this section, we will explore what these buffers are, their roles in rendering, and how to use them effectively.

Vertex Data in Vulkan

Vertex data represents the attributes of a 3D object's vertices, such as position, color, texture coordinates, and normals. This data is crucial for defining the geometry and appearance of 3D objects in a scene. In Vulkan, you store this vertex data in a vertex buffer, which is essentially an array of vertices.

Creating a Vertex Buffer

Creating a vertex buffer involves several steps:

1. **Vertex Data Definition**: You must define the format and structure of your vertex data. This includes specifying the attributes like position, color, and texture coordinates.
2. **Allocate Memory**: Allocate memory on the GPU for your vertex buffer. This memory allocation is done using Vulkan's memory management functions.
3. **Transfer Data**: Copy the vertex data from your CPU to the GPU memory. This step is crucial for efficient

rendering.

4. **Binding**: Bind the vertex buffer to the graphics pipeline, indicating which attributes correspond to the vertex input variables in the vertex shader.

Index Buffers

While vertex buffers contain the attributes of vertices, index buffers help define the order in which vertices are connected to create primitives like triangles. Instead of specifying every vertex for each triangle in a complex mesh, you can reuse vertices by referring to them using indices. This reduces memory consumption and improves rendering efficiency.

Creating an Index Buffer

Creating an index buffer involves these key steps:

1. **Index Data Definition**: Define the indices that reference vertices in your vertex buffer to create triangles or other primitives.
2. **Allocate Memory**: Allocate GPU memory for your index buffer.
3. **Transfer Data**: Copy the index data from CPU to GPU memory.
4. **Binding**: Bind the index buffer, along with the vertex buffer, to the graphics pipeline. This tells Vulkan how to use the index data during rendering.

Efficient Rendering with Vertex and Index Buffers

Using vertex and index buffers efficiently is crucial for rendering performance. Vulkan provides several mechanisms to optimize this process:

- **Vertex and Index Buffer Management**: Vulkan allows you to create and manage multiple vertex and index buffers. This is useful when rendering complex scenes with many objects.

- **Dynamic Buffers**: Vulkan supports dynamic vertex and index buffers, which can be updated frequently for objects with changing geometry or appearance.

- **Buffer Memory Pools**: You can allocate memory from memory pools, which can be more efficient than individual memory allocations.

- **Memory Transfer Optimization**: Vulkan provides mechanisms like memory barriers and memory queues to optimize data transfers between CPU and GPU memory.

In summary, vertex buffers store vertex data, while index buffers define the order in which vertices are connected to create primitives. These buffers play a crucial role in rendering 3D scenes efficiently. Vulkan offers tools for managing and optimizing these buffers, allowing you to render complex and detailed scenes with high performance.

Section 10.2: Uniform Buffers and Push Constants

In the world of 3D graphics and Vulkan, achieving realism and interactivity often requires dynamically updating data during rendering. Uniform buffers and push constants are mechanisms in Vulkan that allow you to send such data to your shaders efficiently. In this section, we'll explore these two concepts in detail.

Uniform Buffers

Uniform buffers are a way to pass constant data to your shaders. These buffers typically contain information that remains constant for a frame but may change between frames. Common examples include transformation matrices, camera parameters, and material properties.

Creating a Uniform Buffer

Creating and using a uniform buffer involves the following steps:

1. **Define Data Structure**: Define a struct in your application code that matches the data you want to send to the shader. This struct will be mirrored in your shader code as a uniform block.
2. **Allocate Memory**: Allocate GPU memory for your uniform buffer. This memory is often managed by Vulkan's memory allocation functions.
3. **Update Data**: Update the data in your uniform buffer as needed. This might involve updating the transformation matrix for a moving object or changing the camera position.
4. **Binding**: Bind the uniform buffer to your shader. This

associates the buffer with a uniform block in your shader code.

Dynamic Uniform Buffers

For data that changes frequently, you can use dynamic uniform buffers. These are allocated from a memory pool and are designed for frequent updates. They are particularly useful for objects with animated transformations.

Push Constants

Push constants are a lightweight alternative to uniform buffers for small amounts of data that change frequently. They allow you to send a limited amount of data directly to a shader without the need for a buffer. Push constants are suitable for parameters like material properties or per-object data.

Declaring Push Constants

To use push constants, you declare a push constant block in your shader code. This block specifies the data structure and size of the push constants.

Updating Push Constants

Push constants are updated on a per-draw call basis. Before each draw call, you set the push constant values in your command buffer. This allows you to send different data for each draw call without the overhead of updating a buffer.

Choosing Between Uniform Buffers and Push Constants

The choice between uniform buffers and push constants depends on your specific use case:

- **Uniform Buffers**: Use uniform buffers when you need to send larger amounts of data that change infrequently or per frame. They are suitable for global scene data.

- **Push Constants**: Use push constants for small, frequently changing data, typically on a per-object or per-draw basis. They are more lightweight but have size limitations.

In summary, uniform buffers and push constants are essential tools for passing data to your shaders in Vulkan. Uniform buffers are suitable for larger, less frequently changing data, while push constants are ideal for small, frequently changing data. Choosing the right mechanism ensures efficient and flexible communication between your application code and shaders, enabling you to create dynamic and interactive 3D scenes.

Section 10.3: Descriptor Sets

In Vulkan, descriptor sets play a pivotal role in binding resources such as uniform buffers, textures, and samplers to your shaders. They provide a flexible way to manage and access resources within your rendering pipeline. This section delves into the details of descriptor sets and how they are used in Vulkan.

Descriptor Set Layouts

A descriptor set layout defines the structure and binding points for the resources that your shaders will access. Each descriptor set layout is associated with a specific shader stage (vertex, fragment, etc.) and reflects the expected types and locations of resources.

Creating Descriptor Set Layouts

Creating a descriptor set layout involves specifying the types of resources (uniform buffers, images, samplers, etc.) and their binding points in your shader code. Vulkan then maps these bindings to specific locations.

Descriptor Pools

Descriptor pools are responsible for allocating and managing descriptor sets. They define the maximum number of descriptor sets of each type that can be allocated from the pool.

Allocating Descriptor Sets

To allocate descriptor sets, you first create a descriptor pool, specifying the maximum number of sets you expect to allocate. Then, you request sets from this pool. Descriptor sets are typically allocated per frame or per object, depending on your rendering needs.

Updating Descriptor Sets

Once you have allocated a descriptor set, you can update it to bind specific resources, like uniform buffers, images, or samplers.

Descriptor Set Updates

Updating a descriptor set involves specifying the resources you want to bind to it. For example, you would update a descriptor set to bind a uniform buffer containing transformation data.

Binding Descriptor Sets

In your rendering pipeline, you must bind the descriptor sets to the appropriate shader stages before drawing.

Binding Descriptor Sets in the Pipeline

To bind descriptor sets, you specify which set to bind for each shader stage in your graphics pipeline. This linkage ensures that the resources are accessible when the shader code is executed.

Descriptor Set Layouts and Compatibility

Descriptor set layouts must be compatible with the pipeline layout used when creating the graphics pipeline. Compatibility ensures that the resources specified in the shader code match the ones bound to the descriptor sets.

Efficient Resource Management

Vulkan's use of descriptor sets offers flexibility and efficiency in resource management. You can allocate descriptor sets for different objects, scenes, or frames, and efficiently update them when needed. This fine-grained control allows you to optimize resource usage and achieve the best performance for your rendering tasks.

In summary, descriptor sets are a fundamental part of Vulkan's resource management and binding system. They enable efficient communication between your shaders and resources, allowing you to dynamically and flexibly bind uniform buffers, textures, and samplers. Properly configuring and managing descriptor sets is essential for achieving efficient and performant rendering in Vulkan.

Section 10.4: Basic Rendering Pipeline

The rendering pipeline in Vulkan is a sequence of stages and operations that transform vertex data into the final pixel colors on the screen. Understanding the basics of the rendering pipeline is crucial for creating visually appealing graphics in Vulkan. This section explores the key components and stages of the rendering pipeline.

Vertex Input

The first stage of the rendering pipeline is the Vertex Input stage. Here, you specify the format and layout of your vertex data. Vulkan allows you to define custom vertex attribute formats and bind them to vertex buffers. This flexibility is essential for accommodating various types of vertex data, such as positions, normals, and texture coordinates.

Vertex Shader

After the Vertex Input stage, vertex data is processed by the Vertex Shader. This shader is responsible for transforming vertex positions and performing other per-vertex calculations. It is a programmable stage, allowing you to implement custom transformations and lighting models.

Input Assembly

The Input Assembly stage assembles vertices into primitives, such as points, lines, or triangles, based on the specified primitive topology. This stage defines how vertices are connected to create geometry.

Tesselation

The Tesselation stage, if enabled, further subdivides primitives into smaller segments. This can be useful for adding detail to curved surfaces or dynamically adjusting the level of detail based on distance.

Geometry Shader

The Geometry Shader is an optional stage that operates on entire primitives. It allows you to generate additional vertices or primitives, making it suitable for tasks like procedural geometry generation or particle systems.

Vertex Post-processing

After the vertex processing stages, you can perform additional per-vertex calculations, such as transforming normals or calculating tangent vectors, in the Vertex Post-processing stage.

Primitive Assembly

The Primitive Assembly stage assembles primitives into larger structures, such as triangles into triangle strips or fans, ready for rasterization.

Rasterization

Rasterization is a critical stage where the 3D geometry is converted into 2D fragments or pixels on the screen. This process involves determining which pixels are covered by the primitive and interpolating attributes across those pixels.

Fragment Shader

The Fragment Shader operates on individual fragments generated during rasterization. It is responsible for calculating the final color of each fragment, applying lighting models, and texturing.

Color Blending

After fragment shading, Color Blending combines the fragment colors with the colors already in the framebuffer. This stage allows for various blending operations, such as alpha blending or additive blending.

Depth and Stencil Testing

Depth and Stencil Testing determine whether a fragment should be written to the framebuffer based on its depth and stencil values. These tests help achieve realistic rendering of overlapping objects and complex scenes.

Output Merger

The final stage, Output Merger, combines the fragment colors, depth, and stencil values into the framebuffer. This stage also includes operations like frame buffer attachments and resolve operations for multisampling.

Pipeline Configuration

Configuring the rendering pipeline involves specifying shader modules, pipeline layout, and rendering passes. Vulkan offers extensive control over pipeline configuration, allowing you to tailor it to your specific rendering needs.

Understanding the rendering pipeline in Vulkan is essential for creating efficient and visually stunning graphics. By comprehending each stage's role and customization options, you can develop graphics applications that leverage Vulkan's power and flexibility to the fullest extent.

Section 10.5: Rendering a Textured Triangle

In this section, we'll walk through the process of rendering a textured triangle using Vulkan. Textured rendering adds another layer of complexity to the rendering pipeline, as it involves loading and sampling textures. Let's break down the steps involved in rendering a textured triangle.

Vertex Data and Shaders

To render a textured triangle, you need vertex data that includes not only vertex positions but also texture coordinates. Texture coordinates specify how texture pixels map to vertices. You'll typically have a vertex buffer with positions and texture coordinates.

```
// Vertex data structure

struct Vertex {

glm::vec2 position; // Vertex position

glm::vec2 texCoord; // Texture coordinate
```

```
};
```

// *Vertex positions and texture coordinates*

```
Vertex vertices[] = {
```

```
{{-0.5f, -0.5f}, {0.0f, 0.0f}}, // Bottom-left
```

```
{{0.5f, -0.5f}, {1.0f, 0.0f}}, // Bottom-right
```

```
{{0.0f, 0.5f}, {0.5f, 1.0f}} // Top
```

```
};
```

Your vertex shader needs to accept both position and texture coordinates as inputs. It should pass the texture coordinates to the fragment shader.

Loading Textures

Before rendering with textures, you need to load image data into Vulkan images. You can use libraries like STB Image or Vulkan-specific libraries like Khronos' KTX for texture loading. Once loaded, create a Vulkan image and copy the image data into it.

// *Load texture using STB Image*

```
int texWidth, texHeight, texChannels;
```

```
stbi_uc* pixels = stbi_load("texture.jpg", &texWidth, &texHeight, &texChannels, STBI_rgb_alpha);
```

// *Create Vulkan image and image view*

```
VkImage textureImage;
```

```
VkImageView textureImageView;
```

CreateTextureImage(pixels, texWidth, texHeight, textureImage, textureImageView);

// Clean up STB Image data

stbi_image_free(pixels);

Texture Sampler

To sample textures in the fragment shader, you need a texture sampler. Create a sampler object to control how textures are sampled, including filtering and addressing modes.

// Create texture sampler

VkSampler textureSampler;

VkSamplerCreateInfo samplerInfo = {};

samplerInfo.sType = VK_STRUCTURE_TYPE_SAMPLER_CREATE_INFO;

samplerInfo.magFilter = VK_FILTER_LINEAR;

samplerInfo.minFilter = VK_FILTER_LINEAR;

samplerInfo.addressModeU = VK_SAMPLER_ADDRESS_MODE_REPEAT;

samplerInfo.addressModeV = VK_SAMPLER_ADDRESS_MODE_REPEAT;

samplerInfo.addressModeW = VK_SAMPLER_ADDRESS_MODE_REPEAT;

samplerInfo.anisotropyEnable = VK_TRUE;

samplerInfo.maxAnisotropy = 16;

samplerInfo.borderColor   =
VK_BORDER_COLOR_INT_OPAQUE_BLACK;

samplerInfo.unnormalizedCoordinates = VK_FALSE;

samplerInfo.compareEnable = VK_FALSE;

samplerInfo.compareOp = VK_COMPARE_OP_ALWAYS;

samplerInfo.mipmapMode   =
VK_SAMPLER_MIPMAP_MODE_LINEAR;

if   (vkCreateSampler(device,   &samplerInfo,   nullptr,
&textureSampler) != VK_SUCCESS) {

throw std::runtime_error("Failed to create texture sampler!");

}

Fragment Shader

In the fragment shader, use the texture coordinates passed from the vertex shader to sample the texture and determine the fragment color.

#version 450

layout(set = 0, binding = 0) **uniform** sampler2D textureSampler;

layout(location = 0) in vec2 fragTexCoord;

layout(location = 0) out vec4 fragColor;

void main() {

fragColor = texture(textureSampler, fragTexCoord);

}

Pipeline Configuration

Finally, when configuring your graphics pipeline, ensure that the fragment shader reads from the correct texture image and sampler.

```
// Configure fragment shader stage

VkPipelineShaderStageCreateInfo fragShaderStageInfo = {};

fragShaderStageInfo.sType                                    =
VK_STRUCTURE_TYPE_PIPELINE_SHADER_STAGE_CREA

fragShaderStageInfo.stage                                    =
VK_SHADER_STAGE_FRAGMENT_BIT;

fragShaderStageInfo.module                                   =
CreateShaderModule("fragment_shader.spv"); // Load fragment
shader

fragShaderStageInfo.pName = "main";

// ...

VkPipelineLayoutCreateInfo pipelineLayoutInfo = {};

// Set layout for texture sampler

pipelineLayoutInfo.setLayoutCount = 1;

pipelineLayoutInfo.pSetLayouts = &descriptorSetLayout;

if (vkCreatePipelineLayout(device, &pipelineLayoutInfo, nullptr,
&pipelineLayout) != VK_SUCCESS) {

throw std::runtime_error("Failed to create pipeline layout!");

}
```

With these steps in place, you can render a textured triangle in Vulkan. This basic example can serve as a starting point for more complex texture rendering in your Vulkan applications.

Chapter 11: Depth and Stencil Testing

Section 11.1: Understanding Depth Testing

Depth testing is a fundamental concept in 3D computer graphics and plays a crucial role in creating realistic and visually appealing scenes. In Vulkan, depth testing is an essential part of the rendering pipeline, allowing you to determine which fragments should be visible based on their depth values.

The Z-Buffer

Depth testing relies on a data structure called the Z-buffer (or depth buffer). The Z-buffer is a two-dimensional array that has the same dimensions as the framebuffer or the image being rendered to. Each element in the Z-buffer stores a depth value for the corresponding pixel in the framebuffer.

When rendering a 3D scene, every fragment (pixel) generated by the rasterization process has an associated depth value. This depth value represents the distance from the camera to the object being rendered. Depth testing compares this depth value with the value stored in the Z-buffer for the same pixel.

Depth Testing Operations

Depth testing involves several operations, and the most common one is called the "depth test." The depth test is a comparison between the depth value of the current fragment and the value stored in the Z-buffer. Depending on the outcome of this comparison, the fragment may be discarded or written to the framebuffer.

The two most commonly used depth testing operations are:

- **Less Than (LT)**: If the depth value of the current fragment is less than the value in the Z-buffer, the fragment is considered closer to the camera and is written to the framebuffer.

- **Less Than or Equal (LE)**: If the depth value of the current fragment is less than or equal to the value in the Z-buffer, the fragment is written to the framebuffer. This operation is often used to avoid "z-fighting," a graphical artifact where two surfaces with very close depth values flicker and fight for visibility.

Depth Buffer Precision

The precision of the depth buffer is essential for accurate depth testing. In Vulkan, you can configure the bit depth of the depth buffer when creating the render pass. Common bit depths include 16-bit and 32-bit, with 24-bit depth and 8-bit stencil being a common combination.

Choosing an appropriate depth buffer precision depends on the specific requirements of your application. In some cases, a higher bit depth may be necessary to handle scenes with extreme depth ranges accurately, while in others, a lower bit depth may suffice to save memory.

Depth Testing in the Rendering Pipeline

Depth testing occurs in the later stages of the Vulkan rendering pipeline, typically in the fragment shader stage. Before the fragment shader is executed, vertices are transformed and projected onto the screen, generating fragments. Each fragment has a calculated depth value based on its position in 3D space.

During the fragment shader stage, you have the option to modify the depth value of fragments, which can be useful for effects like fog or underwater distortion. However, the depth test typically operates on the original depth value unless explicitly modified in the shader.

Conclusion

Depth testing is a crucial technique in 3D rendering that allows Vulkan applications to determine which fragments should be visible in the final image. Understanding depth testing and configuring the depth buffer correctly are essential steps in creating visually accurate and appealing graphics. In the next sections, we'll delve deeper into depth testing and explore various related concepts and techniques.

Stay tuned for more in-depth discussions on depth buffer formats, stencil testing, and combining depth and stencil operations in Vulkan.

Section 11.2: Depth Buffer and Depth Testing

In Section 11.1, we discussed the fundamentals of depth testing and how it determines the visibility of fragments in a 3D scene. Now, let's dive deeper into the concepts of the depth buffer and how depth testing is implemented in Vulkan.

Depth Buffer

The depth buffer, also known as the Z-buffer, is a crucial component of depth testing in Vulkan. It is a two-dimensional array of depth values that has the same dimensions as the framebuffer being rendered to. Each element in the depth buffer corresponds to a pixel in the framebuffer and stores a depth value.

When a fragment is generated during rendering, it has an associated depth value, representing its distance from the camera. This depth value is compared to the value stored in the depth buffer to determine whether the fragment should be rendered.

Depth Testing in Vulkan

Depth testing in Vulkan is configured through the render pass and pipeline settings. Let's explore the key aspects:

Render Pass Configuration

When defining a render pass, you specify the format and usage of the depth buffer attachment using the VkAttachmentDescription structure. You can choose the bit depth (e.g., 16-bit or 32-bit) and whether the depth values should be cleared at the beginning of rendering.

Here's a simplified example of configuring a depth buffer attachment in a render pass:

VkAttachmentDescription depthAttachment = {};

depthAttachment.format = VK_FORMAT_D32_SFLOAT; // *32-bit depth format* depthAttachment.samples = VK_SAMPLE_COUNT_1_BIT; // *No multi-sampling*

depthAttachment.loadOp = VK_ATTACHMENT_LOAD_OP_CLEAR; // *Clear depth buffer at start*

depthAttachment.storeOp = VK_ATTACHMENT_STORE_OP_STORE; // *Store depth values*

depthAttachment.stencilLoadOp = VK_ATTACHMENT_LOAD_OP_DONT_CARE;

depthAttachment.stencilStoreOp = VK_ATTACHMENT_STORE_OP_DONT_CARE;

Pipeline Configuration

In the graphics pipeline, depth testing is enabled by setting the depthTestEnable field to VK_TRUE in the VkPipelineDepthStencilStateCreateInfo structure.

Here's an example of enabling depth testing in a Vulkan pipeline:

VkPipelineDepthStencilStateCreateInfo depthStencilCreateInfo = {};

depthStencilCreateInfo.sType = VK_STRUCTURE_TYPE_PIPELINE_DEPTH_STENCIL_STATE_C

depthStencilCreateInfo.depthTestEnable = VK_TRUE; // *Enable depth testing*

depthStencilCreateInfo.depthWriteEnable = VK_TRUE; // *Allow writing to the depth buffer*

depthStencilCreateInfo.depthCompareOp   =
VK_COMPARE_OP_LESS; // *Use the "Less Than" depth test*

Depth Testing Operations

Vulkan supports various depth testing operations, including:

- **Less Than (LT)**: Fragments with depth values less than the depth buffer are rendered.

- **Less Than or Equal (LE)**: Fragments with depth values less than or equal to the depth buffer are rendered.

- **Greater Than (GT)**: Fragments with depth values greater than the depth buffer are rendered.

- **Greater Than or Equal (GE)**: Fragments with depth values greater than or equal to the depth buffer are rendered.

The specific depth testing operation is determined by the depthCompareOp field in the pipeline configuration.

Practical Considerations

When configuring depth testing, you should consider factors such as the precision of the depth buffer, the range of depth values in your scene, and the chosen depth testing operation. These choices impact the visual quality and performance of your application.

In conclusion, depth testing and the depth buffer are essential concepts in Vulkan for determining the visibility of fragments in 3D scenes. Properly configuring the depth buffer and depth testing operations is crucial for achieving accurate and visually pleasing rendering results. In the next section, we'll explore stencil testing and its role in advanced rendering techniques.

Section 11.3: Stencil Buffer and Stencil Testing

In Section 11.2, we discussed depth testing, which is crucial for determining the visibility of fragments in a 3D scene based on their depths. Now, let's explore another essential component of rendering in Vulkan: the stencil buffer and stencil testing.

Stencil Buffer

The stencil buffer, often referred to as the "S-buffer," is a 2D array of stencil values, which are typically 8 bits each. It has the same dimensions as the framebuffer and is used alongside the depth buffer. Each stencil value corresponds to a pixel in the framebuffer.

The stencil buffer is primarily used for more advanced rendering techniques, such as masking and selective rendering. It allows you to perform conditional rendering based on certain conditions, providing greater control over the rendering process.

Stencil Testing in Vulkan

Stencil testing in Vulkan involves comparing stencil values in the stencil buffer to a reference value and performing operations based on the result of this comparison. Key aspects of stencil testing include:

Stencil State Configuration

In the graphics pipeline, you configure stencil testing through the VkPipelineDepthStencilStateCreateInfo structure. You set the stencilTestEnable field to VK_TRUE to enable stencil testing.

Here's an example of enabling stencil testing in a Vulkan pipeline:

VkPipelineDepthStencilStateCreateInfo depthStencilCreateInfo = {};

depthStencilCreateInfo.sType   = VK_STRUCTURE_TYPE_PIPELINE_DEPTH_STENCIL_STAT

depthStencilCreateInfo.stencilTestEnable = VK_TRUE; // *Enable stencil testing*

depthStencilCreateInfo.front = {}; // *Stencil settings for front-facing triangles*

depthStencilCreateInfo.back = {}; // *Stencil settings for back-facing triangles*

Stencil Operations

Vulkan supports various stencil operations, including:

- **Stencil Fail (SFail)**: Specifies the action to take if the stencil test fails.

- **Depth Fail (DFail)**: Specifies the action to take if the depth test fails.

- **Depth Pass (DPass)**: Specifies the action to take if both the stencil and depth tests pass.

You define these operations for both front-facing and back-facing triangles in the VkStencilOpState structures within the front and back fields.

Here's an example of configuring stencil operations:

VkStencilOpState stencilOpState = {};

stencilOpState.failOp = VK_STENCIL_OP_KEEP; // *Keep the existing stencil value*

stencilOpState.depthFailOp   = VK_STENCIL_OP_INCREMENT_AND_CLAMP;   // *Increment stencil on depth fail*

stencilOpState.passOp = VK_STENCIL_OP_KEEP; // *Keep stencil on depth pass*

stencilOpState.compareOp = VK_COMPARE_OP_EQUAL; // *Compare stencil values for equality*

stencilOpState.compareMask = 0xFF; // *Stencil mask*

stencilOpState.writeMask = 0xFF; // *Stencil write mask*

stencilOpState.reference = 1; // *Reference value for stencil tests*

Stencil Reference Value

The reference value used in stencil testing is specified in the reference field of the VkStencilOpState structure. This value is compared to the stencil values in the stencil buffer to determine whether the stencil test passes or fails.

Practical Applications

Stencil testing is employed in various rendering techniques, such as shadow mapping, reflections, and masking. It allows you to selectively render parts of the scene based on complex conditions, providing the flexibility needed for advanced visual effects.

In summary, the stencil buffer and stencil testing are important components of Vulkan rendering. They enable you to perform conditional rendering and implement advanced rendering techniques by selectively controlling which fragments are rendered based on stencil values. In the next section, we'll explore how depth and stencil testing can be combined to achieve more complex rendering operations.

Section 11.4: Combining Depth and Stencil Testing

In the previous sections, we discussed depth testing and stencil testing as separate processes. Now, we'll explore how depth and stencil testing can be combined to achieve more complex and versatile rendering operations.

Depth and Stencil Together

Combining depth and stencil testing allows you to create advanced rendering effects that require fine-grained control over which fragments are drawn. Here's how they can work together:

Stencil Masking

Stencil masking is a technique where you use the stencil buffer to mark specific areas of the framebuffer as "masked" or "unmasked."

This is often used in complex rendering scenarios, like shadow mapping or rendering reflections.

1. **Stencil Test**: You configure the stencil test to pass when specific stencil conditions are met. For example, you can set it to pass when the stencil value is equal to a certain reference value.
2. **Stencil Operation**: When the stencil test passes, you can modify the stencil value for that fragment using stencil operations. This is where you mark certain pixels in the stencil buffer as "masked."
3. **Depth Test**: Following the stencil test, you perform the depth test. The depth test ensures that only unmasked pixels, as determined by the stencil test, go through depth testing.

By combining stencil masking with depth testing, you can achieve effects like shadows, reflections, and more. For example, in shadow mapping, you use the stencil buffer to determine which parts of the scene are in shadow and then apply the appropriate shadow calculations during rendering.

Complex Scene Rendering

In complex 3D scenes, you may need to render objects in specific orders or apply different rendering techniques to different parts of the scene. Depth and stencil testing allow you to control the rendering order and apply different shaders or techniques selectively.

1. **Stencil Operations**: You can use stencil operations to increment or decrement the stencil values based on certain conditions. This can help you keep track of rendering order or apply different techniques to objects.

2. **Depth Testing**: After stencil operations, depth testing ensures that fragments are drawn in the correct order, preventing issues like Z-fighting.

Practical Example: Rendering Order

Consider a scene with transparent objects that need to be rendered in a specific order. You can use stencil testing to mark the pixels of transparent objects during the first pass and then render them in the correct order during subsequent passes.

// First pass: Stencil mask transparent objects

StencilTestEnable = VK_TRUE;

StencilOpState = { /*... *configure stencil operations ... */* };

DepthTestEnable = VK_FALSE; *// Disable depth testing*

// Subsequent passes: Render transparent objects in the desired order

StencilTestEnable = VK_TRUE;

StencilOpState = { /*... *configure stencil operations ... */* };

DepthTestEnable = VK_TRUE; *// Enable depth testing*

Conclusion

Combining depth and stencil testing in Vulkan allows you to create sophisticated rendering effects and manage complex scenes effectively. By controlling the stencil buffer and integrating it with depth testing, you can achieve effects such as shadows, reflections, and selective rendering of objects in complex 3D scenes. Understanding how to leverage both depth and stencil testing opens up a wide range of possibilities for advanced graphics rendering. In the next section, we'll explore practical depth and stencil operations commonly used in Vulkan applications.

Section 11.5: Practical Depth and Stencil Operations

In this section, we'll delve into practical depth and stencil operations commonly used in Vulkan applications. These operations are essential for achieving specific rendering effects and maintaining rendering correctness in complex scenes.

Clearing the Depth and Stencil Buffers

Before rendering a new frame or pass, it's often necessary to clear the depth and stencil buffers to their initial values. Vulkan provides the vkCmdClearDepthStencilImage command for this purpose.

VkClearDepthStencilValue clearValue = { 1.0f, 0 }; // *Clear depth to 1.0 and stencil to 0*

VkImageSubresourceRange subresourceRange = {

VK_IMAGE_ASPECT_DEPTH_BIT |
VK_IMAGE_ASPECT_STENCIL_BIT, // *Specify the aspects to clear*

0, // *Base mip level*

1, // *Level count*

0, // *Base array layer*

1 // *Layer count*

};

```
VkImage imageToClear = /* The depth-stencil image to clear */;

VkClearDepthStencilImageCmd clearCmd = {};

clearCmd.sType                                    =
VK_STRUCTURE_TYPE_CLEAR_DEPTH_STENCIL_IMAGE

clearCmd.pNext = nullptr;

clearCmd.image = imageToClear;

clearCmd.imageLayout                              =
VK_IMAGE_LAYOUT_TRANSFER_DST_OPTIMAL;

clearCmd.pRanges = &subresourceRange;

clearCmd.rangeCount = 1;

clearCmd.clearValue = clearValue;

vkCmdClearDepthStencilImage(commandBuffer,    imageToClear,
VK_IMAGE_LAYOUT_TRANSFER_DST_OPTIMAL,
&clearValue, 1, &subresourceRange);
```

Stencil Buffer Masking

Stencil buffer masking is a technique to selectively render parts of an object based on their stencil values. Here's how you can configure stencil operations to achieve this:

```
VkStencilOpState stencilOp = {};

stencilOp.failOp = VK_STENCIL_OP_KEEP; // Stencil operation
on stencil test failure

stencilOp.passOp = VK_STENCIL_OP_REPLACE; // Stencil
operation on stencil test pass
```

stencilOp.depthFailOp = VK_STENCIL_OP_KEEP; // *Stencil operation on depth test failure*

stencilOp.compareOp = VK_COMPARE_OP_ALWAYS; // *Comparison operation*

stencilOp.compareMask = 0xFF; // *Bit mask for comparison*

stencilOp.writeMask = 0xFF; // *Bit mask for writing stencil values*

stencilOp.reference = 1; // *Reference value for comparison*

In this example, we configure stencil operations to replace the stencil value with a reference value when the stencil test passes.

Depth Range Adjustments

Vulkan allows you to adjust the depth range during rendering. This can be useful for special effects or when you want to render objects with a different depth range.

VkViewport viewport = {};

viewport.x = 0.0f;

viewport.y = 0.0f;

viewport.width = (float)swapchainExtent.width;

viewport.height = (float)swapchainExtent.height;

viewport.minDepth = 0.0f; // *Adjust the minimum depth*

viewport.maxDepth = 1.0f; // *Adjust the maximum depth*

vkCmdSetViewport(commandBuffer, 0, 1, &viewport);

In this code snippet, we adjust the minimum and maximum depth values of the viewport. This can be handy for effects like fog or rendering specific objects with a different depth range.

Conclusion

Understanding practical depth and stencil operations is crucial for fine-tuning rendering effects and maintaining correctness in Vulkan applications. Whether you need to clear the depth and stencil buffers, apply stencil buffer masking, or adjust the depth range, Vulkan provides the necessary tools to control these aspects of rendering. These operations play a significant role in achieving advanced graphics effects and creating visually appealing scenes. In the next chapter, we will explore the concept of framebuffers and render passes in Vulkan, which are fundamental for efficient and flexible rendering.

Chapter 12: Framebuffer and Render Pass

Section 12.1: Framebuffer Attachments

In Vulkan, framebuffers play a crucial role in rendering. A framebuffer represents a collection of attachments, such as color buffers, depth buffers, and stencil buffers, that define the rendering targets. Framebuffers are essential for rendering to images and presenting the final result on the screen. In this section, we'll explore the concept of framebuffer attachments and their role in Vulkan rendering.

What Are Framebuffer Attachments?

Framebuffer attachments are images or image views that are attached to a framebuffer. They serve as the rendering targets where the output of rendering operations is stored. The most common types of framebuffer attachments are:

1. **Color Attachments:** These attachments store the color information of the rendered scene. Multiple color attachments can be used for various rendering passes, such as deferred rendering.
2. **Depth Attachment:** The depth attachment stores the depth information of the rendered scene. It's crucial for depth testing and determining the visibility of objects.
3. **Stencil Attachment:** The stencil attachment stores stencil information, which can be used for advanced rendering techniques, like shadow mapping or stencil buffer operations.
4. **Resolve Attachment:** In case of multisampling (antialiasing), a resolve attachment is used to downsample the multisampled image to a non-multisampled image.

Creating Framebuffer Attachments

To create framebuffer attachments, you'll typically follow these steps:

1. **Create Image(s):** You'll create Vulkan images to serve as the attachments. These images represent the actual memory where the pixel data will be stored.
2. **Create Image Views:** For each image, you'll create an image view, which specifies how to interpret the image data. Image views define aspects like the image format, usage, and subresource range.
3. **Create Framebuffer:** Finally, you'll create the framebuffer, attaching the image views as framebuffer attachments. The

framebuffer also specifies the dimensions and layers of the attachments.

Let's take a look at some example code for creating framebuffer attachments:

```
// 1. Create Image(s)
```

```
VkImageCreateInfo imageCreateInfo = {};
```

```
imageCreateInfo.sType = VK_STRUCTURE_TYPE_IMAGE_CREATE_INFO;
```

```
imageCreateInfo.imageType = VK_IMAGE_TYPE_2D;
```

```
imageCreateInfo.format = VK_FORMAT_R8G8B8A8_UNORM;
```

```
imageCreateInfo.extent.width = framebufferWidth;
```

```
imageCreateInfo.extent.height = framebufferHeight;
```

```
imageCreateInfo.extent.depth = 1;
```

```
imageCreateInfo.mipLevels = 1;
```

```
imageCreateInfo.arrayLayers = 1;
```

```
imageCreateInfo.samples = VK_SAMPLE_COUNT_1_BIT;
```

```
imageCreateInfo.tiling = VK_IMAGE_TILING_OPTIMAL;
```

```
imageCreateInfo.usage = VK_IMAGE_USAGE_COLOR_ATTACHMENT_BIT;
```

```
VkImage colorImage;
```

```
vkCreateImage(device, &imageCreateInfo, nullptr, &colorImage);
```

```
// 2. Create Image Views

VkImageViewCreateInfo imageViewCreateInfo = {};

imageViewCreateInfo.sType                                    =
VK_STRUCTURE_TYPE_IMAGE_VIEW_CREATE_INFO;

imageViewCreateInfo.image = colorImage;

imageViewCreateInfo.viewType                                 =
VK_IMAGE_VIEW_TYPE_2D;

imageViewCreateInfo.format                                   =
VK_FORMAT_R8G8B8A8_UNORM;

imageViewCreateInfo.subresourceRange.aspectMask             =
VK_IMAGE_ASPECT_COLOR_BIT;

imageViewCreateInfo.subresourceRange.baseMipLevel = 0;

imageViewCreateInfo.subresourceRange.levelCount = 1;

imageViewCreateInfo.subresourceRange.baseArrayLayer = 0;

imageViewCreateInfo.subresourceRange.layerCount = 1;

VkImageView colorImageView;

vkCreateImageView(device,      &imageViewCreateInfo,      nullptr,
&colorImageView);

// 3. Create Framebuffer

VkFramebufferCreateInfo framebufferCreateInfo = {};

framebufferCreateInfo.sType                                  =
VK_STRUCTURE_TYPE_FRAMEBUFFER_CREATE_INFO;
```

```
framebufferCreateInfo.renderPass = renderPass;

framebufferCreateInfo.attachmentCount = 1; // Number of attachments

framebufferCreateInfo.pAttachments = &colorImageView;

framebufferCreateInfo.width = framebufferWidth;

framebufferCreateInfo.height = framebufferHeight;

framebufferCreateInfo.layers = 1;

VkFramebuffer framebuffer;

vkCreateFramebuffer(device, &framebufferCreateInfo, nullptr, &framebuffer);
```

In this example, we create a color attachment for the framebuffer. Similar steps can be followed for other types of attachments like depth and stencil attachments. Understanding how to create and manage framebuffer attachments is fundamental to Vulkan rendering.

Conclusion

Framebuffer attachments are a critical concept in Vulkan, serving as the rendering targets for graphics operations. They include color attachments, depth attachments, stencil attachments, and resolve attachments, depending on the rendering needs. Creating and managing framebuffer attachments correctly is essential for efficient and flexible Vulkan rendering. In the next sections, we'll explore the creation of render passes and subpasses, which define how attachments are used in rendering operations.

Section 12.2: Creating a Render Pass

In Vulkan, a render pass is a fundamental concept that defines how rendering operations interact with framebuffer attachments. A render pass specifies the number and types of attachments, how they are used in rendering operations, and the order in which these operations occur. Understanding render passes is crucial for efficient and flexible rendering in Vulkan.

What Is a Render Pass?

A render pass consists of a collection of subpasses, each of which defines a set of rendering operations that read from and write to framebuffer attachments. These operations include drawing commands, clear operations, and load/store operations for attachments.

The primary components of a render pass are as follows:

1. **Attachments:** These are the images (framebuffer attachments) used as rendering targets. Attachments can be color images, depth images, stencil images, or multisampled images.
2. **Subpasses:** Subpasses are individual rendering operations within a render pass. They define the set of attachments used as input and output and the operations that occur during that subpass.
3. **Dependencies:** Dependencies define the ordering constraints between subpasses. They specify which subpasses must finish before others can begin and control how data is synchronized between subpasses.
4. **Load and Store Operations:** For each attachment, you can specify whether to load or clear the attachment at the start of a subpass and whether to store its contents at the

end of the subpass. This allows for optimizations like tile-based rendering.

Creating a Render Pass

Creating a render pass in Vulkan involves the following steps:

1. **Attachment Descriptions:** Describe the format, sample count, load/store operations, and final layout of each attachment.
2. **Subpass Descriptions:** Define the attachments used by each subpass and specify the layout transitions that occur at the start and end of each subpass.
3. **Subpass Dependencies:** Set up dependencies between subpasses to control their execution order.
4. **Render Pass Creation:** Combine the attachment descriptions, subpass descriptions, and subpass dependencies to create the render pass.

Here's a simplified example of creating a render pass in Vulkan:

```
// 1. Attachment Descriptions

VkAttachmentDescription colorAttachment = {};

colorAttachment.format = swapchainImageFormat;

colorAttachment.samples = VK_SAMPLE_COUNT_1_BIT;

colorAttachment.loadOp                          =
VK_ATTACHMENT_LOAD_OP_CLEAR;

colorAttachment.storeOp                         =
VK_ATTACHMENT_STORE_OP_STORE;
```

```
colorAttachment.initialLayout                        =
VK_IMAGE_LAYOUT_UNDEFINED;

colorAttachment.finalLayout                          =
VK_IMAGE_LAYOUT_PRESENT_SRC_KHR;

// 2. Subpass Descriptions

VkSubpassDescription subpass = {};

subpass.pipelineBindPoint                            =
VK_PIPELINE_BIND_POINT_GRAPHICS;

subpass.colorAttachmentCount = 1;

subpass.pColorAttachments = &colorAttachmentRef;

// 3. Subpass Dependencies

VkSubpassDependency dependency = {};

dependency.srcSubpass = VK_SUBPASS_EXTERNAL;

dependency.dstSubpass = 0;

dependency.srcStageMask                              =
VK_PIPELINE_STAGE_COLOR_ATTACHMENT_OUTPUT_BIT;

dependency.srcAccessMask = 0;

dependency.dstStageMask                              =
VK_PIPELINE_STAGE_COLOR_ATTACHMENT_OUTPUT_BIT;

dependency.dstAccessMask                             =
VK_ACCESS_COLOR_ATTACHMENT_WRITE_BIT;

// 4. Render Pass Creation
```

```
VkRenderPassCreateInfo renderPassInfo = {};

renderPassInfo.sType                    =
VK_STRUCTURE_TYPE_RENDER_PASS_CREATE_INFO;

renderPassInfo.attachmentCount = 1;

renderPassInfo.pAttachments = &colorAttachment;

renderPassInfo.subpassCount = 1;

renderPassInfo.pSubpasses = &subpass;

renderPassInfo.dependencyCount = 1;

renderPassInfo.pDependencies = &dependency;

VkRenderPass renderPass;

if  (vkCreateRenderPass(device,    &renderPassInfo,    nullptr,
&renderPass) != VK_SUCCESS) {

// Handle render pass creation failure

}
```

In this example, we create a simple render pass with one color attachment and one subpass. The subpass specifies that it uses the color attachment for rendering operations. Subpass dependencies ensure proper synchronization between subpasses.

Conclusion

Render passes are a critical part of Vulkan's rendering pipeline. They define the structure and order of rendering operations, including how data is read from and written to framebuffer attachments. Properly defining render passes is essential for achieving optimal performance and visual quality in Vulkan applications. In the next section, we'll explore subpasses in more detail and see how they enable advanced rendering techniques.

Section 12.3: Subpasses in Render Passes

In Vulkan, subpasses are a crucial concept within the context of a render pass. They define individual rendering operations that occur within the render pass and how they interact with framebuffer attachments. Understanding subpasses is essential for optimizing and structuring rendering operations efficiently.

What Are Subpasses?

A subpass is a sequence of rendering operations that read from and write to framebuffer attachments. Subpasses define the following:

1. **Attachments:** Each subpass specifies a set of framebuffer attachments that are used as input and output for the rendering operations within that subpass. These attachments can include color images, depth-stencil images, or multisampled images.
2. **Render Pass Operations:** Subpasses define the actual rendering operations that occur. These operations typically include drawing commands, clear operations, and load/store operations for attachments.
3. **Dependency on Previous Subpasses:** Subpasses can have dependencies on previous subpasses within the render pass. These dependencies ensure the correct ordering of subpasses and proper synchronization of data.

Benefits of Using Subpasses

Subpasses offer several advantages in Vulkan:

1. **Optimization:** Subpasses enable optimizations like tile-based rendering by allowing load and store operations for framebuffer attachments to be specified per subpass. This can result in more efficient memory access patterns.
2. **Resolve Operations:** When working with multisampled images, subpasses allow for automatic resolve operations, reducing the need for manual resolve code.
3. **Attachment Reuse:** Subpasses can reuse framebuffer attachments between different subpasses, which can be useful for effects like post-processing.

Creating Subpasses

To create subpasses in Vulkan, you need to define a VkSubpassDescription structure for each subpass. This structure specifies the pipeline bind point (graphics or compute), the attachments used by the subpass, and the operations that occur within the subpass.

Here's a simplified example of creating a subpass:

VkSubpassDescription subpass = {};

subpass.pipelineBindPoint   =
VK_PIPELINE_BIND_POINT_GRAPHICS;

subpass.colorAttachmentCount = 1;

subpass.pColorAttachments = &colorAttachmentRef;

subpass.pDepthStencilAttachment = &depthAttachmentRef;

// Optional: Input attachments, preserve attachments, etc.

In this example, colorAttachmentRef and depthAttachmentRef are references to the attachments used by the subpass. You can also specify input attachments, preserve attachments, and other parameters as needed.

Subpass Dependencies

Subpasses can have dependencies that control their execution order and data synchronization. These dependencies are defined using VkSubpassDependency structures and help ensure that one subpass finishes before another begins.

Conclusion

Subpasses are a fundamental concept in Vulkan's render passes. They allow you to structure rendering operations efficiently, optimize memory access patterns, and specify attachment operations on a per-subpass basis. By understanding how to create and use subpasses, you can harness the full power of Vulkan for advanced graphics rendering. In the next section, we'll explore framebuffer creation, which is closely tied to render passes.

Section 12.4: Framebuffer Creation

In Vulkan, framebuffers are essential objects that represent the rendering targets for each subpass within a render pass. Framebuffers provide the association between framebuffer attachments (such as color images, depth-stencil images, or multisampled images) and the specific render pass that will use them. This section discusses framebuffer creation in Vulkan.

What Is a Framebuffer?

A framebuffer in Vulkan is a collection of one or more attachments, each representing a specific image that the render pass will write to or read from. These attachments are associated with particular subpasses in the render pass. Framebuffers define the rendering targets and their layouts for each subpass.

Framebuffer Attachments

Framebuffer attachments are images that serve as the targets for rendering operations. They can include:

- **Color Images:** These are typically the images where the final color output of rendering operations is stored.

- **Depth-Stencil Images:** These are used for depth and stencil testing and can store depth and stencil information.

- **Multisampled Images:** When using multisampling for anti-aliasing, these images store multiple samples per pixel.

Framebuffer Creation

Creating a framebuffer in Vulkan involves specifying the following:

1. **Render Pass:** You must specify the render pass to which the framebuffer belongs. The framebuffer is compatible with a particular render pass, and the attachments must match the render pass's attachment descriptions.
2. **Attachments:** Define the attachments that will be used by the framebuffer. These attachments should correspond to the attachments defined in the render pass.
3. **Width and Height:** Specify the width and height of the framebuffer, which should match the dimensions of the attachments.
4. **Layers:** If working with layered attachments (e.g., for

stereoscopic rendering), you can specify the number of layers.

Here's a simplified example of creating a framebuffer in Vulkan:

```
VkFramebufferCreateInfo framebufferInfo = {};

framebufferInfo.sType                        =
VK_STRUCTURE_TYPE_FRAMEBUFFER_CREATE_INFO;

framebufferInfo.renderPass = renderPass;

framebufferInfo.attachmentCount = attachmentCount;

framebufferInfo.pAttachments = attachments;

framebufferInfo.width = width;

framebufferInfo.height = height;

framebufferInfo.layers = 1;

VkFramebuffer framebuffer;

if (vkCreateFramebuffer(device, &framebufferInfo, nullptr,
&framebuffer) != VK_SUCCESS) {

throw std::runtime_error("Failed to create framebuffer!");

}
```

In this code, renderPass refers to the render pass to which the framebuffer belongs. attachments is an array of image views corresponding to the framebuffer attachments. The width and height should match the dimensions of the attachments.

Framebuffer Compatibility

Framebuffers are tied to a specific render pass. It's crucial to ensure that the attachments in the framebuffer match the attachments described in the render pass's subpasses. Mismatched attachments can lead to runtime errors.

Conclusion

Framebuffers in Vulkan play a critical role in defining rendering targets and their associated attachments within a render pass. Understanding how to create and manage framebuffers is essential for constructing efficient rendering pipelines in Vulkan. In the next section, we'll dive deeper into the concept of render passes in Vulkan.

Section 12.5: Render Passes in Vulkan

In Vulkan, a render pass is a crucial concept that defines the structure of rendering operations. It specifies how input attachments, color attachments, depth/stencil attachments, and subpasses are used in a rendering operation. Understanding render passes is essential for efficiently managing rendering resources and achieving optimal performance. This section provides an in-depth look at render passes in Vulkan.

What Is a Render Pass?

A render pass in Vulkan defines a series of rendering operations that produce a final image. It encompasses:

- **Attachments:** Images or memory regions used as rendering targets, including color, depth, and stencil attachments.

• **Subpasses:** Each render pass can consist of multiple subpasses. Subpasses define a portion of the rendering operations and specify which attachments are read from and written to.

• **Dependencies:** Specifies dependencies between subpasses, ensuring correct synchronization between them.

Key Components of a Render Pass

1. Attachments

Attachments define the images or memory regions used for rendering. There are several types of attachments:

• **Color Attachments:** These typically store the final color output of rendering operations.

• **Depth Attachments:** Used for depth testing and can store depth information.

• **Stencil Attachments:** Used for stencil testing and can store stencil values.

• **Input Attachments:** These allow reading from previous subpass attachments.

Attachments are described by VkAttachmentDescription structures, specifying their format, sample count, and how they are used.

2. Subpasses

Subpasses define a portion of the rendering operations within the render pass. Each subpass includes:

- **Attachment References:** These specify which attachments are used as inputs, outputs, and resolves within the subpass.

- **Pipeline Bind Points:** Subpasses also specify whether the graphics pipeline or compute pipeline is used.

3. Dependencies

Dependencies define the execution order and synchronization between subpasses. They ensure that subpasses are executed in the correct order and that their dependencies are satisfied.

Render Pass Creation

Creating a render pass in Vulkan involves specifying:

- **Attachments:** Attachments are described using VkAttachmentDescription structures.

- **Subpasses:** Subpasses are defined using VkSubpassDescription structures, including attachment references.

- **Dependencies:** Dependencies are specified using VkSubpassDependency structures.

Here's a simplified example of creating a render pass in Vulkan:

```
VkRenderPassCreateInfo renderPassInfo = {};

renderPassInfo.sType                        = VK_STRUCTURE_TYPE_RENDER_PASS_CREATE_INFO;

renderPassInfo.attachmentCount = attachmentCount;

renderPassInfo.pAttachments = attachments;

renderPassInfo.subpassCount = subpassCount;

renderPassInfo.pSubpasses = subpasses;

renderPassInfo.dependencyCount = dependencyCount;

renderPassInfo.pDependencies = dependencies;

VkRenderPass renderPass;

if   (vkCreateRenderPass(device,   &renderPassInfo,   nullptr, &renderPass) != VK_SUCCESS) {

throw std::runtime_error("Failed to create render pass!");

}
```

In this code, attachments describe the attachments, subpasses define the subpasses, and dependencies specify dependencies between subpasses.

Render Passes and Performance

Render passes are crucial for optimizing rendering performance in Vulkan. They allow the GPU to perform optimizations such as tile-based rendering, reducing memory bandwidth usage and improving efficiency. Properly designed render passes can significantly impact the performance of your Vulkan application.

Conclusion

Render passes in Vulkan are fundamental for structuring rendering operations efficiently. They define attachments, subpasses, and dependencies, enabling the GPU to perform optimizations for improved performance. Understanding render passes is vital for creating high-performance Vulkan applications.

Chapter 13: Multisampling and Anti-aliasing

Section 13.1: Introduction to Multisampling

Multisampling is a technique used in computer graphics to improve the visual quality of rendered images. It is particularly useful in reducing the visual artifacts known as "jaggies" or aliasing, which occur when a diagonal line or an edge appears jagged or stair-stepped due to limited pixel resolution. In this section, we will explore the concept of multisampling, its benefits, and how it is implemented in Vulkan.

What is Aliasing?

Aliasing is a visual artifact that occurs when the pixel grid of a display or an image sensor does not provide sufficient resolution to accurately represent the details of a scene. When rendering an image, this can lead to jagged edges, shimmering, or flickering, especially in high-contrast areas or on diagonal lines. Aliasing can significantly degrade the visual quality of computer-generated images.

The Need for Multisampling

Multisampling is a solution to the aliasing problem. It works by sampling multiple points within each pixel and using the average or weighted values to determine the final pixel color. This approach reduces the jagged appearance of edges and produces smoother, more visually pleasing results.

How Multisampling Works

Here's a simplified explanation of how multisampling works:

1. **Sample Locations:** Instead of sampling only one point at the center of each pixel, multisampling selects multiple sample points within the pixel. The number of samples per pixel is determined by the level of multisampling used (e.g., 2x, 4x, 8x).
2. **Sample Coverage:** For each sample point, the GPU checks whether it is inside or outside the geometry being rendered. This is called "sample coverage."
3. **Sample Computation:** The color and depth values of the covered samples are computed and averaged or weighted according to their coverage. This results in a single color and depth value for the pixel.
4. **Final Pixel Color:** The computed pixel color is then used for rendering.

Benefits of Multisampling

Multisampling offers several benefits:

• **Anti-aliasing:** It reduces aliasing artifacts, resulting in smoother and more natural-looking images.

• **Improved Image Quality:** Multisampling enhances the overall visual quality of rendered scenes.

• **Higher Rendering Resolutions:** It allows you to achieve higher effective resolutions without the need for super-sampling the entire scene.

• **Performance:** While multisampling adds some computational overhead, it is generally more efficient than super-sampling the entire image.

Implementing Multisampling in Vulkan

In Vulkan, implementing multisampling involves configuring the pipeline and render pass to enable multisample anti-aliasing (MSAA). This includes specifying the number of samples per pixel, enabling multisampling in the framebuffer attachments, and configuring the shader pipeline.

Here's a simplified example of enabling 4x multisampling in Vulkan:

```
// Create a render pass with multisample attachments.

VkAttachmentDescription colorAttachment = {};

colorAttachment.format = swapChainImageFormat;

colorAttachment.samples = VK_SAMPLE_COUNT_4_BIT; // 4x multisampling

colorAttachment.loadOp                                    =
VK_ATTACHMENT_LOAD_OP_CLEAR;

colorAttachment.storeOp                                   =
VK_ATTACHMENT_STORE_OP_STORE;

// Create a pipeline with multisample state.

VkPipelineMultisampleStateCreateInfo multisampling = {};

multisampling.sType                                       =
VK_STRUCTURE_TYPE_PIPELINE_MULTISAMPLE_STATE_CR

multisampling.rasterizationSamples                        =
VK_SAMPLE_COUNT_4_BIT; // 4x multisampling

multisampling.sampleShadingEnable = VK_FALSE;

// Configure the pipeline with multisample state.
```

```
VkPipelineDepthStencilStateCreateInfo depthStencil = {};

depthStencil.sType                    =
VK_STRUCTURE_TYPE_PIPELINE_DEPTH_STENCIL_STAT

depthStencil.depthTestEnable = VK_TRUE;

depthStencil.depthWriteEnable = VK_TRUE;

depthStencil.depthCompareOp = VK_COMPARE_OP_LESS;

// Create the graphics pipeline with these configurations.
```

In this example, we specify 4x multisampling for both the color attachment and the pipeline. Additionally, the depth and stencil state is configured to work with multisampling.

Conclusion

Multisampling is a powerful technique in computer graphics that addresses aliasing artifacts, improving the visual quality of rendered images. In Vulkan, you can enable multisampling by configuring the render pass, framebuffer attachments, and pipeline settings. Understanding and implementing multisampling is essential for achieving high-quality and visually pleasing graphics in Vulkan applications.

Section 13.2: Enabling Multisampling

In the previous section, we introduced the concept of multisampling and discussed its importance in reducing aliasing artifacts in computer graphics. Now, let's delve deeper into enabling multisampling in Vulkan and understand how to configure it for your rendering needs.

Vulkan Sample Counts

In Vulkan, multisampling is specified using the VkSampleCountFlagBits enumeration, which represents the number of samples per pixel. Common sample counts include VK_SAMPLE_COUNT_1_BIT (no multisampling), VK_SAMPLE_COUNT_2_BIT, VK_SAMPLE_COUNT_4_BIT, VK_SAMPLE_COUNT_8_BIT, and more. The choice of sample count depends on the desired level of anti-aliasing and the capabilities of the graphics hardware.

Enabling Multisampling in the Render Pass

To enable multisampling in Vulkan, you need to configure the render pass to use multisample attachments. Multisample attachments have a similar structure to regular attachments but with a specified sample count. Here's an example of how to create a multisample color attachment for a render pass:

VkAttachmentDescription colorAttachment = {};

colorAttachment.format = swapChainImageFormat;

colorAttachment.samples = VK_SAMPLE_COUNT_4_BIT; // *4x multisampling*

colorAttachment.loadOp   =
VK_ATTACHMENT_LOAD_OP_CLEAR;

colorAttachment.storeOp   =
VK_ATTACHMENT_STORE_OP_STORE;

colorAttachment.initialLayout   =
VK_IMAGE_LAYOUT_UNDEFINED;

colorAttachment.finalLayout   =
VK_IMAGE_LAYOUT_PRESENT_SRC_KHR;

In this code, we set the samples field of VkAttachmentDescription to
VK_SAMPLE_COUNT_4_BIT to specify 4x multisampling for
the color attachment. You should configure other attachment
properties as needed for your application.

Multisampling in the Graphics Pipeline

Enabling multisampling in the graphics pipeline involves
configuring the VkPipelineMultisampleStateCreateInfo structure.
This structure controls aspects of the multisampling process,
including sample shading and sample mask.

VkPipelineMultisampleStateCreateInfo multisampling = {};

multisampling.sType   =
VK_STRUCTURE_TYPE_PIPELINE_MULTISAMPLE_STATE

multisampling.rasterizationSamples   =
VK_SAMPLE_COUNT_4_BIT; // *4x multisampling*

multisampling.sampleShadingEnable = VK_FALSE; // *Disable
sample shading*

multisampling.minSampleShading = 1.0f; // *Optional*

multisampling.pSampleMask = nullptr; // *Optional*

multisampling.alphaToCoverageEnable = VK_FALSE; // *Optional*

multisampling.alphaToOneEnable = VK_FALSE; // *Optional*

- rasterizationSamples specifies the sample count to use for rasterization. It should match the sample count of the render pass attachment.

- sampleShadingEnable controls whether sample shading is enabled. Sample shading can be used to perform per-sample shading calculations.

- minSampleShading specifies the minimum fraction of samples that must pass the sample shading test. It's relevant when sampleShadingEnable is set to VK_TRUE.

- pSampleMask allows you to specify a custom sample mask. If nullptr is provided, the default sample mask is used.

- alphaToCoverageEnable and alphaToOneEnable control optional features related to alpha testing and coverage calculations.

Resolving Multisample Images

After rendering to multisample attachments, you may need to resolve them to single-sample images for presentation. This is done using a resolve attachment in the subpass description of the render pass. The resolve attachment specifies the target single-sample image to which the multisample data is resolved.

Conclusion

Enabling multisampling in Vulkan involves configuring the render pass and the graphics pipeline to use the desired sample count. By using multisampling, you can significantly improve the visual quality of your rendered images by reducing aliasing artifacts. The choice of sample count and other multisampling settings should be made based on your application's requirements and the capabilities of the target hardware.

Section 13.3: Sample Shading and Sample Masks

Sample shading is a technique in Vulkan that allows you to perform per-sample shading calculations, enhancing the accuracy of your rendering. In this section, we will explore sample shading and how to use it in your Vulkan applications.

Sample Shading Basics

In traditional shading models, shading calculations are performed once per pixel. However, in a multisample rendering scenario, each pixel can have multiple samples, and traditional shading may not accurately represent the true shading behavior. Sample shading solves this problem by performing shading calculations for each sample within a pixel.

To enable sample shading in Vulkan, you need to set the sampleShadingEnable field in the VkPipelineMultisampleStateCreateInfo structure to VK_TRUE. Additionally, you can specify the minSampleShading parameter to control the minimum fraction of samples that must pass the sample shading test.

Here's how you can configure sample shading in the pipeline state:

```
VkPipelineMultisampleStateCreateInfo multisampling = {};

multisampling.sType                                =
VK_STRUCTURE_TYPE_PIPELINE_MULTISAMPLE_STATE
```

```
multisampling.rasterizationSamples                    =
VK_SAMPLE_COUNT_4_BIT; // Sample count
```

```
multisampling.sampleShadingEnable = VK_TRUE; // Enable
sample shading
```

```
multisampling.minSampleShading = 0.25f; // Minimum fraction of
samples to shade
```

In this example, sampleShadingEnable is set to VK_TRUE, indicating that sample shading is enabled. The minSampleShading parameter is set to 0.25, which means that at least 25% of the samples within a pixel must pass the sample shading test to execute the shading calculations.

Sample Masks

Sample masks allow you to specify which samples within a pixel should be shaded. You can use sample masks to skip shading for certain samples, improving performance or achieving specific rendering effects.

Sample masks are specified using the pSampleMask field in the VkPipelineMultisampleStateCreateInfo structure. This field should point to an array of 32-bit integers, where each bit corresponds to a sample. By setting specific bits, you can control which samples are shaded.

```
VkPipelineMultisampleStateCreateInfo multisampling = {};
```

```
multisampling.sType                                   =
VK_STRUCTURE_TYPE_PIPELINE_MULTISAMPLE_STATE_CR
```

```
multisampling.rasterizationSamples                    =
VK_SAMPLE_COUNT_4_BIT; // Sample count
```

multisampling.sampleShadingEnable = VK_FALSE; // *Disable sample shading*

multisampling.pSampleMask = &sampleMask; // *Pointer to sample mask*

In the code above, we disable sample shading (sampleShadingEnable = VK_FALSE) and specify a sample mask using the sampleMask variable. The sample mask is an integer where each bit corresponds to a sample, and you can set or clear bits to control which samples are shaded.

Use Cases

Sample shading and sample masks are useful in various scenarios:

- **Performance Optimization:** You can use sample masks to skip shading for certain samples, reducing computational overhead for less important samples.

- **Custom Anti-Aliasing:** By selectively shading samples based on their positions or other factors, you can implement custom anti-aliasing techniques.

- **Artistic Effects:** Sample shading can be used creatively to achieve specific artistic effects in your rendering.

Conclusion

Sample shading and sample masks are powerful tools in Vulkan for achieving accurate shading and optimizing rendering performance. By enabling sample shading and configuring sample masks, you can control how shading calculations are performed for each sample within a pixel. This flexibility allows you to enhance the quality of your rendered images and implement custom rendering effects.

Section 13.4: Anti-aliasing Techniques

Anti-aliasing is a crucial technique in computer graphics to reduce aliasing artifacts, such as jagged edges and flickering, in rendered images. In this section, we'll explore anti-aliasing techniques in Vulkan and how to improve the visual quality of your renderings.

What is Aliasing?

Aliasing occurs when a high-frequency signal is sampled or rendered at a lower resolution, leading to incorrect representation of details in the image. In computer graphics, aliasing artifacts manifest as jagged edges, moiré patterns, and shimmering in moving objects.

Multisampling Anti-aliasing (MSAA)

Multisampling anti-aliasing (MSAA) is a widely used technique in Vulkan to combat aliasing. MSAA works by sampling each pixel at multiple points within the pixel's area and averaging the results. This reduces the appearance of jagged edges.

To enable MSAA in Vulkan, you need to configure the VkPipelineMultisampleStateCreateInfo structure:

```
VkPipelineMultisampleStateCreateInfo multisampling = {};

multisampling.sType                                 =
VK_STRUCTURE_TYPE_PIPELINE_MULTISAMPLE_STATE_CRE

multisampling.rasterizationSamples                  =
VK_SAMPLE_COUNT_4_BIT; // Sample count (adjust as
needed)
```

In this example, rasterizationSamples is set to VK_SAMPLE_COUNT_4_BIT, indicating that four samples are taken per pixel. You can adjust the sample count based on your quality/performance requirements.

Supersampling Anti-aliasing (SSAA)

Supersampling anti-aliasing (SSAA) is a more computationally intensive technique than MSAA. It involves rendering the scene at a higher resolution and then downsampling to the target resolution. This approach provides better anti-aliasing results but at the cost of increased GPU load.

SSAA can be implemented in Vulkan by rendering to a higher-resolution framebuffer and then resizing the image to the target resolution using image scaling techniques.

Post-processing Anti-aliasing

Another anti-aliasing approach is post-processing anti-aliasing, where anti-aliasing is applied as a post-processing step after the scene is rendered. Techniques like FXAA (Fast Approximate Anti-aliasing) and SMAA (Subpixel Morphological Anti-aliasing) are popular choices. These techniques analyze the final rendered image and apply blurring and smoothing to reduce aliasing artifacts.

Implementing post-processing anti-aliasing in Vulkan involves rendering the scene to a framebuffer, then applying the anti-aliasing filter in a separate pass.

Conclusion

Anti-aliasing is essential for improving the visual quality of your Vulkan applications. Vulkan provides various anti-aliasing techniques, such as MSAA, SSAA, and post-processing anti-aliasing, to choose from based on your project's requirements and performance constraints. Implementing anti-aliasing effectively can significantly enhance the overall appeal and realism of your rendered images.

Section 13.5: Configuring Multisampling

In Vulkan, configuring multisampling involves specifying how many samples are taken per pixel and how the fragment shader's output is resolved to a single color value. Multisampling helps in reducing aliasing artifacts, such as jagged edges, by averaging multiple samples for each pixel.

Multisampling Setup

To configure multisampling in Vulkan, you'll need to make several adjustments in your pipeline and framebuffer setup:

1. **Multisample State**: Configure the VkPipelineMultisampleStateCreateInfo structure to specify the sample count. For example:

VkPipelineMultisampleStateCreateInfo multisampling = {};

multisampling.sType   =
VK_STRUCTURE_TYPE_PIPELINE_MULTISAMPLE_STATE_

multisampling.rasterizationSamples   =
VK_SAMPLE_COUNT_4_BIT; // *Sample count (adjust as needed)*

In this example, VK_SAMPLE_COUNT_4_BIT indicates that four samples are taken per pixel. Adjust the sample count based on your quality and performance requirements.

1. **Framebuffer Attachment**: Ensure that the framebuffer attachments, such as color and depth attachments, are created with the same sample count as specified in the VkPipelineMultisampleStateCreateInfo.

VkImageCreateInfo colorImageInfo = {};

colorImageInfo.sType   =
VK_STRUCTURE_TYPE_IMAGE_CREATE_INFO;

colorImageInfo.samples   =
VK_SAMPLE_COUNT_4_BIT; // *Sample count (must match pipeline)*

1. **Resolve Attachment**: If you want to resolve the multisampled image to a single sample image, you'll need to create a separate resolve attachment:

VkAttachmentDescription colorAttachmentResolve =
{};

colorAttachmentResolve.format   =
swapChainImageFormat;

colorAttachmentResolve.samples   =
VK_SAMPLE_COUNT_1_BIT; // *Single sample*

colorAttachmentResolve.loadOp   =
VK_ATTACHMENT_LOAD_OP_DONT_CARE;

colorAttachmentResolve.storeOp   =
VK_ATTACHMENT_STORE_OP_STORE;

colorAttachmentResolve.stencilLoadOp   =
VK_ATTACHMENT_LOAD_OP_DONT_CARE;

```
colorAttachmentResolve.stencilStoreOp        =
VK_ATTACHMENT_STORE_OP_DONT_CARE;
```

```
colorAttachmentResolve.initialLayout         =
VK_IMAGE_LAYOUT_UNDEFINED;
```

```
colorAttachmentResolve.finalLayout           =
VK_IMAGE_LAYOUT_PRESENT_SRC_KHR;
```

1. **Subpass**: Modify the subpass description to specify that the multisampled color attachment is resolved to the resolve attachment:

```
VkAttachmentReference  colorAttachmentResolveRef =
{};
```

```
colorAttachmentResolveRef.attachment = 2; // Index of
the resolve attachment
```

```
colorAttachmentResolveRef.layout             =
VK_IMAGE_LAYOUT_COLOR_ATTACHMENT_OPTIMAL;
```

```
VkSubpassDescription subpass = {};
```

```
subpass.colorAttachmentCount = 1;
```

```
subpass.pColorAttachments = &colorAttachmentRef;
```

```
subpass.pResolveAttachments                  =
&colorAttachmentResolveRef; // Resolve attachment
```

Rendering with Multisampling

When rendering with multisampling enabled, Vulkan will automatically take multiple samples per pixel and apply the fragment shader to each sample. The results are then averaged, reducing aliasing artifacts.

Remember that enabling multisampling comes with an additional performance cost due to the increased number of samples. You should choose the sample count carefully based on your application's requirements and hardware capabilities. Multisampling is particularly beneficial for improving the visual quality of your rendered images, especially in scenes with fine details and high-contrast edges.

Chapter 14: Dynamic State and Viewports

Section 14.1: Dynamic State in Vulkan

In Vulkan, dynamic state allows you to change certain aspects of the pipeline state without recreating the entire pipeline. This can be particularly useful when you want to modify rendering parameters frequently or efficiently switch between different rendering configurations. Dynamic state is an optimization feature that can help reduce the overhead of pipeline creation and management.

Dynamic State Objects

Dynamic state in Vulkan is managed through dynamic state objects, which are set independently of the pipeline state. The following aspects of the pipeline can be made dynamic:

1. **Viewport**: The viewport defines the transformation from normalized device coordinates (NDC) to the framebuffer. You can set the viewport dynamically, allowing you to efficiently change the area of the framebuffer that is visible.
2. **Scissor**: Scissors are rectangles that can be used to clip the rendering area. Like viewports, you can set scissors dynamically to control which parts of the framebuffer are affected by rendering.
3. **Line Width**: The line width affects the thickness of lines when rendering primitives. Dynamic line width allows you to change the line thickness on the fly.
4. **Depth Bias**: Depth bias is used to adjust the depth values of fragments. This is often used to avoid z-fighting artifacts. Dynamic depth bias allows you to change this bias as

needed.

5. **Blend Constants**: Blend constants are used in blending operations. Dynamic blend constants enable you to modify the constants used in blending equations.

6. **Stencil Reference**: Stencil reference values are used in stencil tests. Dynamic stencil reference allows you to change these reference values when needed.

Dynamic State Commands

To set dynamic state in Vulkan, you use the vkCmdSetViewport, vkCmdSetScissor, and other similar commands within a command buffer. Here's an example of how to set the viewport dynamically:

VkViewport viewport = {};

viewport.x = 0.0f;

viewport.y = 0.0f;

viewport.width = static_cast<float>(swapChainExtent.width);

viewport.height = static_cast<float>(swapChainExtent.height);

viewport.minDepth = 0.0f;

viewport.maxDepth = 1.0f;

vkCmdSetViewport(commandBuffer, 0, 1, &viewport);

In this example, we're setting the viewport to cover the entire framebuffer. You can update the viewport as needed based on your rendering requirements.

Dynamic state provides flexibility while avoiding the need to create multiple pipelines for slight variations in rendering. However, not all aspects of the pipeline can be made dynamic, so you'll need to choose the appropriate rendering technique based on your specific use case.

Section 14.2: Dynamic Viewport and Scissor

In Vulkan, dynamic viewport and scissor settings provide powerful tools for controlling the rendering area and how it's displayed. These features are particularly useful when you need to change the rendering region or apply different viewport and scissor configurations within a single render pass.

Dynamic Viewport

Dynamic viewport allows you to modify the region of the framebuffer that should be visible without recreating the entire pipeline. This feature is valuable when you want to adapt rendering to different screen sizes, zoom levels, or split-screen scenarios.

Here's an example of setting a dynamic viewport:

VkViewport viewport = {};

viewport.x = 0.0f; // *X-coordinate of the top-left corner*

viewport.y = 0.0f; // *Y-coordinate of the top-left corner*

viewport.width = float(swapChainExtent.width); // *Width of the viewport*

viewport.height = float(swapChainExtent.height); // *Height of the viewport*

viewport.minDepth = 0.0f; // *Minimum depth value*

viewport.maxDepth = 1.0f; // *Maximum depth value*

vkCmdSetViewport(commandBuffer, 0, 1, &viewport);

In this example, we set a dynamic viewport that covers the entire framebuffer. You can update the viewport structure with different values to change the rendering region dynamically.

Dynamic Scissor

Dynamic scissor settings complement dynamic viewports by defining a rectangular area where rendering is limited. This is often used to apply effects to specific regions of the framebuffer or to render UI elements within a defined area.

Here's an example of setting a dynamic scissor:

VkRect2D scissor = {};

scissor.offset = { 0, 0 }; // *Offset of the top-left corner*

scissor.extent = swapChainExtent; // *Extent of the scissor rectangle*

vkCmdSetScissor(commandBuffer, 0, 1, &scissor);

In this example, we set a dynamic scissor that matches the extent of the framebuffer. You can adjust the scissor structure to change the area affected by rendering.

Combining Dynamic Viewport and Scissor

Dynamic viewport and scissor settings can be combined to achieve more complex rendering effects. For instance, in a split-screen game, you can use dynamic viewport and scissor to render different portions of the framebuffer for each player.

// *Set dynamic viewport and scissor for player 1*

SetViewportAndScissor(player1Viewport, player1Scissor);

// Render player 1's view

// Set dynamic viewport and scissor for player 2

SetViewportAndScissor(player2Viewport, player2Scissor);

// Render player 2's view

By leveraging dynamic viewport and scissor settings, you can efficiently adapt your Vulkan application to various scenarios and create visually appealing and interactive graphics. These features are particularly valuable when implementing complex rendering techniques and optimizations.

Section 14.3: Viewport Transformations

Viewport transformations play a crucial role in Vulkan, allowing you to define how 3D scenes are projected onto the 2D screen. Understanding viewport transformations is essential for controlling the rendering aspect ratio, depth range, and projection type.

The Viewport and Projection Matrix

In Vulkan, the viewport transformation is closely related to the projection matrix, which is used to project 3D coordinates onto the 2D screen. The viewport transformation involves defining the following parameters:

- **Viewport Dimensions**: These specify the size and position of the viewport on the screen, usually in normalized device coordinates. You set this information using the VkViewport structure.

- **Projection Matrix**: The projection matrix determines how the 3D scene is projected onto the 2D viewport. It can be orthographic or perspective, depending on your rendering requirements.

Setting Up the Viewport

To set up the viewport in Vulkan, you use the vkCmdSetViewport command within a command buffer. Here's a brief example of setting up a viewport:

VkViewport viewport = {};

viewport.x = 0.0f; // *X-coordinate of the top-left corner*

viewport.y = 0.0f; // *Y-coordinate of the top-left corner*

viewport.width = float(width); // *Width of the viewport*

viewport.height = float(height); // *Height of the viewport*

viewport.minDepth = 0.0f; // *Minimum depth value*

viewport.maxDepth = 1.0f; // *Maximum depth value*

vkCmdSetViewport(commandBuffer, 0, 1, &viewport);

In this example, we create a VkViewport structure and specify its properties. The vkCmdSetViewport function is then called to set the viewport within a command buffer. This command defines the portion of the framebuffer to which rendering will occur.

Using the Projection Matrix

The projection matrix is a critical component of the viewport transformation. Depending on whether you choose an orthographic or perspective projection, the projection matrix will vary. You typically multiply this matrix with your model-view matrix to project your 3D vertices onto the 2D screen.

Here's an example of setting up a perspective projection matrix:

```
glm::mat4                    projectionMatrix              =
glm::perspective(glm::radians(45.0f), aspectRatio, 0.1f, 10.0f);
```

In this example, we use the GLM library to create a perspective projection matrix. It's important to calculate the aspect ratio based on the viewport's dimensions to ensure that the rendered scene appears correctly.

Adapting Viewport Transformations

Dynamic viewport transformations are useful when you need to adapt the viewport's parameters during rendering, such as implementing zoom or rendering multiple views. You can modify the viewport dimensions or projection matrix as needed to achieve the desired effect.

Understanding viewport transformations and projection matrices is fundamental for rendering realistic and visually appealing 3D scenes in Vulkan. Properly configuring these settings is key to controlling the projection of your 3D world onto the 2D screen and ensuring that your graphics look as intended.

Section 14.4: Using Dynamic State

Dynamic state in Vulkan allows you to change certain pipeline state settings on a per-draw or per-command basis without recreating the entire pipeline. This flexibility is valuable for optimizing rendering performance and implementing various rendering effects. In this section, we will explore how to use dynamic state in Vulkan.

Understanding Dynamic State

Dynamic state in Vulkan includes a set of pipeline state objects that you can modify dynamically at render time, such as viewport, scissor, line width, and blend constants. Instead of specifying these values when creating a pipeline, you set them before executing a command buffer. This means you can change these settings between draws without re-creating pipelines, which can be especially beneficial for performance.

Enabling Dynamic State

To enable dynamic state for specific pipeline state objects, you need to specify them when creating a graphics pipeline. For example, to enable dynamic viewport and scissor state, you can do the following:

VkPipelineDynamicStateCreateInfo dynamicStateInfo = {};

dynamicStateInfo.sType   =
VK_STRUCTURE_TYPE_PIPELINE_DYNAMIC_STATE_CRF

dynamicStateInfo.dynamicStateCount = 2; // *Number of dynamic states to enable*

dynamicStateInfo.pDynamicStates = dynamicStates; // *Array of dynamic states to enable*

VkPipelineViewportStateCreateInfo viewportStateInfo = {};

// *... (other viewport and scissor configuration)*

viewportStateInfo.pDynamicState = &dynamicStateInfo; // *Enable dynamic state*

// *Attach viewportStateInfo to VkGraphicsPipelineCreateInfo*

In this example, dynamicStates is an array of dynamic states you want to enable, which includes VK_DYNAMIC_STATE_VIEWPORT and VK_DYNAMIC_STATE_SCISSOR. By specifying these dynamic states, you indicate that you want to change the viewport and scissor settings dynamically.

Setting Dynamic State

Once dynamic state is enabled, you can set the dynamic state values before drawing. Here's an example of how to set dynamic viewport and scissor values in a command buffer:

VkViewport viewport = {}; // *Set your desired viewport parameters*

VkRect2D scissor = {}; // *Set your desired scissor parameters*

vkCmdSetViewport(commandBuffer, 0, 1, &viewport);

vkCmdSetScissor(commandBuffer, 0, 1, &scissor);

In this code snippet, we use vkCmdSetViewport and vkCmdSetScissor to set the viewport and scissor dynamically within a command buffer. These changes will affect the rendering for the subsequent draw calls.

Use Cases for Dynamic State

Dynamic state is particularly useful in scenarios where you need to change rendering parameters for different objects or frames, such as implementing zoom functionality or rendering multiple views in a single render pass. It can also improve performance by reducing the need to create and manage multiple pipelines for minor variations in state settings.

In conclusion, dynamic state in Vulkan provides a powerful mechanism for altering certain pipeline state objects on a per-draw or per-command basis, offering flexibility and performance benefits in various rendering scenarios. Understanding when and how to use dynamic state can lead to more efficient Vulkan applications.

Section 14.5: Multiple Viewports and Scissors

In Vulkan, you can take advantage of multiple viewports and scissors to render complex scenes efficiently. Multiple viewports allow you to render from different perspectives or regions in a single pass, while multiple scissors help define different clipping regions. This section explores how to utilize multiple viewports and scissors effectively in your Vulkan application.

Enabling Multiple Viewports and Scissors

To enable multiple viewports and scissors, you need to create a graphics pipeline with the appropriate settings. Here's how you can do it:

VkPipelineViewportStateCreateInfo viewportStateInfo = {};

viewportStateInfo.sType   = VK_STRUCTURE_TYPE_PIPELINE_VIEWPORT_STATE_CF

viewportStateInfo.viewportCount = 2; // *Set the number of viewports*

viewportStateInfo.pViewports = viewports; // *An array of viewport configurations*

viewportStateInfo.scissorCount = 2; // *Set the number of scissors*

viewportStateInfo.pScissors = scissors; // *An array of scissor configurations*

// *Attach viewportStateInfo to VkGraphicsPipelineCreateInfo*

In this example, we specify that we want to use two viewports and two scissors by setting viewportCount and scissorCount accordingly. You also need to provide arrays of viewport and scissor configurations in pViewports and pScissors, respectively.

Configuring Multiple Viewports and Scissors

Now that you have enabled multiple viewports and scissors, you can configure them according to your rendering needs. For instance, you might want to set up a top-down and a side view for your scene. Here's how you can configure two viewports and scissors:

```
// Define viewport configurations

VkViewport viewports[2] = {};

viewports[0].x = 0.0f;

viewports[0].y = 0.0f;

viewports[0].width = static_cast<float>(windowWidth) / 2.0f; //
Half of the window width

viewports[0].height = static_cast<float>(windowHeight);

viewports[0].minDepth = 0.0f;

viewports[0].maxDepth = 1.0f;

viewports[1].x = static_cast<float>(windowWidth) / 2.0f; // Second
viewport starts from the middle

viewports[1].y = 0.0f;

viewports[1].width = static_cast<float>(windowWidth) / 2.0f; //
Half of the window width
```

viewports[1].height = static_cast<float>(windowHeight);

viewports[1].minDepth = 0.0f;

viewports[1].maxDepth = 1.0f;

// Define scissor configurations

VkRect2D scissors[2] = {};

scissors[0].offset = {0, 0};

scissors[0].extent = {windowWidth / 2, windowHeight}; *// Same as the first viewport*

scissors[1].offset = {windowWidth / 2, 0}; *// Start from the middle*

scissors[1].extent = {windowWidth / 2, windowHeight}; *// Same as the second viewport*

In this code snippet, we define two viewports and two scissor regions. The first viewport covers the left half of the window, while the second viewport covers the right half. The scissors are set accordingly to match the viewport regions.

Rendering with Multiple Viewports and Scissors

Once configured, you can use these multiple viewports and scissors when rendering commands. When binding a graphics pipeline, make sure that it's compatible with the number of viewports and scissors you've enabled. Then, you can render objects with different viewports and scissor regions in a single pass.

// Bind your graphics pipeline that supports multiple viewports and scissors

// Bind descriptor sets, vertex buffers, and other resources

```
// Set viewport and scissor dynamically for each draw

for (int i = 0; i < 2; ++i) {

vkCmdSetViewport(commandBuffer, i, 1, &viewports[i]);

vkCmdSetScissor(commandBuffer, i, 1, &scissors[i]);

// Issue draw commands for objects in this viewport-scissor pair

}
```

In this code, we loop through the two viewports and scissors, setting them dynamically for each draw operation. You can issue draw commands for objects in different regions or perspectives, and Vulkan will handle rendering them accordingly.

Multiple viewports and scissors are powerful tools in Vulkan, allowing you to efficiently render complex scenes, implement split-screen views, or achieve other multi-perspective effects. By understanding how to enable, configure, and use them, you can enhance your Vulkan application's rendering capabilities.

Chapter 15: Command Buffers and Rendering

Section 15.1: Command Buffer Basics

In Vulkan, command buffers are essential for submitting rendering commands to the GPU. A command buffer is a data structure that holds a sequence of rendering commands, such as drawing objects, binding resources, and setting pipeline states. These commands are executed by the GPU in the order they appear in the command buffer, allowing you to control the rendering process precisely.

Creating Command Buffers

Before you can start recording rendering commands, you need to create command buffers. Command buffers in Vulkan are allocated from a command pool. A command pool manages the memory used for command buffers and ensures efficient allocation and reuse.

Here's how you can create a command pool and allocate command buffers:

VkCommandPoolCreateInfo poolInfo = {};

poolInfo.sType   =
VK_STRUCTURE_TYPE_COMMAND_POOL_CREATE_INF

poolInfo.queueFamilyIndex = graphicsQueueFamilyIndex;

VkCommandPool commandPool;

if   (vkCreateCommandPool(device,   &poolInfo,   nullptr,
&commandPool) != VK_SUCCESS) {

throw std::runtime_error("Failed to create command pool!");

```
}

std::vector<VkCommandBuffer>
commandBuffers(swapchainImages.size());

VkCommandBufferAllocateInfo allocInfo = {};

allocInfo.sType                                        =
VK_STRUCTURE_TYPE_COMMAND_BUFFER_ALLOCATE_INF

allocInfo.commandPool = commandPool;

allocInfo.level                                        =
VK_COMMAND_BUFFER_LEVEL_PRIMARY;

allocInfo.commandBufferCount                           =
static_cast<uint32_t>(commandBuffers.size());

if        (vkAllocateCommandBuffers(device,        &allocInfo,
commandBuffers.data()) != VK_SUCCESS) {

throw std::runtime_error("Failed to allocate command buffers!");

}
```

In this code snippet, we first create a command pool suitable for the graphics queue family. Then, we allocate a set of primary command buffers. Primary command buffers are the main command buffers used for rendering operations.

Recording Commands

Once you have allocated command buffers, you can start recording rendering commands into them. Command buffer recording is typically done within a render loop for each frame. Here's a simplified example of how to record rendering commands:

```
VkCommandBufferBeginInfo beginInfo = {};

beginInfo.sType                                    =
VK_STRUCTURE_TYPE_COMMAND_BUFFER_BEGIN_INI

beginInfo.flags                                    =
VK_COMMAND_BUFFER_USAGE_SIMULTANEOUS_USE_

for (size_t i = 0; i < commandBuffers.size(); i++) {

if (vkBeginCommandBuffer(commandBuffers[i], &beginInfo) !=
VK_SUCCESS) {

throw std::runtime_error("Failed to begin recording command
buffer!");

}

// Set pipeline state, bind resources, and issue drawing commands here

if        (vkEndCommandBuffer(commandBuffers[i])        !=
VK_SUCCESS) {

throw std::runtime_error("Failed to record command buffer!");

}

}
```

In this example, we begin recording each command buffer, set up the rendering state, bind resources, and issue drawing commands. Finally, we end the recording of each command buffer.

Executing Command Buffers

Once you have recorded rendering commands into command buffers, you can submit these command buffers to the graphics queue for execution. Command buffer submission is typically synchronized with the presentation of images. Here's how you can submit command buffers:

```
VkSubmitInfo submitInfo = {};

submitInfo.sType                                        =
VK_STRUCTURE_TYPE_SUBMIT_INFO;

submitInfo.commandBufferCount                           =
static_cast<uint32_t>(commandBuffers.size());

submitInfo.pCommandBuffers = commandBuffers.data();

if    (vkQueueSubmit(graphicsQueue,    1,    &submitInfo,
VK_NULL_HANDLE) != VK_SUCCESS) {

throw std::runtime_error("Failed to submit command buffer to the
queue!");

}
```

In this code, we specify the command buffers to submit and the graphics queue to which they should be submitted.

Conclusion

Command buffers are a fundamental concept in Vulkan, allowing you to control the rendering process by recording and submitting rendering commands. In the next sections, we will explore more advanced topics related to command buffers and rendering in Vulkan.

Please note that this is a simplified overview, and the actual implementation may vary depending on your Vulkan application's structure and complexity.

Section 15.2: Recording Command Buffers

Recording command buffers in Vulkan is a critical step in the rendering process. Command buffers capture a sequence of rendering commands that will be executed by the GPU. In this section, we'll delve deeper into the process of recording command buffers and explore some advanced techniques.

Command Buffer Lifecycle

Command buffers in Vulkan have a well-defined lifecycle:

1. **Recording**: This is the phase where you record the commands that should be executed by the GPU. You can record multiple command buffers simultaneously, each for a specific frame or rendering task.
2. **Execution**: Once you've recorded the commands, you can submit the command buffers to a queue for execution. Vulkan allows you to have multiple command buffers in flight at the same time, making it suitable for multi-threaded rendering.
3. **Resetting**: After a command buffer has been executed, you can reset it to record new commands. Resetting can be either a full reset, which clears all recorded commands, or a partial reset, which allows you to reuse some of the recorded commands.

Recording Basic Commands

Recording commands in Vulkan is done in a straightforward manner. You start by calling vkBeginCommandBuffer with a VkCommandBufferBeginInfo struct, specifying flags like VK_COMMAND_BUFFER_USAGE_ONE_TIME_SUBMIT if the command buffer will only be used once. After that, you issue rendering commands such as binding a pipeline, setting viewport and scissor state, binding vertex and index buffers, and drawing objects.

Here's an example of recording basic commands to draw a triangle:

VkCommandBufferBeginInfo beginInfo = {};

beginInfo.sType   =
VK_STRUCTURE_TYPE_COMMAND_BUFFER_BEGIN_INFO;

beginInfo.flags   =
VK_COMMAND_BUFFER_USAGE_SIMULTANEOUS_USE_BIT;

*//   You   can   use
VK_COMMAND_BUFFER_USAGE_ONE_TIME_SUBMIT if
it's a one-time submit*

if (vkBeginCommandBuffer(commandBuffer, &beginInfo) !=
VK_SUCCESS) {

throw std::runtime_error("Failed to begin recording command buffer!");

}

// Bind the graphics pipeline

vkCmdBindPipeline(commandBuffer,
VK_PIPELINE_BIND_POINT_GRAPHICS, graphicsPipeline);

// Set viewport and scissor state

vkCmdSetViewport(commandBuffer, 0, 1, &viewport);

vkCmdSetScissor(commandBuffer, 0, 1, &scissor);

// Bind vertex and index buffers

```
const VkBuffer vertexBuffers[] = {vertexBuffer};

const VkDeviceSize offsets[] = {0};

vkCmdBindVertexBuffers(commandBuffer, 0, 1, vertexBuffers, offsets);

vkCmdBindIndexBuffer(commandBuffer, indexBuffer, 0, VK_INDEX_TYPE_UINT16);

// Draw the triangle

vkCmdDrawIndexed(commandBuffer,
static_cast<uint32_t>(indices.size()), 1, 0, 0, 0);

if (vkEndCommandBuffer(commandBuffer) != VK_SUCCESS) {

throw std::runtime_error("Failed to record command buffer!");

}
```

In this example, we begin recording the command buffer, bind the graphics pipeline, set viewport and scissor states, bind vertex and index buffers, and issue a draw command. Finally, we end the command buffer recording.

Secondary Command Buffers

Vulkan also supports secondary command buffers, which can be recorded separately and then included in primary command buffers. This is useful for organizing rendering tasks and reducing CPU overhead.

```
// Create secondary command buffer

VkCommandBufferAllocateInfo allocInfo = {};
```

```
allocInfo.sType                                =
VK_STRUCTURE_TYPE_COMMAND_BUFFER_ALLOCATE_INF

allocInfo.level                                =
VK_COMMAND_BUFFER_LEVEL_SECONDARY;

allocInfo.commandPool = commandPool;

allocInfo.commandBufferCount = 1;

VkCommandBuffer secondaryCommandBuffer;

if       (vkAllocateCommandBuffers(device,        &allocInfo,
&secondaryCommandBuffer) != VK_SUCCESS) {

throw std::runtime_error("Failed to allocate secondary command
buffer!");

}

// Recording the secondary command buffer

VkCommandBufferBeginInfo secondaryBeginInfo = {};

secondaryBeginInfo.sType                                =
VK_STRUCTURE_TYPE_COMMAND_BUFFER_BEGIN_INFO;

if       (vkBeginCommandBuffer(secondaryCommandBuffer,
&secondaryBeginInfo) != VK_SUCCESS) {

throw std::runtime_error("Failed to begin recording secondary
command buffer!");

}

// Record commands for the secondary command buffer

// ...
```

```
if     (vkEndCommandBuffer(secondaryCommandBuffer)     !=
VK_SUCCESS) {
```

```
throw std::runtime_error("Failed to record secondary command
buffer!");
```

```
}
```

```
// Including the secondary command buffer in a primary command
buffer
```

```
vkCmdExecuteCommands(primaryCommandBuffer,           1,
&secondaryCommandBuffer);
```

In this example, we allocate a secondary command buffer, record commands into it, and then include it in a primary command buffer using vkCmdExecuteCommands.

Conclusion

Recording command buffers in Vulkan is a fundamental part of rendering. It allows you to precisely control the GPU's actions and can be used for various rendering tasks. Whether you're rendering simple shapes or complex scenes, mastering command buffer recording is essential for Vulkan development. In the next sections, we'll explore more advanced topics related to command buffers and rendering techniques.

Section 15.3: Submitting Command Buffers

Submitting command buffers is the process of dispatching recorded rendering commands to the GPU for execution. In Vulkan, this involves several steps, including synchronization and presentation. In this section, we will explore how to submit command buffers effectively.

Queue Families and Queues

Before submitting command buffers, it's important to understand Vulkan's queue system. Vulkan supports multiple queue families, each specialized for different types of operations. Common queue families include graphics, compute, and transfer.

When creating a logical device, you can specify the number of queues and the queue families it should belong to. It's typical to create separate queues for graphics and presentation. To submit a command buffer, you need a handle to a queue from the appropriate queue family.

```
// Assuming you have created a logical device and retrieved queue handles

VkQueue graphicsQueue;

VkQueue presentQueue;

vkGetDeviceQueue(device,      graphicsQueueFamilyIndex,      0,
&graphicsQueue);

vkGetDeviceQueue(device,      presentQueueFamilyIndex,      0,
&presentQueue);
```

Semaphore and Fence

In Vulkan, synchronization is crucial to ensure that command buffers are executed in the correct order and that rendering is synchronized with presentation. Two primary synchronization mechanisms are semaphores and fences.

- **Semaphore**: Semaphores are used to signal and wait for events between different command queues. They ensure that rendering operations are properly synchronized.

- **Fence**: Fences are used to synchronize between the CPU and the GPU. They can be used to determine when a submitted set of command buffers has finished execution.

Submitting Command Buffers

To submit a command buffer, you need to create a VkSubmitInfo structure that describes the command buffers and synchronization objects involved in the submission.

Here's a simplified example:

VkSubmitInfo submitInfo = {};

submitInfo.sType   = VK_STRUCTURE_TYPE_SUBMIT_INFO;

// Wait semaphores: signals when the command buffer can start execution

VkSemaphore waitSemaphores[] = {imageAvailableSemaphore};

VkPipelineStageFlags   waitStages[]   = {VK_PIPELINE_STAGE_COLOR_ATTACHMENT_OUTPUT

submitInfo.waitSemaphoreCount = 1;

submitInfo.pWaitSemaphores = waitSemaphores;

submitInfo.pWaitDstStageMask = waitStages;

// Command buffers to submit

submitInfo.commandBufferCount = 1;

submitInfo.pCommandBuffers = &commandBuffer;

// Signal semaphores: signals when rendering is complete

VkSemaphore signalSemaphores[] = {renderFinishedSemaphore};

submitInfo.signalSemaphoreCount = 1;

submitInfo.pSignalSemaphores = signalSemaphores;

// Submit the command buffer

if (vkQueueSubmit(graphicsQueue, 1, &submitInfo, inFlightFences[currentFrame]) != VK_SUCCESS) {

throw std::runtime_error("Failed to submit command buffer!");

}

In this example, we specify wait semaphores that indicate when the command buffer can start execution (typically, when the image is available for rendering). After execution, the command buffer signals the renderFinishedSemaphore. We also associate the command buffer with a fence (inFlightFences[currentFrame]), allowing us to determine when it has finished executing.

Presentation

After submitting command buffers, we need to ensure that the rendered image is presented to the screen. Presentation is often synchronized with rendering using semaphores.

VkPresentInfoKHR presentInfo = {};

presentInfo.sType = VK_STRUCTURE_TYPE_PRESENT_INFO_KHR;

// Wait semaphores: wait for rendering to complete

```
presentInfo.waitSemaphoreCount = 1;

presentInfo.pWaitSemaphores = signalSemaphores;

// Swapchain to present images from

VkSwapchainKHR swapChains[] = {swapChain};

presentInfo.swapchainCount = 1;

presentInfo.pSwapchains = swapChains;

presentInfo.pImageIndices = &imageIndex;

// Present the image

vkQueuePresentKHR(presentQueue, &presentInfo);
```

In this code snippet, we specify the semaphore signaled by the rendering process as a wait semaphore. We also specify the swapchain and image index for presentation.

Conclusion

Submitting command buffers in Vulkan involves synchronization, queue management, and presentation. Proper synchronization using semaphores and fences ensures that rendering commands are executed correctly and that the results are presented to the screen. Understanding this process is essential for building efficient Vulkan applications. In the next sections, we'll explore more advanced rendering techniques and optimizations.

Section 15.4: Command Buffer Pools

In Vulkan, command buffers are objects that contain rendering commands, and they are allocated from command buffer pools.

Understanding command buffer pools is essential for efficient Vulkan applications.

Command Buffer Allocation

Command buffers are allocated from command buffer pools associated with a specific queue family. Vulkan provides two types of command buffer pools: primary and secondary.

- **Primary Command Buffers**: These are the main command buffers that contain the primary sequence of rendering commands. They can be submitted directly to a queue for execution.

- **Secondary Command Buffers**: These are used for more specialized tasks, such as reusing common sequences of rendering commands across multiple frames. They cannot be submitted directly but can be executed within primary command buffers.

Creating a Command Buffer Pool

To create a command buffer pool, you need to specify the queue family and the type of command buffers you want to allocate.

VkCommandPoolCreateInfo poolInfo = {};

poolInfo.sType = VK_STRUCTURE_TYPE_COMMAND_POOL_CREATE_INFO;

poolInfo.queueFamilyIndex = graphicsQueueFamilyIndex; // *Specify the queue family index*

```
poolInfo.flags                                        =
VK_COMMAND_POOL_CREATE_RESET_COMMAND_BU
// Optional

VkCommandPool commandPool;

if    (vkCreateCommandPool(device,    &poolInfo,    nullptr,
&commandPool) != VK_SUCCESS) {

throw std::runtime_error("Failed to create command pool!");

}
```

In the code snippet above, we create a command pool associated
with the graphics queue family and specify the
VK_COMMAND_POOL_CREATE_RESET_COMMAND_BU
flag, which allows us to reset individual command buffers later.

Allocating Command Buffers

Once you have a command pool, you can allocate command buffers
from it. The number of command buffers to allocate is typically
based on your application's requirements.

```
VkCommandBufferAllocateInfo allocInfo = {};

allocInfo.sType                                       =
VK_STRUCTURE_TYPE_COMMAND_BUFFER_ALLOCAT

allocInfo.commandPool = commandPool; // Specify the command
pool

allocInfo.level                                       =
VK_COMMAND_BUFFER_LEVEL_PRIMARY; // Use primary
command buffers
```

```
allocInfo.commandBufferCount = 1; // Specify the number of
command buffers to allocate

VkCommandBuffer commandBuffer;

if        (vkAllocateCommandBuffers(device,        &allocInfo,
&commandBuffer) != VK_SUCCESS) {

throw std::runtime_error("Failed to allocate command buffer!");

}
```

In this code snippet, we allocate a primary command buffer from the command pool. You can change the VK_COMMAND_BUFFER_LEVEL_PRIMARY to VK_COMMAND_BUFFER_LEVEL_SECONDARY if you need a secondary command buffer.

Resetting Command Buffers

It's often necessary to reset command buffers before recording new commands. This is where the command pool's reset flag becomes useful.

```
vkResetCommandBuffer(commandBuffer,
VK_COMMAND_BUFFER_RESET_RELEASE_RESOURCES_BIT);
```

In this example, we reset the commandBuffer and release the associated resources, making it ready for new commands. This step is essential before recording commands into a command buffer.

Conclusion

Command buffer pools are crucial for managing command buffer allocation in Vulkan. Understanding the distinction between primary and secondary command buffers, creating command pools, and properly resetting command buffers are fundamental concepts when building Vulkan applications. Efficient use of command buffers and pools can lead to better performance and resource management in your Vulkan rendering pipeline.

Section 15.5: Rendering Multiple Objects

Rendering multiple objects is a common requirement in graphics applications. In Vulkan, this involves creating and managing resources for each object and issuing draw commands for each of them. Let's explore how to render multiple objects efficiently in Vulkan.

Object Representations

Before rendering multiple objects, you need to represent each object in your application. This typically involves defining structures or classes to hold the object's geometry, materials, transformation matrices, and other relevant data.

struct Object {

VkBuffer vertexBuffer; // *Vertex buffer for object geometry*

VkBuffer indexBuffer; // *Index buffer for object geometry*

uint32_t vertexCount;

uint32_t indexCount;

glm::mat4 transform; // *Transformation matrix for positioning*

};

In this example, we define an Object structure to represent each object, storing its vertex and index buffers, counts, and transformation matrix.

Creating and Managing Objects

You'll need to create and manage objects based on your application's requirements. This involves allocating memory, copying data to buffers, and potentially loading textures.

```
std::vector<Object> objects;
```

```
// Create and populate objects (vertex and index buffers, textures, etc.)
```

```
for (size_t i = 0; i < numObjects; ++i) {
```

```
Object object;
```

```
// Initialize and fill the object structure here
```

```
objects.push_back(object);
```

```
}
```

Rendering Loop

In your rendering loop, iterate over the objects and issue draw commands for each of them.

```
for (const Object& object : objects) {
```

```
// Bind the object's vertex and index buffers
```

```
vkCmdBindVertexBuffers(commandBuffer,          0,          1,
&object.vertexBuffer, offsets);
```

```
vkCmdBindIndexBuffer(commandBuffer,   object.indexBuffer,   0,
VK_INDEX_TYPE_UINT32);
```

// Set the object's transformation matrix as a uniform buffer or push constant

```
vkCmdPushConstants(commandBuffer, pipelineLayout,
VK_SHADER_STAGE_VERTEX_BIT, 0, sizeof(glm::mat4),
&object.transform);
```

// Issue a draw command for the object

```
vkCmdDrawIndexed(commandBuffer, object.indexCount, 1, 0, 0,
0);
```

```
}
```

In the rendering loop, you bind the vertex and index buffers for each object, set the object's transformation matrix using either a uniform buffer or push constants, and issue a draw command. This process is repeated for each object in your scene.

Object Culling and Optimization

To optimize rendering performance, consider implementing object culling techniques to determine which objects are visible in the current frame. Additionally, you can explore Vulkan's multi-threading capabilities to parallelize object rendering for better CPU utilization.

Rendering multiple objects efficiently in Vulkan involves proper resource management and issuing draw commands for each object in your scene. By organizing and optimizing your code, you can achieve high-performance rendering in Vulkan-based applications.

Chapter 16: Syncing Frames and Presentation

Section 16.1: Semaphore and Fence Usage

In Vulkan, synchronization is critical to ensure that various parts of the rendering process, such as command buffer execution and presentation, happen in the correct order and don't produce graphical artifacts or crashes. Two important synchronization objects in Vulkan are semaphores and fences.

Semaphores

Semaphores are synchronization primitives that are used to signal and block execution of queues. They are typically employed to synchronize operations between the graphics queue (used for rendering) and the presentation queue (used for displaying images on the screen).

In Vulkan, there are two types of semaphores:

1. **Image Semaphores**: These are used to signal that an image is available for rendering or presentation. When rendering to an image is complete, the semaphore is signaled, allowing the presentation to begin.
2. **Render Semaphores**: These are used to signal that rendering operations (e.g., command buffer submission) are complete. They ensure that rendering commands don't start until the previous frame's rendering is finished.

Here's how you would use semaphores in Vulkan:

VkSemaphore imageAvailableSemaphore;

```
VkSemaphore renderFinishedSemaphore;

VkSemaphoreCreateInfo semaphoreInfo = {};

semaphoreInfo.sType                              =
VK_STRUCTURE_TYPE_SEMAPHORE_CREATE_INFO;

if   (vkCreateSemaphore(device,   &semaphoreInfo,   nullptr,
&imageAvailableSemaphore) != VK_SUCCESS ||

vkCreateSemaphore(device,       &semaphoreInfo,       nullptr,
&renderFinishedSemaphore) != VK_SUCCESS) {

throw std::runtime_error("Failed to create semaphores!");

}
```

You create two semaphores, one for signaling image availability (imageAvailableSemaphore) and another for signaling rendering completion (renderFinishedSemaphore).

Fences

Fences are synchronization primitives that are used to signal and block host operations. They are useful for ensuring that the CPU doesn't proceed with rendering operations until the GPU has finished previous work.

```
VkFence renderFence;

VkFenceCreateInfo fenceInfo = {};

fenceInfo.sType                                 =
VK_STRUCTURE_TYPE_FENCE_CREATE_INFO;

fenceInfo.flags = 0; // Flags can be used for special behavior, but 0 is
fine for basic usage.
```

```
if (vkCreateFence(device, &fenceInfo, nullptr, &renderFence) !=
VK_SUCCESS) {

throw std::runtime_error("Failed to create fence!");

}
```

You create a fence (renderFence) to control CPU-GPU synchronization. After submitting a command buffer for execution, you can wait on this fence to ensure that the GPU has completed its work before proceeding with CPU operations.

Semaphores and fences are essential for coordinating rendering and presentation in Vulkan, ensuring smooth and synchronized frame rendering and display. Proper usage of these synchronization primitives is crucial for efficient and artifact-free graphics applications.

Section 16.2: Acquiring Swapchain Images

Once we've set up semaphores and fences for synchronization in Vulkan, the next step is to acquire swapchain images. This process involves retrieving the images that will be used as rendering targets in the current frame.

The Swapchain Image Acquisition Process

1. **Retrieving Swapchain Images**: To acquire swapchain images, you need to call the vkAcquireNextImageKHR function. This function waits until an image becomes available and returns the index of the acquired image. You specify the semaphore that will be signaled when the image is acquired.

```cpp
uint32_t imageIndex;

VkResult result = vkAcquireNextImageKHR(device,
swapchain, UINT64_MAX, imageAvailableSemaphore,
VK_NULL_HANDLE, &imageIndex);

if (result == VK_ERROR_OUT_OF_DATE_KHR) {

// Handle swapchain recreation here

} else if (result != VK_SUCCESS && result !=
VK_SUBOPTIMAL_KHR) {

throw std::runtime_error("Failed to acquire swapchain
image!");

}
```

In this code, imageIndex will contain the index of the acquired image, and we specify the imageAvailableSemaphore for signaling when the image is ready.

1. **Waiting for Fence**: Before rendering to the acquired image, you should wait for the fence that corresponds to the acquired image. This ensures that the GPU has finished rendering to the image from the previous frame.

```cpp
if          (vkWaitForFences(device,          1,
&inFlightFences[currentFrame],          VK_TRUE,
UINT64_MAX) != VK_SUCCESS) {

throw std::runtime_error("Failed to wait for fence!");

}
```

// Reset the fence for the next use.

```
vkResetFences(device,                                    1,
&inFlightFences[currentFrame]);
```

Here, inFlightFences[currentFrame] corresponds to the fence associated with the current frame.

1. **Recording and Submitting Commands**: Once the image is acquired and the fence is ready, you can proceed to record rendering commands into the command buffer. After recording, you submit the command buffer for execution. The semaphore imageAvailableSemaphore is used for signaling when the image is available for rendering.
2. **Presentation**: Finally, you use the acquired image for presentation by calling vkQueuePresentKHR. This operation involves specifying the acquired image, the presentation queue, and the semaphore that signals when rendering is complete.

Handling Swapchain Recreation

It's important to note that the vkAcquireNextImageKHR function may return VK_ERROR_OUT_OF_DATE_KHR, indicating that the swapchain needs to be recreated. This can occur if the window is resized or other events require a swapchain update. When you receive this error, you should recreate the swapchain and all associated resources.

In summary, acquiring swapchain images is a crucial step in the rendering process in Vulkan. It involves synchronization with semaphores and fences to ensure that rendering and presentation occur in the correct order. Proper handling of swapchain recreation is essential for robust Vulkan applications that adapt to changes in the rendering environment.

Section 16.3: Submitting Command Buffers

Once we've acquired swapchain images and recorded rendering commands into command buffers, the next step in the Vulkan rendering process is submitting these command buffers for execution. This section explores the submission process and how it ties into synchronization.

Submission to the Graphics Queue

In Vulkan, command buffers are submitted to queues for execution. For rendering, you typically use the graphics queue. The submission process involves the following steps:

1. **Specifying Submit Information**: You create a VkSubmitInfo structure that specifies the command buffers to be submitted and the synchronization primitives to be used.

VkSubmitInfo submitInfo = {};

submitInfo.sType   = VK_STRUCTURE_TYPE_SUBMIT_INFO;

submitInfo.commandBufferCount = 1;

submitInfo.pCommandBuffers   = &commandBuffers[imageIndex]; // *Command buffer to submit*

1. **Semaphore Signaling**: You specify semaphores for

signaling and waiting in the VkSubmitInfo structure. The semaphore signaled at the end of rendering is the one we previously used to acquire the image (imageAvailableSemaphore).

```
VkSemaphore        waitSemaphores[]    =    {
imageAvailableSemaphore };
```

```
VkPipelineStageFlags      waitStages[]    =    {
VK_PIPELINE_STAGE_COLOR_ATTACHMENT_OUTPUT_]
};
```

```
submitInfo.waitSemaphoreCount = 1;
```

```
submitInfo.pWaitSemaphores = waitSemaphores;
```

```
submitInfo.pWaitDstStageMask = waitStages;
```

Here, we wait for the VK_PIPELINE_STAGE_COLOR_ATTACHMENT_OUTPUT_] stage, indicating that the image is available for color attachment.

1. **Fence for Synchronization**: You can specify a fence that will be signaled when the submitted commands are finished executing. This fence is used to synchronize the CPU with the GPU.

```
submitInfo.signalSemaphoreCount = 1;
```

```
submitInfo.pSignalSemaphores                =
&renderFinishedSemaphore; // Semaphore for signaling
when rendering is complete
```

1. **Queue Submission**: You submit the command buffers to the graphics queue for execution.

```
if (vkQueueSubmit(graphicsQueue, 1, &submitInfo,
inFlightFences[currentFrame]) != VK_SUCCESS) {

throw std::runtime_error("Failed to submit draw
command buffer!");

}
```

Here, graphicsQueue is the graphics queue, and inFlightFences[currentFrame] is the fence associated with the current frame.

Presentation Semaphore

After submitting the command buffer, the final step is presenting the rendered image. For this, you use the vkQueuePresentKHR function, which takes the following parameters:

- The presentation queue

- The VkPresentInfoKHR structure specifying the swapchain, the index of the image to present, and the semaphore indicating when rendering is complete.

```
VkPresentInfoKHR presentInfo = {};

presentInfo.sType                                    =
VK_STRUCTURE_TYPE_PRESENT_INFO_KHR;

presentInfo.waitSemaphoreCount = 1;
```

presentInfo.pWaitSemaphores = &renderFinishedSemaphore; // *Wait for rendering to complete*

presentInfo.swapchainCount = 1;

presentInfo.pSwapchains = &swapchain;

presentInfo.pImageIndices = &imageIndex; // *Index of the image to present*

// *Present the image*

VkResult result = vkQueuePresentKHR(presentationQueue, &presentInfo);

Frame Synchronization

Frame synchronization is essential to ensure that rendering and presentation are correctly ordered. Semaphores and fences play a crucial role in coordinating the CPU and GPU. By using them effectively, you can achieve smooth and synchronized rendering in Vulkan applications.

Section 16.4: Presentation and Syncing

Presentation in Vulkan involves displaying the rendered image to the screen, and synchronization is key to ensuring that this process occurs smoothly. In this section, we'll explore presentation and how synchronization ensures that the image is displayed at the right time.

The vkQueuePresentKHR Function

To present an image, you use the vkQueuePresentKHR function. This function takes the following parameters:

- The presentation queue: This is typically the queue associated with presenting images.

- The VkPresentInfoKHR structure: This structure specifies the swapchain, the index of the image to present, and semaphores to synchronize with rendering.

Here's an example of how to use vkQueuePresentKHR:

```
VkPresentInfoKHR presentInfo = {};

presentInfo.sType                                        = VK_STRUCTURE_TYPE_PRESENT_INFO_KHR;

presentInfo.waitSemaphoreCount = 1;

presentInfo.pWaitSemaphores = &renderFinishedSemaphore; // Wait for rendering to complete

presentInfo.swapchainCount = 1;

presentInfo.pSwapchains = &swapchain;

presentInfo.pImageIndices = &imageIndex; // Index of the image to present

// Present the image

VkResult result = vkQueuePresentKHR(presentationQueue, &presentInfo);
```

In this example, renderFinishedSemaphore is the semaphore that signals when rendering is complete. This semaphore is waited upon before presentation.

Frame Synchronization

Frame synchronization in Vulkan ensures that rendering and presentation are properly coordinated. It's essential to avoid visual artifacts like tearing or flickering. Semaphores and fences play a crucial role in this synchronization.

- **Acquiring Swapchain Images**: Before rendering, you acquire an image from the swapchain using a semaphore (imageAvailableSemaphore). This semaphore ensures that the rendering process waits for an available image before proceeding.

- **Submitting Command Buffers**: After recording rendering commands into a command buffer, you submit it to the graphics queue. You can specify wait semaphores to ensure that the rendering commands wait until the acquired image is available for writing.

- **Signaling Rendering Completion**: When rendering is complete, a semaphore (renderFinishedSemaphore) is signaled. This semaphore is used by the presentation process to know when the image is ready to be presented.

- **Presentation**: The presentation process uses vkQueuePresentKHR to present the image to the screen. It specifies the semaphore to wait on before presentation to ensure that the image is displayed at the right time.

Fences for CPU-GPU Synchronization

Fences are used for CPU-GPU synchronization. They are signaled by the GPU when the submitted command buffers are executed. By waiting on a fence in the CPU code, you can ensure that the CPU doesn't proceed until the GPU has finished executing the rendering commands. This is particularly important when recycling resources between frames.

// Wait for the fence to be signaled (CPU-GPU synchronization)

```
vkWaitForFences(device, 1, &inFlightFences[currentFrame], VK_TRUE, UINT64_MAX);
```

// Reset the fence for the next frame

```
vkResetFences(device, 1, &inFlightFences[currentFrame]);
```

In this code, vkWaitForFences waits for the specified fence to be signaled. Once it's signaled, the CPU can proceed, and the fence is reset to be used in the next frame.

In summary, proper synchronization using semaphores and fences ensures that rendering and presentation are coordinated, preventing visual glitches and artifacts in Vulkan applications.

Section 16.5: Practical Frame Synchronization

In this section, we'll discuss practical approaches to frame synchronization in Vulkan. Proper synchronization is crucial for maintaining smooth and artifact-free rendering. We'll explore some common synchronization patterns used in Vulkan applications.

Triple Buffering

Triple buffering is a technique used to minimize the effects of input lag and screen tearing. Unlike double buffering, where you have two frame buffers (front and back), triple buffering uses three frame buffers: two for rendering and one for presentation.

1. **Front Buffer**: This is the buffer currently displayed on the screen.
2. **Back Buffer**: This is the buffer where rendering commands are executed.
3. **Rendering Buffer**: This is an additional buffer where rendering commands can be queued.

Triple buffering works as follows:

- When a frame is rendered, it goes to the rendering buffer (if available).

- The rendering buffer is presented to the screen only if it's complete and ready.

- If the rendering buffer is not ready, the back buffer is presented instead.

Triple buffering reduces input lag because the CPU can work ahead of the GPU. However, it increases memory usage as it requires an extra frame buffer.

Double Buffering with V-Sync

Double buffering is the simplest synchronization technique. It uses two frame buffers: one for rendering and one for presentation. Synchronization with vertical synchronization (V-Sync) ensures that frames are presented only during the vertical blanking period of the monitor.

// Enabling V-Sync

VkSurfaceCapabilitiesKHR surfaceCapabilities;

vkGetPhysicalDeviceSurfaceCapabilitiesKHR(physicalDevice, surface, &surfaceCapabilities);

VkPresentModeKHR   desiredPresentMode   = VK_PRESENT_MODE_FIFO_KHR; // *V-Sync*

Using VK_PRESENT_MODE_FIFO_KHR (the default) enforces V-Sync. While this reduces screen tearing, it may introduce input lag, as frames are presented only during vertical blanking intervals.

Adaptive Sync

Adaptive sync technologies like NVIDIA G-Sync and AMD FreeSync dynamically adjust the monitor's refresh rate to match the frame rate of the GPU. This eliminates screen tearing without introducing input lag associated with V-Sync.

To use adaptive sync, you should:

1. Ensure the monitor and GPU support adaptive sync.
2. Choose the appropriate present mode that supports adaptive sync if available.

Dynamic Frame Rate Control

Dynamic frame rate control adjusts the frame rate based on the GPU workload. It can be implemented manually or by using Vulkan extensions like VK_EXT_variable_pointers. With dynamic frame rate control, you can reduce GPU power consumption and heat generation when high frame rates aren't necessary, such as in menu screens.

Implementing dynamic frame rate control involves:

- Measuring GPU workload.

- Adjusting the frame rate dynamically.

- Using Vulkan extensions or driver-specific APIs for controlling frame rate.

Conclusion

Frame synchronization is a critical aspect of Vulkan applications. The choice of synchronization technique depends on factors like input lag tolerance, screen tearing, and hardware support. Triple buffering, double buffering with V-Sync, adaptive sync, and dynamic frame rate control are some common approaches to achieving smooth and artifact-free rendering in Vulkan applications. The choice should align with your application's specific requirements and target hardware capabilities.

Chapter 17: Resource Cleanup and Validation

Section 17.1: Cleaning Up Vulkan Resources

Cleaning up Vulkan resources is a crucial aspect of developing Vulkan applications. Failing to release resources properly can lead to memory leaks and resource exhaustion. In this section, we'll explore best practices for cleaning up Vulkan resources.

RAII (Resource Acquisition Is Initialization)

Vulkan does not provide automatic memory management like some higher-level languages. It's the developer's responsibility to release resources when they are no longer needed. One common approach to achieve resource cleanup is using the RAII (Resource Acquisition Is Initialization) pattern.

RAII is based on the principle that resource management should be tied to object lifetimes. When a Vulkan object is created, its destructor can be used to automatically release associated resources when the object goes out of scope. This ensures that resources are cleaned up properly, even in the presence of exceptions or early function returns.

Here's an example of using RAII for a Vulkan buffer:

```
class VulkanBuffer {

public:

VulkanBuffer(VkDevice device, VkBuffer buffer)

: device_(device), buffer_(buffer) {}
```

```
~VulkanBuffer() {

vkDestroyBuffer(device_, buffer_, nullptr);

}
```

// Other member functions...

private:

```
VkDevice device_;

VkBuffer buffer_;

};
```

With this approach, when the VulkanBuffer object is destroyed, the associated Vulkan buffer is automatically released.

Cleanup Order

In Vulkan, resources can have dependencies, meaning that some resources must be destroyed before others. It's essential to manage the cleanup order correctly to avoid errors and crashes.

A common order for cleaning up Vulkan resources is as follows:

1. Command buffers and pools.
2. Framebuffers and render passes.
3. Pipeline objects (graphics and compute).
4. Descriptor set layouts and pools.
5. Shader modules.
6. Images, image views, and samplers.
7. Buffers.
8. Semaphores and fences.

Ensure that you destroy resources in the reverse order of their creation. Additionally, don't forget to clean up resources allocated by Vulkan loaders, validation layers, and extensions.

Validation Layers

Vulkan validation layers are invaluable during development as they can help detect resource leaks and incorrect cleanup. Ensure that you enable validation layers when developing your application. The layers will provide feedback and warnings about resource cleanup issues.

Resource Management Libraries

To simplify resource management, you can also consider using resource management libraries built on top of Vulkan. These libraries provide higher-level abstractions for managing Vulkan resources, making it easier to avoid common cleanup mistakes.

In conclusion, cleaning up Vulkan resources is a critical part of Vulkan application development. The RAII pattern, proper cleanup order, validation layers, and resource management libraries are valuable tools for ensuring that resources are released correctly and efficiently, reducing the risk of memory leaks and other resource-related issues.

Section 17.2: Resource Management Best Practices

Managing resources efficiently in a Vulkan application is crucial for optimal performance and stability. In this section, we'll discuss some best practices for resource management in Vulkan.

1. Resource Reuse

Creating and destroying Vulkan resources, such as buffers and images, can be costly operations. Whenever possible, reuse existing resources instead of recreating them. Vulkan provides mechanisms like memory barriers and image layout transitions that allow you to reuse resources efficiently.

2. Descriptor Sets

Descriptor sets in Vulkan define how resources are bound to shaders. When designing your Vulkan application, carefully plan the layout of descriptor sets to minimize descriptor set changes during rendering. Frequent descriptor set changes can impact performance. Group resources that are frequently used together into the same descriptor set.

3. Descriptor Pooling

Descriptor pools are used to allocate descriptor sets. Avoid creating and destroying descriptor pools frequently. Instead, allocate a pool with a sufficient number of descriptors at the beginning of your application and reuse it throughout the program's lifetime.

4. Memory Allocation

Vulkan allows you to manage memory explicitly. Be mindful of how memory is allocated and used. Use memory heaps and memory types that are suitable for your application's needs. Vulkan's memory management can be complex, so consider using memory allocation libraries like Vulkan Memory Allocator (VMA) to simplify memory management.

5. Pipeline Caching

Pipeline creation in Vulkan can be expensive. To optimize pipeline creation, use pipeline caching. Vulkan provides mechanisms to serialize and deserialize pipelines, allowing you to reuse them across application runs.

6. Resource Tracking

Implement a resource tracking system that helps you keep track of resource allocations and deallocations. This can be particularly useful for debugging and profiling your Vulkan application. You can create custom tracking tools or use existing profiling tools that support Vulkan.

7. Multi-threading

If your application utilizes multi-threading, ensure that resource access is properly synchronized to avoid data corruption and crashes. Vulkan provides synchronization primitives like semaphores and fences for this purpose.

8. Validation Layers

Validation layers are essential during development to detect resource-related issues. Keep validation layers enabled during development and testing to catch errors early.

9. Resource Release Order

As mentioned in the previous section, pay attention to the order in which resources are released. Releasing resources in the correct order prevents validation layer warnings and errors. Using RAII (Resource Acquisition Is Initialization) for Vulkan objects is a good practice to ensure timely and correct resource cleanup.

10. Testing and Profiling

Thoroughly test your application's resource management under different scenarios, including heavy workloads and low-memory conditions. Profiling tools can help identify resource bottlenecks and memory leaks.

In summary, efficient resource management is vital for Vulkan application development. By following these best practices, you can improve your application's performance, stability, and maintainability while minimizing the risk of resource-related issues. Additionally, thorough testing and profiling will help you identify and address resource management issues effectively.

Section 17.3: Vulkan Validation Layers Revisited

Validation layers are a critical component of Vulkan development, aiding in the debugging and validation of your Vulkan applications. In this section, we'll revisit Vulkan validation layers and discuss their importance and usage in Vulkan development.

Importance of Validation Layers

Validation layers are tools provided by the Vulkan SDK that help developers detect errors, validate API usage, and ensure that their Vulkan applications adhere to the specification. They serve several crucial purposes:

1. **Error Detection:** Validation layers catch common programming mistakes and misuse of the Vulkan API. This includes checking function parameters, object lifetimes, and state transitions.
2. **Validation of Best Practices:** They help enforce best

practices and conventions recommended by the Vulkan specification, ensuring that your application follows Vulkan's guidelines.

3. **Debugging Assistance:** Validation layers provide detailed error messages and debugging information when issues are detected, making it easier to identify and fix problems in your code.

4. **Cross-Platform Compatibility:** By running validation layers during development, you can identify platform-specific issues and ensure that your application works consistently across different Vulkan implementations.

Enabling Validation Layers

To use Vulkan validation layers effectively, you must enable them during Vulkan instance creation. Here's a brief overview of the steps:

1. **Specify Validation Layers:** Create an array of validation layer names you want to enable. Common layers include VK_LAYER_KHRONOS_validation, VK_LAYER_LUNARG_standard_validation, and VK_LAYER_RENDERDOC_Capture.

2. **Enable Validation Layers During Instance Creation:** Pass the validation layer names to the VkInstanceCreateInfo structure when creating a Vulkan instance. The Vulkan loader will ensure that these layers are enabled during instance creation.

```
const char* validationLayers[] = {

"VK_LAYER_KHRONOS_validation"

};
```

VkInstanceCreateInfo createInfo = {};

createInfo.enabledLayerCount = **sizeof**(validationLayers) /
sizeof(validationLayers[0]);

createInfo.ppEnabledLayerNames = validationLayers;

vkCreateInstance(&createInfo, nullptr, &instance);

1. **Check Layer Availability:** Before enabling validation
    layers, check if they are available on the current system
    using vkEnumerateInstanceLayerProperties. If a requested
    layer is not available, you should handle it gracefully.

Validation Layer Messages

Validation layers generate messages categorized into different
severity levels, including information, warning, and error. These
messages are useful for identifying issues in your application's Vulkan
usage.

You can control the behavior of validation layers, such as enabling
or disabling specific messages or adjusting their verbosity, using
environment variables or layer-specific settings. Refer to the Vulkan
SDK documentation for details on configuring validation layers.

Disabling Validation Layers in Release Builds

While validation layers are invaluable during development, they can
introduce overhead and should be disabled in release builds for
optimal performance. Ensure that you provide a mechanism in your
application to toggle validation layer usage based on a build
configuration or command-line arguments.

In conclusion, Vulkan validation layers are essential tools for developing robust and reliable Vulkan applications. By enabling and using these layers during development, you can catch errors early, validate best practices, and ensure cross-platform compatibility. However, remember to disable validation layers in release builds to achieve optimal performance.

Section 17.4: Debugging and Validation Tips

Debugging Vulkan applications can be challenging due to its low-level nature and the potential complexity of the code. In this section, we'll explore some valuable debugging and validation tips to help you identify and resolve issues in your Vulkan projects efficiently.

1. Vulkan Validation Layers

As mentioned earlier, validation layers are your best friends when debugging Vulkan applications. They can catch common errors and provide detailed error messages. Always enable validation layers during development, and pay close attention to the messages they generate. Use environment variables or layer-specific settings to control the verbosity of these messages.

2. Vulkan Debugging Tools

Utilize Vulkan-specific debugging tools and libraries like RenderDoc and NVIDIA Nsight Graphics. These tools provide invaluable insights into your application's behavior, including frame captures, shader debugging, and GPU performance analysis. Integrate these tools into your debugging workflow to visualize and analyze Vulkan commands and resources.

3. Vulkan Memory Debugging

Memory management can be a significant source of issues in Vulkan applications. Implement a robust memory allocation and tracking system, and use tools like Vulkan Memory Allocator (VMA) to assist in debugging memory-related problems. VMA can provide information about memory leaks and misuse.

4. Vulkan Validation Layers Tweaks

Customize the behavior of Vulkan validation layers to suit your needs. You can enable or disable specific validation checks, adjust message verbosity, and filter messages based on your application's requirements. Experiment with different settings to focus on the issues most relevant to your project.

5. Thorough Error Checking

Check the return values of Vulkan functions diligently. Vulkan functions often return a result code, and failing to check these codes can lead to silent errors in your code. Implement error-checking mechanisms and log any issues to aid in debugging.

```
VkResult result = vkCreateDevice(device, &createInfo, nullptr,
&logicalDevice);

if (result != VK_SUCCESS) {

// Handle error and log details

printf("Failed to create Vulkan logical device with error code %d\n",
result);

}
```

6. Validation Callbacks

Vulkan validation layers allow you to register custom validation callback functions. Use these callbacks to intercept and analyze validation layer messages. This can be helpful for implementing custom debugging features, such as logging specific types of messages or tracking resource usage.

7. Vulkan Validation Reports

Some Vulkan implementations provide validation reports that can be accessed through the Vulkan SDK or GPU vendor-specific tools. These reports can offer additional insights into issues not caught by validation layers. Check these reports for any warnings or errors related to your application.

8. Incremental Testing

When developing a complex Vulkan application, adopt an incremental testing approach. Start with a minimal working example and gradually add features and complexity. Test each new feature thoroughly before moving on to the next. This way, you can isolate issues and identify their sources more easily.

9. Version Compatibility

Ensure that your Vulkan application and the installed Vulkan runtime or drivers are compatible. Mismatched versions can lead to unexpected behavior. Always target a specific Vulkan version and communicate the version requirements to users or testers.

10. Documentation and Community Resources

Refer to the Vulkan specification, official documentation, and online community resources for guidance when debugging. The Vulkan community is active and can provide valuable insights and solutions to common problems.

In conclusion, debugging Vulkan applications requires a combination of thorough error checking, the use of validation layers, specialized debugging tools, and a systematic approach to testing and development. By following these tips and best practices, you can streamline the debugging process and create stable and performant Vulkan applications.

Section 17.5: Finalizing Your Vulkan Application

As you reach the final stages of your Vulkan application development, it's essential to focus on finalization tasks that ensure your application is robust, user-friendly, and ready for deployment. In this section, we'll explore the key steps involved in finalizing your Vulkan application.

1. Memory and Resource Cleanup

Properly releasing Vulkan resources is crucial for preventing memory leaks and ensuring the efficient use of system resources. Implement a cleanup routine to release Vulkan objects, such as buffers, images, and descriptor sets, when they are no longer needed. Be especially mindful of cleanup when handling dynamic or frequently allocated resources.

Here's an example of cleaning up a Vulkan buffer:

// Destroy a Vulkan buffer

```
vkDestroyBuffer(device, buffer, nullptr);
```

2. Error Handling and Graceful Failure

Ensure that your application gracefully handles errors and failures. Implement error-handling mechanisms that provide meaningful error messages to the user or log error details for debugging. Consider including a mechanism for error recovery or fallback strategies when possible.

3. User Interface (UI) and User Experience (UX)

If your Vulkan application includes a user interface, pay close attention to the UI design and overall user experience. Make sure the UI is intuitive, responsive, and visually appealing. Test your application with real users or gather feedback to identify and address usability issues.

4. Performance Optimization

Optimize your Vulkan application for performance. Profile your code to identify bottlenecks and areas where optimization is needed. Utilize Vulkan's performance counters and debugging tools to analyze GPU and CPU performance. Optimize rendering pipelines, shader code, and resource management to achieve smooth and efficient performance.

5. Testing and Quality Assurance

Thoroughly test your Vulkan application on different hardware configurations and platforms to ensure compatibility and stability. Create test cases that cover various usage scenarios and edge cases. Consider automated testing frameworks and regression testing to catch potential issues during development.

6. Documentation

Prepare comprehensive documentation for your Vulkan application. This documentation should include user guides, installation instructions, and developer documentation. Clearly explain how to use your application, its features, and any configuration options. Well-documented code is also essential for maintainability.

7. Licensing and Legal Considerations

Determine the licensing terms for your Vulkan application. Specify whether it's open-source or proprietary, and include the appropriate licensing information in your documentation. Ensure that your application complies with Vulkan's licensing terms and any third-party libraries or components you've used.

8. Packaging and Distribution

Plan how you'll package and distribute your Vulkan application. Create installer packages for different platforms if necessary. Consider using platform-specific package managers or app stores for distribution. Provide clear download links and installation instructions for users.

9. Versioning and Updates

Implement versioning for your Vulkan application to track changes and updates. Consider incorporating an automatic update mechanism to deliver bug fixes and feature enhancements to users seamlessly. Notify users of available updates to keep them using the latest version.

10. User Support and Feedback

Establish a support channel for users to report issues and seek assistance. Respond promptly to user feedback and bug reports. Engage with the user community to build trust and improve your application based on user needs and suggestions.

By following these finalization steps, you can ensure that your Vulkan application is polished, reliable, and well-prepared for deployment. Taking the time to address these aspects will contribute to a positive user experience and the success of your Vulkan project.

Chapter 18: Beyond the Basics

In this chapter, we will delve into advanced Vulkan features and techniques that go beyond the fundamentals covered earlier in this book. These advanced topics are essential for developing complex and high-performance graphics applications using Vulkan. While they may be more challenging, they provide greater flexibility and control over the rendering pipeline and can lead to more impressive and efficient graphics applications.

Section 18.1: Advanced Vulkan Features

Vulkan offers a wide range of advanced features and capabilities that can take your graphics applications to the next level. In this section, we'll explore some of the most notable advanced features of Vulkan.

1. Compute Shaders

Compute shaders are a powerful addition to Vulkan, allowing you to perform general-purpose computing tasks on the GPU. With compute shaders, you can offload complex calculations and data processing to the GPU, taking advantage of its parallel processing capabilities. This is particularly useful for tasks like physics simulations, image processing, and numerical computations.

Here's a simplified example of a compute shader in Vulkan:

#version 450

layout(local_size_x = 16, local_size_y = 16) in;

layout(set = 0, binding = 0, rgba8) **buffer** InputBuffer {

vec4 data[];

```
} input;

layout(set = 0, binding = 1, rgba8) buffer OutputBuffer {

vec4 data[];

} output;

void main() {

uvec2 gid = gl_GlobalInvocationID.xy;

output.data[gid.x   +   gid.y   *   gl_NumWorkGroups.x]   =
input.data[gid.x + gid.y * gl_NumWorkGroups.x] * 2.0;

}
```

2. Multi-threading with Vulkan

Vulkan provides support for multi-threading, allowing you to take advantage of modern multi-core processors. By using Vulkan's multi-threading capabilities, you can parallelize various tasks, such as command buffer recording, rendering, and resource loading. Properly designed multi-threaded Vulkan applications can achieve significant performance improvements.

3. Vulkan Extensions

Vulkan extensions offer additional functionality beyond the core Vulkan API. These extensions are often platform-specific or provide access to advanced hardware features. You can use extensions to access ray tracing capabilities, machine learning acceleration, and more. Be sure to check the documentation for your target platform to discover available extensions and their usage.

4. Exploring Vulkan Ecosystem

The Vulkan ecosystem is rich and diverse, with numerous tools, libraries, and resources available to assist developers. Explore the Vulkan ecosystem to find tools for debugging, profiling, and optimizing your applications. Additionally, consider using high-level graphics libraries built on top of Vulkan, which can simplify complex tasks and accelerate development.

5. Advanced Rendering Techniques

With Vulkan's flexibility, you can implement advanced rendering techniques like physically-based rendering (PBR), global illumination, and shadow mapping. These techniques require a deep understanding of graphics programming principles, but they can result in stunning visual effects in your applications.

As you advance in your Vulkan journey, these advanced features and techniques will become valuable tools in your toolkit. They empower you to create cutting-edge graphics applications that push the boundaries of real-time rendering and simulation. However, with great power comes great responsibility, so be prepared for the complexity and challenges that come with these advanced topics.

Section 18.2: Compute Shaders in Vulkan

Compute shaders are a vital component of modern graphics programming, and Vulkan provides robust support for them. These shaders enable developers to perform general-purpose computing tasks on the GPU, leveraging the massive parallel processing capabilities of modern graphics hardware. In this section, we'll dive deeper into compute shaders in Vulkan.

Understanding Compute Shaders

Compute shaders are a type of shader in Vulkan that focus on data processing rather than rendering graphics. They are well-suited for tasks such as physics simulations, image processing, and numerical computations, where parallelism is key. Unlike vertex or fragment shaders, compute shaders don't have predefined input or output stages; instead, they operate on data buffers.

Here's a simplified example of a compute shader written in GLSL, the shading language used in Vulkan:

```glsl
#version 450

layout(local_size_x = 16, local_size_y = 16) in;

layout(set = 0, binding = 0, rgba8) buffer InputBuffer {

vec4 data[];

} input;

layout(set = 0, binding = 1, rgba8) buffer OutputBuffer {

vec4 data[];

} output;

void main() {

uvec2 gid = gl_GlobalInvocationID.xy;

output.data[gid.x + gid.y * gl_NumWorkGroups.x] = input.data[gid.x + gid.y * gl_NumWorkGroups.x] * 2.0;

}
```

Key Components of a Compute Shader

- **Layout Specifiers**: In Vulkan, compute shaders use layout specifiers to define the size and layout of the workgroup. These specifiers determine how the work is divided and executed across the GPU's cores.

- **Buffers**: Compute shaders often operate on data stored in buffers. In the example above, we have input and output buffers defined. These buffers hold data that the shader processes, and they can be read from and written to.

- **Main Function**: The main() function is the entry point of the compute shader. It processes data based on the shader's logic. In our example, we're doubling the values in the input buffer and storing the results in the output buffer.

Dispatching Compute Shaders

To execute a compute shader, you need to dispatch it. Dispatching a compute shader means specifying the number of workgroups and workgroup size. Workgroups are groups of threads, and the workgroup size determines how many threads are in each workgroup. The Vulkan API provides functions like vkCmdDispatch to dispatch compute shaders.

Synchronization

Synchronization in compute shaders is essential because multiple workgroups may be executing in parallel. Vulkan provides synchronization mechanisms like barriers and memory fences to ensure correct memory access and ordering of operations.

Use Cases

Compute shaders are versatile and can be used for various purposes, including:

- **Physics Simulations**: Simulating physical phenomena like fluid dynamics or particle systems.

- **Image Processing**: Applying filters, effects, or transformations to images.

- **Numerical Computations**: Solving mathematical problems that benefit from parallel processing.

In summary, compute shaders are a powerful tool in Vulkan for performing general-purpose computing on the GPU. They are integral to many modern graphics and compute applications, enabling efficient parallel processing and expanding the capabilities of your Vulkan-powered software.

Section 18.3: Multi-threading with Vulkan

Multi-threading is a fundamental technique for maximizing the performance of modern applications, and Vulkan provides excellent support for multi-threaded rendering and compute tasks. In this section, we'll explore how Vulkan enables you to harness the power of multi-threading to achieve efficient parallelism.

Vulkan and Multi-threading

Vulkan was designed with multi-threading in mind from the ground up. It allows you to perform tasks like rendering, data processing, and resource management concurrently, taking full advantage of multi-core CPUs.

One of the key concepts in multi-threading with Vulkan is the use of multiple command buffers and threads. Vulkan command buffers are used to record rendering commands, and they can be recorded on multiple threads simultaneously. This enables you to distribute rendering work across CPU cores, reducing the CPU bottleneck and improving overall performance.

Multi-threaded Command Buffer Recording

Vulkan's multi-threaded command buffer recording works by creating multiple secondary command buffers, each associated with a different thread. These secondary command buffers can be recorded independently and then combined into a primary command buffer for execution. This approach allows you to efficiently parallelize rendering tasks across multiple CPU cores.

Here's a simplified example of how you can record command buffers on multiple threads:

```
// Pseudo-code illustrating multi-threaded command buffer recording

std::vector<std::thread> threads;

std::vector<VkCommandBuffer> secondaryCommandBuffers;

for (int i = 0; i < numThreads; ++i) {

threads.emplace_back([i, &secondaryCommandBuffers]() {

// Each thread records commands into its own secondary command buffer

VkCommandBufferBeginInfo        beginInfo        =        {
VK_STRUCTURE_TYPE_COMMAND_BUFFER_BEGIN_INFO
};
```

```
vkBeginCommandBuffer(secondaryCommandBuffers[i],
&beginInfo);
```

// *Record rendering commands for this thread's portion of the scene*

```
RecordRenderingCommands(secondaryCommandBuffers[i], i);
```

```
vkEndCommandBuffer(secondaryCommandBuffers[i]);
```

```
});
```

```
}
```

// *Wait for all threads to finish recording*

```
for (auto& thread : threads) {
```

```
thread.join();
```

```
}
```

// *Combine secondary command buffers into a primary command buffer*

```
vkBeginCommandBuffer(primaryCommandBuffer, ...);
```

```
for (const auto& secondaryCmdBuffer : secondaryCommandBuffers) {
```

```
vkCmdExecuteCommands(primaryCommandBuffer, 1, &secondaryCmdBuffer);
```

```
}
```

```
vkEndCommandBuffer(primaryCommandBuffer);
```

In the above example, each thread records rendering commands into its own secondary command buffer. Once all threads have finished recording, the secondary command buffers are combined into a primary command buffer for execution.

Thread Safety and Synchronization

Multi-threading in Vulkan requires careful management of synchronization to avoid data races and ensure thread safety. Vulkan provides synchronization primitives like semaphores, fences, and memory barriers to coordinate access to resources and ensure correct order of execution between threads.

When using multiple threads with Vulkan, it's crucial to synchronize access to resources such as buffers, images, and pipelines to prevent conflicts. Vulkan's synchronization mechanisms allow you to control memory access and ensure that multiple threads interact with resources in a safe and predictable manner.

Benefits of Multi-threading in Vulkan

The primary benefits of multi-threading in Vulkan include:

- **Improved CPU Utilization**: Multi-threading allows Vulkan applications to take full advantage of multi-core CPUs, distributing rendering and compute workloads across available cores.

- **Reduced CPU Bottleneck**: By parallelizing command buffer recording and other tasks, Vulkan can reduce the CPU bottleneck often encountered in single-threaded applications.

- **Responsive Applications**: Multi-threaded Vulkan applications can remain responsive to user input even during resource-intensive rendering or compute operations.

- **Scalability**: Multi-threading makes it easier to scale your application's performance across a wide range of hardware, from entry-level systems to high-end GPUs.

In conclusion, multi-threading with Vulkan is a powerful technique for achieving high performance in graphics and compute applications. By leveraging the parallelism offered by multi-core CPUs, Vulkan enables you to create responsive and efficient applications that make the most of modern hardware capabilities.

Section 18.4: Vulkan Extensions

Vulkan extensions are additional features and functionalities that can be added to the core Vulkan API. These extensions enable developers to access advanced capabilities, experimental features, and vendor-specific optimizations that may not be part of the core Vulkan specification. In this section, we'll delve into Vulkan extensions, how to use them, and their significance in Vulkan development.

What Are Vulkan Extensions?

Vulkan extensions are modules of functionality that can be dynamically loaded into a Vulkan application to enhance its capabilities. These extensions can provide a wide range of features, from advanced rendering techniques to platform-specific optimizations. Some common categories of Vulkan extensions include:

- **Vendor Extensions**: These extensions are provided by GPU vendors (e.g., NVIDIA, AMD, Intel) to expose unique hardware features or optimizations specific to their GPUs. Developers can use vendor extensions to access hardware-accelerated functionality.

• **KHR Extensions**: Extensions with the "KHR" suffix are ratified by the Khronos Group, the organization behind Vulkan. These extensions are widely supported across different platforms and serve as a standard for certain features.

• **EXT Extensions**: EXT extensions are experimental or provisional extensions, and they might not be as widely supported as KHR extensions. They often expose features that are still in development or testing.

• **MoltenVK**: MoltenVK is an extension that allows Vulkan applications to run on macOS and iOS devices, which don't natively support Vulkan. It acts as a translation layer between Vulkan and Apple's Metal API.

Using Vulkan Extensions

To use Vulkan extensions in your application, you need to follow these steps:

1. **Query Extension Support**: Determine which extensions are supported by the Vulkan implementation on the target system. This can be done using the vkEnumerateInstanceExtensionProperties function for instance extensions or vkEnumerateDeviceExtensionProperties for device extensions.

2. **Enable the Extensions**: Once you've identified the extensions you want to use, you need to enable them when

creating the Vulkan instance or device. This is typically done by specifying the extension names in the VkInstanceCreateInfo or VkDeviceCreateInfo structures during initialization.

3. **Use Extension Features**: Once an extension is enabled, you can make use of the additional features and functionality it provides. This may involve creating specific Vulkan objects or using extension-specific functions.

Here's an example of how you might enable a Vulkan extension during instance creation:

```
VkInstanceCreateInfo createInfo = {};

createInfo.sType                          =
VK_STRUCTURE_TYPE_INSTANCE_CREATE_INFO;

// Enable the desired extension(s)

const        char*       extensions[]        =        {
VK_EXT_DEBUG_UTILS_EXTENSION_NAME,
VK_KHR_SURFACE_EXTENSION_NAME };

createInfo.enabledExtensionCount  =  sizeof(extensions)  /
sizeof(extensions[0]);

createInfo.ppEnabledExtensionNames = extensions;

// Create the Vulkan instance

VkInstance instance;

if   (vkCreateInstance(&createInfo,   nullptr,   &instance)   !=
VK_SUCCESS) {

// Handle instance creation failure
```

}

Extension Examples

Some practical examples of Vulkan extensions include:

- **VK_KHR_swapchain**: This extension provides cross-platform support for creating and managing swapchains, which are crucial for presenting images to the screen.

- **VK_KHR_ray_tracing**: An extension that enables hardware-accelerated ray tracing, allowing developers to implement advanced rendering techniques like ray tracing for realistic lighting and reflections.

- **VK_EXT_debug_utils**: A useful extension for debugging Vulkan applications, it offers enhanced debugging capabilities, such as validation layers and debug messenger callbacks.

- **Vendor-Specific Extensions**: GPU vendors often provide extensions for accessing proprietary hardware features or optimizations. For example, NVIDIA offers the VK_NV_ray_tracing extension for ray tracing on NVIDIA GPUs.

Considerations When Using Extensions

When working with Vulkan extensions, consider the following:

- **Portability**: While Vulkan extensions can unlock powerful capabilities, they may not be available on all platforms or GPUs. Be mindful of portability if you plan to target multiple platforms.

- **Versioning**: Vulkan extensions may have multiple versions, so ensure that your code is compatible with the specific version of the extension you're using.

- **Validation**: When using extensions, it's essential to test your application thoroughly to ensure correctness and performance. Vulkan validation layers can help identify issues related to extension usage.

In conclusion, Vulkan extensions are a valuable tool for extending the capabilities of the Vulkan API. They enable developers to access advanced features, optimizations, and experimental functionality. However, using extensions should be done carefully to ensure compatibility and maintain portability across different platforms and hardware configurations.

Section 18.5: Exploring Vulkan Ecosystem

The Vulkan ecosystem extends beyond the core API, offering a wide range of tools, libraries, and resources that enhance the development experience and streamline the creation of Vulkan applications. In this section, we'll explore the Vulkan ecosystem and the various resources available to Vulkan developers.

Vulkan SDK

The Vulkan Software Development Kit (SDK) is a comprehensive package provided by the Khronos Group. It includes essential tools, libraries, and documentation for Vulkan development. Some key components of the Vulkan SDK are:

- **Validation Layers**: These are crucial for debugging Vulkan applications. They help identify errors, ensure correct API usage, and provide useful diagnostic messages.

- **SPIR-V Tools**: Tools for working with SPIR-V, the intermediate shader language used in Vulkan. You can compile and optimize shaders using these tools.

- **GLSLang**: The GLSLang compiler, which converts GLSL shaders into SPIR-V, facilitating shader development.

- **Vulkan Headers and Loader**: The Vulkan headers and loader are necessary for interacting with the Vulkan API. The loader manages loading the appropriate Vulkan library for the target platform.

- **Documentation**: The Vulkan SDK includes extensive documentation, including specifications, guides, and tutorials, which are valuable resources for developers.

Vulkan Libraries

Several libraries built on top of Vulkan simplify various aspects of graphics programming. These libraries offer abstractions, utilities, and additional functionality to speed up development. Some notable Vulkan libraries include:

- **Vulkan-Hpp**: A C++ binding for Vulkan, which makes Vulkan programming more accessible and idiomatic for C++ developers.

- **Vulkan Memory Allocator (VMA)**: VMA is a library for managing memory allocations in Vulkan. It helps with memory pool management, allocation strategies, and defragmentation.

- **VulkanSceneGraph**: A scene graph library that simplifies scene management and rendering in Vulkan applications.

- **Vulkan Cookbook**: While not a library per se, the Vulkan Cookbook is a collection of practical code examples and recipes for common Vulkan tasks.

- **RenderDoc**: Although not specific to Vulkan, RenderDoc is a popular open-source graphics debugger and profiler that supports Vulkan. It allows you to capture and inspect frames of your Vulkan application to identify performance bottlenecks and issues.

Community Resources

The Vulkan community is active and provides valuable resources for developers:

- **Vulkan Forums**: The Vulkan community forums are a place to ask questions, share experiences, and seek assistance from other developers and experts.

- **GitHub Repositories**: Numerous Vulkan-related repositories on GitHub contain open-source projects, sample applications, and useful utilities.

- **Tutorials and Blogs**: Many developers and organizations share tutorials, blog posts, and educational content on Vulkan programming. These resources can help you learn and stay up to date with Vulkan developments.

Vulkan on the Web

Various websites and online platforms cater to Vulkan developers:

- **Vulkan Documentation**: The official Vulkan documentation on the Khronos Group website provides in-depth information about Vulkan's specifications and usage.

- **Vulkan API Registry**: The registry contains detailed specifications and documentation for Vulkan extensions.

- **Vulkan Samples**: Websites like the Vulkan Samples repository on GitHub offer a collection of Vulkan code samples and examples covering a wide range of topics.

- **Vulkan Hardware Database**: Some websites and databases provide information about Vulkan support and performance on different GPUs and platforms, helping developers make informed choices.

Conclusion

The Vulkan ecosystem offers a wealth of resources, tools, and libraries to support Vulkan development. Whether you're a beginner or an experienced graphics programmer, these resources can significantly accelerate your development process and help you create high-performance graphics applications with Vulkan. Exploring the Vulkan ecosystem and leveraging these resources can make your journey into Vulkan development more efficient and enjoyable.

Chapter 19: Real-world Vulkan Applications

Section 19.1: Vulkan in Game Development

Vulkan has gained significant attention and adoption in the game development industry due to its performance-oriented design and cross-platform capabilities. In this section, we'll explore how Vulkan is utilized in game development, its advantages, and some practical considerations.

Performance Benefits

One of the primary reasons game developers choose Vulkan is its ability to unlock the full potential of modern GPUs. Vulkan provides lower-level access to the hardware, allowing developers to finely control the rendering pipeline. This level of control can result in improved performance, reduced CPU overhead, and more efficient multi-threading.

Cross-platform Support

Vulkan's cross-platform nature is a significant advantage for game developers. It is supported on various desktop platforms (Windows, Linux, macOS through MoltenVK), mobile platforms (Android), and even emerging platforms like Google Stadia. This enables developers to target multiple platforms with a single codebase, reducing development effort and increasing reach.

Efficient Multi-threading

Modern game engines rely heavily on multi-threading to make the most of available CPU cores. Vulkan's explicit multi-threading capabilities allow developers to manage rendering tasks efficiently across CPU cores. This is essential for maintaining smooth and responsive gameplay while handling complex rendering tasks.

Memory Management

Memory management is a crucial aspect of game development. Vulkan provides explicit control over memory allocation, which is beneficial for managing limited GPU memory efficiently. This control helps developers avoid unexpected memory allocation stalls during gameplay.

Tools and Libraries

Game developers often rely on a combination of Vulkan and game engines that provide Vulkan support. Popular game engines like Unreal Engine and Unity support Vulkan, allowing developers to leverage the power of Vulkan without the need for low-level programming.

Challenges

While Vulkan offers numerous benefits, it also comes with challenges, especially for smaller game development teams. Vulkan's low-level nature can be intimidating, and it may require more development effort compared to higher-level APIs like DirectX or OpenGL. Additionally, debugging Vulkan applications can be complex, although validation layers and debugging tools help mitigate this challenge.

Conclusion

Vulkan has established itself as a viable and attractive option for game developers looking to create high-performance, cross-platform games. Its emphasis on performance, multi-threading, and efficient memory management align well with the demands of modern game development. While adopting Vulkan may require a learning curve, the benefits it offers in terms of performance and platform support make it a valuable choice for game developers aiming to deliver immersive gaming experiences. As Vulkan continues to evolve and gain wider support, its role in the game development industry is likely to grow even further.

Section 19.2: Vulkan in Simulation and Visualization

Vulkan's capabilities extend beyond gaming and have found valuable applications in simulation and visualization fields. In this section, we'll explore how Vulkan is utilized in these domains and the advantages it brings.

Simulation

Vulkan's performance-oriented design makes it an excellent choice for simulation applications. Whether it's simulating physics, fluid dynamics, or any other complex system, Vulkan's low-level control over the GPU enables efficient computation. Simulations often involve heavy parallelism, and Vulkan's multi-threading support can significantly improve the simulation's speed and accuracy.

Scientific Visualization

Scientific visualization often deals with vast datasets, requiring real-time rendering and interaction. Vulkan's ability to handle large amounts of data efficiently is a significant advantage. Applications in fields such as medical imaging, computational fluid dynamics, and geospatial analysis benefit from Vulkan's performance and flexibility.

Virtual Reality (VR) and Augmented Reality (AR)

Vulkan plays a crucial role in the development of VR and AR applications. These applications demand low latency and high frame rates to provide immersive experiences. Vulkan's low-level access to the GPU allows developers to fine-tune rendering to meet these requirements. Additionally, Vulkan's cross-platform support enables VR and AR applications to run on various devices, including PCs, mobile devices, and standalone headsets.

Engineering and Architecture

Architects and engineers use Vulkan for real-time architectural visualization and CAD applications. Vulkan's rendering capabilities allow for the creation of highly detailed and interactive 3D models of buildings, infrastructure, and products. This is invaluable for design review, client presentations, and collaboration among project stakeholders.

Data Visualization

In the realm of data analysis and visualization, Vulkan's GPU computing capabilities are put to good use. From rendering complex graphs to visualizing large datasets, Vulkan's performance and parallelism facilitate the rapid exploration and comprehension of data. This is particularly valuable in scientific research, financial analysis, and business intelligence.

Challenges and Considerations

While Vulkan offers numerous benefits for simulation and visualization applications, it's essential to consider some challenges. Developing with Vulkan may require a steeper learning curve compared to higher-level APIs, and specialized knowledge may be necessary to optimize performance fully.

Moreover, not all hardware and platforms support Vulkan, so compatibility issues may arise. Developers should carefully assess their target platforms and user base when choosing Vulkan for their projects.

Conclusion

Vulkan's versatility and performance make it a compelling choice for applications beyond gaming. In simulation and visualization fields, where real-time rendering and computational efficiency are critical, Vulkan's capabilities shine. As the ecosystem around Vulkan continues to grow, its adoption in these domains is likely to expand, enabling developers to create more sophisticated and interactive simulations and visualizations.

Section 19.3: Vulkan in Scientific Computing

Scientific computing is a diverse field that involves solving complex mathematical problems through numerical simulations and data analysis. Vulkan's capabilities make it a powerful tool in scientific computing applications, aiding researchers and scientists in various domains. In this section, we'll explore how Vulkan is leveraged in scientific computing and the advantages it offers.

High-Performance Computing (HPC)

High-performance computing (HPC) relies on powerful computing systems to solve complex problems. Vulkan's low-level access to the GPU allows scientists to harness the full potential of modern graphics hardware for general-purpose computing tasks. This can significantly accelerate simulations and data processing in fields like physics, chemistry, and engineering.

Parallelism and GPU Acceleration

One of Vulkan's standout features is its support for parallelism. Many scientific simulations involve performing the same computation on a large dataset or running simulations with multiple variables. Vulkan's multithreading capabilities and GPU acceleration can speed up these processes significantly. Researchers can take advantage of Vulkan's parallelism to run simulations faster or process more data in less time.

Machine Learning and Deep Learning

Machine learning (ML) and deep learning (DL) are critical components of scientific computing, especially in fields like artificial intelligence, bioinformatics, and materials science. Vulkan's GPU capabilities can accelerate ML and DL workloads, reducing training times and enabling researchers to experiment with larger and more complex models.

Numerical Libraries and Frameworks

To facilitate the use of Vulkan in scientific computing, several numerical libraries and frameworks have been developed. These libraries provide high-level abstractions and tools for common scientific computing tasks, such as linear algebra operations, numerical integration, and signal processing. Vulkan can be integrated into these libraries to provide GPU acceleration, making them even more efficient.

Data Visualization and Analysis

In scientific research, visualizing data and results is crucial for understanding complex phenomena. Vulkan's rendering capabilities can be harnessed to create interactive and informative data visualizations. Whether it's rendering 3D simulations or generating scientific plots and charts, Vulkan's performance and flexibility make it a valuable tool for data analysis and visualization.

Challenges and Considerations

Despite its advantages, using Vulkan in scientific computing may pose challenges. Developing scientific applications with Vulkan may require specialized knowledge of both the API and GPU architecture. Additionally, not all scientific computing libraries and tools have Vulkan support, which may require custom integration.

Moreover, while Vulkan offers excellent performance, achieving optimal results may require extensive optimization efforts, which can be time-consuming.

Conclusion

Vulkan's capabilities in scientific computing are expanding the horizons of research and discovery. Its ability to accelerate simulations, data processing, machine learning, and data visualization makes it a valuable asset for scientists and researchers across various domains. As Vulkan continues to gain traction in the scientific computing community, it's likely to lead to more breakthroughs and innovations in the years to come.

Section 19.4: Vulkan in Automotive and Aerospace

Vulkan, with its low-level graphics API and emphasis on performance, has found a significant place in the automotive and aerospace industries. These industries require robust and efficient graphics solutions for various applications, from in-vehicle infotainment systems to flight simulators. In this section, we'll explore how Vulkan is making an impact in automotive and aerospace technology.

In-Vehicle Infotainment Systems

Modern vehicles often come equipped with in-vehicle infotainment (IVI) systems that provide entertainment, navigation, and vehicle control functions. Vulkan's efficiency and cross-platform compatibility make it a compelling choice for developing visually appealing and responsive IVI interfaces. It allows developers to create smooth and immersive user experiences while efficiently utilizing the underlying hardware.

Automotive Simulations

The automotive industry relies heavily on simulations for testing and development. Vulkan's capabilities are well-suited for running realistic vehicle simulations, including those related to autonomous driving, crash testing, and aerodynamics. These simulations demand high-performance rendering and physics calculations, where Vulkan's GPU acceleration and multithreading shine.

Aerospace Simulations and Training

In aerospace, where safety and precision are paramount, Vulkan plays a crucial role in simulations and pilot training. Flight simulators, used for training pilots and testing aircraft, benefit from Vulkan's ability to render highly detailed and realistic environments in real-time. Pilots can practice maneuvers and emergency procedures in a realistic virtual environment, enhancing their skills and readiness.

Embedded Systems and Compact Hardware

The automotive and aerospace industries often involve embedded systems with strict size and power constraints. Vulkan's lightweight runtime and efficient resource management are well-suited for these environments. Whether it's an IVI system in a car or a portable flight training device, Vulkan can deliver high-quality graphics on compact hardware.

Cross-Platform Compatibility

Both industries value cross-platform compatibility to reach a wider audience and reduce development costs. Vulkan's ability to run on various operating systems, including Linux, Windows, and Android, makes it an attractive choice. Developers can write code once and deploy it across multiple platforms, ensuring consistent performance and user experiences.

Challenges and Considerations

Implementing Vulkan in automotive and aerospace applications can be challenging due to the complexity of the systems and the need for safety-critical operations. Ensuring real-time responsiveness and reliability is paramount, which requires careful optimization and thorough testing.

Additionally, Vulkan development may demand specialized expertise, particularly in industries with strict safety and certification requirements.

Conclusion

Vulkan's presence in the automotive and aerospace sectors is steadily growing, thanks to its performance, cross-platform capabilities, and suitability for resource-constrained environments. Whether it's enhancing in-vehicle experiences, improving simulations, or enabling realistic training scenarios, Vulkan continues to push the boundaries of what's possible in these industries, contributing to innovation and safety. As technology continues to evolve, Vulkan's role in these sectors is likely to expand even further.

Section 19.5: Vulkan in Cross-platform Development

Vulkan's cross-platform capabilities make it an excellent choice for developers who want to create graphics-intensive applications that run seamlessly on multiple platforms. In this section, we'll explore how Vulkan empowers cross-platform development and discuss its advantages and considerations.

Cross-Platform Development with Vulkan

One of Vulkan's most significant strengths is its ability to work across various operating systems, including Windows, Linux, Android, and more. This cross-platform support allows developers to write their graphics code once and deploy it across different platforms, saving time and effort.

Abstraction Layers

Vulkan's cross-platform compatibility doesn't mean developers have to write platform-specific code for each target. Instead, many developers use abstraction layers or game engines that build upon Vulkan's capabilities. These tools simplify the development process by providing a higher-level interface that abstracts the underlying Vulkan complexity.

Popular abstraction layers and engines that support Vulkan include the Vulkan-Hpp C++ library, the open-source graphics framework called GLFW, and game engines like Unity and Unreal Engine.

Performance and Efficiency

When developing for multiple platforms, performance and efficiency are critical. Vulkan's low-level API allows developers to optimize their code for each platform's unique hardware characteristics. This level of control is especially beneficial when targeting platforms with varying levels of GPU performance.

Considerations for Cross-Platform Vulkan Development

While Vulkan offers numerous advantages for cross-platform development, there are some considerations to keep in mind:

1. **Learning Curve**: Vulkan's low-level nature can be challenging for newcomers. Developers may need time to become proficient in Vulkan's API.
2. **Portability vs. Performance**: Achieving the best performance on each platform often requires platform-specific optimizations. Developers must strike a balance between portability and platform-specific performance

improvements.

3. **Abstraction Layers**: While abstraction layers simplify cross-platform development, they may introduce a slight overhead. Developers should evaluate whether the performance trade-offs are acceptable for their project.

4. **Validation Layers**: Vulkan validation layers help catch errors and issues in code. However, they may impact performance, so developers should consider enabling them for debugging and testing but disabling them in production builds.

Vulkan in Cross-platform Games

One of the most common use cases for Vulkan in cross-platform development is game development. Game developers appreciate Vulkan's performance and efficiency, as well as its ability to target various gaming platforms, including Windows, Linux, Android, and even gaming consoles like the Nintendo Switch.

Conclusion

Vulkan's cross-platform capabilities empower developers to create high-performance, visually stunning applications that can reach a broad audience. While mastering Vulkan may require an initial learning curve, its potential for efficient cross-platform development makes it a valuable tool in the world of graphics programming. Whether you're developing games, simulations, or other graphics-intensive applications, Vulkan's flexibility and performance can help you achieve your goals across multiple platforms.

Chapter 20: Building Your First Vulkan Project

In this final chapter, we will walk through the process of building your first Vulkan project. By this point in the book, you have learned the fundamentals of Vulkan, including how to set up your development environment, create Vulkan instances, work with logical devices, manage memory, render graphics, and more. Now, it's time to put this knowledge into practice and create a complete Vulkan application.

Section 20.1: Planning Your Vulkan Project

Before diving into the code, it's crucial to plan your Vulkan project carefully. Proper planning can save you a lot of time and help you avoid common pitfalls. Here are some essential steps to consider:

1. Define Your Project Goals:

- What is the purpose of your Vulkan application?

- What platforms do you want to target (e.g., Windows, Linux, Android)?

- What kind of graphics and rendering features do you need?

2. Choose Development Tools:

- Decide on the development tools and libraries you'll use, such as an integrated development environment (IDE) and any additional libraries or frameworks.

3. Create a Project Structure:

- Organize your project's source code, assets, and resources in a well-structured directory hierarchy.

4. Design Your Graphics Pipeline:

- Determine how your graphics pipeline will be structured, including the shaders, render passes, and framebuffers you'll use.

5. Plan for User Interaction:

- Consider how users will interact with your application. Will you need input handling for things like keyboard, mouse, or touch input?

6. Handle Resources:

- Think about how you'll manage and load assets like textures, models, and shaders.

7. Performance Considerations:

- Consider performance optimizations for your application, including multithreading, memory management, and resource streaming.

8. Debugging and Error Handling:

- Plan how you'll handle debugging and error reporting in your application, including the use of Vulkan validation layers.

9. Testing and Deployment:

- Define your testing strategy and how you'll deploy your application to different platforms.

10. Documentation:

- Plan for documenting your code, APIs, and user manuals if applicable.

Once you've carefully planned your project, you'll be well-prepared to start coding your Vulkan application. The subsequent sections will guide you through the implementation process, covering various aspects of Vulkan development. Remember that building a Vulkan project can be challenging, but with patience and practice, you can create impressive graphics applications that run efficiently on various platforms.

Section 20.2: Project Setup and Organization

Now that you have a clear plan for your Vulkan project, the next step is to set up your development environment and organize your project structure. A well-structured project will make it easier to manage code, assets, and resources as your application grows.

Development Environment

Before diving into project setup, ensure you have a working development environment for Vulkan:

1. **Install Vulkan SDK:** Download and install the Vulkan SDK provided by the Khronos Group. The SDK includes the Vulkan header files, libraries, and tools needed for development.
2. **IDE Choice:** Choose an integrated development environment (IDE) that supports C/C++ development. Popular choices include Visual Studio, Visual Studio Code, CLion, and others. Configure your IDE to work with Vulkan by setting include and library paths.

Project Structure

A well-organized project structure can significantly simplify development. Here's a typical structure for a Vulkan project:

ProjectRoot/

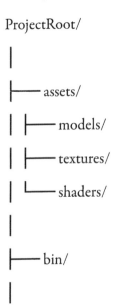

```
ProjectRoot/
│
├── assets/
│   ├── models/
│   ├── textures/
│   └── shaders/
│
├── bin/
│
```

```
├── build/
│
├── src/
│   ├── main.cpp
│   ├── VulkanRenderer.cpp
│   ├── VulkanRenderer.h
│   ├── Shader.cpp
│   ├── Shader.h
│   ├── Model.cpp
│   └── Model.h
│
├── include/
│   └── Vulkan/
│   ├── VulkanHeader.h
│   └── OtherVulkanHeaders.h
│
└── CMakeLists.txt
```

- **assets:** This directory stores all your project assets, including 3D models, textures, and shaders.

- **bin:** This is where the compiled binary executable will be placed after building the project.

- **build:** The build directory is used to generate build files and store intermediate build artifacts. You can use tools like CMake to manage your builds.

- **src:** This is the source code directory. Place your C++ source files here.

- **include:** Include headers required for your project. You may have Vulkan-related headers and any custom headers you create.

- **CMakeLists.txt:** Use CMake or another build system to manage your project's build configuration.

CMake Build System

CMake is a popular choice for managing the build process of Vulkan projects. You can create a CMakeLists.txt file in your project root to define how your project should be built. Here's a simplified example:

cmake_minimum_required(VERSION 3.10)

project(MyVulkanApp)

 # Set C++ standard

set(CMAKE_CXX_STANDARD 17)

 # Add Vulkan package

find_package(**Vulkan** REQUIRED)

 # Add your source files

add_executable(MyVulkanApp   src/main.cpp   src/VulkanRenderer.cpp src/Shader.cpp src/Model.cpp)

 # Link Vulkan libraries

target_link_libraries(MyVulkanApp Vulkan::Vulkan)

This CMake configuration sets the C++ standard, finds the Vulkan package, and specifies your source files. Adjust it according to your project's needs.

Version Control

Consider using a version control system (e.g., Git) to manage your project's source code. This ensures that you can track changes, collaborate with others, and maintain a history of your project's development.

With your development environment set up and project organized, you're ready to start implementing your Vulkan application. The next sections will cover the implementation details, including creating Vulkan instances, logical devices, and rendering graphics.

Section 20.3: Implementing Your Application

With your Vulkan project set up and organized, it's time to dive into the implementation of your Vulkan application. This section will guide you through the key steps in creating a Vulkan application.

Vulkan Initialization

The first step in your application is initializing Vulkan. This involves creating a Vulkan instance and setting up debugging tools. Here's a simplified code snippet for initializing Vulkan:

// Include Vulkan headers

#define GLFW_INCLUDE_VULKAN

```cpp
#include <GLFW/glfw3.h>

int main() {
// Initialize GLFW
if (!glfwInit()) {
// Handle initialization error
return -1;
}
// Create a window
GLFWwindow* window = glfwCreateWindow(800, 600, "My Vulkan App", nullptr, nullptr);

// Initialize Vulkan
if (window) {
VkInstance instance;
VkApplicationInfo appInfo{};
appInfo.sType = VK_STRUCTURE_TYPE_APPLICATION_INFO;
appInfo.pApplicationName = "My Vulkan App";
appInfo.applicationVersion = VK_MAKE_VERSION(1, 0, 0);
appInfo.pEngineName = "No Engine";
appInfo.engineVersion = VK_MAKE_VERSION(1, 0, 0);
appInfo.apiVersion = VK_API_VERSION_1_2;
```

```
VkInstanceCreateInfo createInfo{};

createInfo.sType = VK_STRUCTURE_TYPE_INSTANCE_CREATE_INFO;

createInfo.pApplicationInfo = &appInfo;

// Enable Vulkan validation layers if needed

const char* validationLayers[] = { "VK_LAYER_KHRONOS_validation" };

createInfo.enabledLayerCount = 1;

createInfo.ppEnabledLayerNames = validationLayers;

// Create Vulkan instance

if (vkCreateInstance(&createInfo, nullptr, &instance) != VK_SUCCESS) {

// Handle instance creation error

return -1;

}

// Continue with Vulkan setup

// Cleanup Vulkan instance

vkDestroyInstance(instance, nullptr);

}

// Continue with GLFW window and Vulkan setup

// Main loop and rendering
```

```
// Cleanup GLFW

glfwDestroyWindow(window);

glfwTerminate();

return 0;

}
```

This code initializes GLFW for window creation and sets up a Vulkan instance. Don't forget to handle error cases gracefully.

GLFW Window and Main Loop

Once Vulkan is initialized, you can create a GLFW window and set up the main rendering loop. GLFW provides a simple way to create windows and manage user input. Here's a basic example:

```
// Create a Vulkan window

if (window) {

// Main loop

while (!glfwWindowShouldClose(window)) {

// Poll for and process events

glfwPollEvents();

// Rendering code goes here

// Swap buffers

glfwSwapBuffers(window);

}
```

}

In the main loop, you can implement your rendering code, which includes creating Vulkan objects like command buffers and rendering graphics.

Vulkan Rendering

Implementing Vulkan rendering involves creating Vulkan objects such as command buffers, pipelines, and render passes. The specifics of rendering depend on your application's requirements. Ensure you have a clear understanding of Vulkan rendering concepts, as discussed in previous chapters.

Resource Management

Effective resource management is crucial in Vulkan applications. You'll need to manage buffers, textures, shaders, and more efficiently. Consider using Vulkan memory allocation libraries like VmaMalloc or building your custom resource management system.

Error Handling and Validation

Throughout your application, handle errors gracefully and use Vulkan validation layers for debugging. Validation layers help catch common mistakes and ensure your Vulkan code is correct.

Cleanup

Don't forget to clean up Vulkan resources, such as command buffers, images, and framebuffers, before exiting your application. Proper cleanup prevents resource leaks.

With these fundamental steps, you can start implementing your Vulkan application. Keep in mind that Vulkan development can be complex, but breaking it down into manageable tasks and referring to Vulkan documentation and tutorials will help you succeed.

Section 20.4: Testing and Debugging

Testing and debugging are essential phases of Vulkan application development. Ensuring that your Vulkan application works correctly and efficiently is crucial before deploying it. In this section, we'll explore various testing and debugging techniques for your Vulkan project.

Vulkan Validation Layers

Throughout your development process, you should have enabled Vulkan validation layers, as discussed in Chapter 2. These layers help catch common mistakes and issues in your Vulkan code. Validation layers provide detailed error messages and warnings to assist you in identifying and resolving problems.

Debugging Tools

In addition to validation layers, Vulkan provides debugging tools and extensions that can aid in identifying issues. These tools include RenderDoc, NVIDIA Nsight Graphics, and AMD Radeon GPU Profiler. These tools allow you to inspect your application's behavior, performance, and resource usage. They are particularly useful for diagnosing rendering problems and optimizing your application.

Error Handling

Effective error handling is crucial in Vulkan development. When Vulkan functions return an error, it's essential to check the result and handle errors gracefully. This includes cleaning up resources and notifying the user or developer of the issue.

Here's an example of error handling in Vulkan:

```
VkResult result = vkCreateBuffer(device, &bufferCreateInfo,
nullptr, &buffer);

if (result != VK_SUCCESS) {

// Handle buffer creation error

std::cerr << "Failed to create buffer. Error code: " << result <<
std::endl;

return;

}
```

Validation and Debug Callbacks

Vulkan allows you to set up validation and debug callbacks to receive notifications about validation layer messages and debug output. This can be particularly helpful for tracking down issues and understanding the behavior of your application. Here's a simplified example of setting up a validation callback:

```
VkDebugUtilsMessengerCreateInfoEXT createInfo{};

createInfo.sType                                    =
VK_STRUCTURE_TYPE_DEBUG_UTILS_MESSENGER_CREATE

createInfo.messageSeverity                          =
VK_DEBUG_UTILS_MESSAGE_SEVERITY_WARNING_BIT_EXT
|

VK_DEBUG_UTILS_MESSAGE_SEVERITY_ERROR_BIT_EXT;
```

```
createInfo.messageType                                    =
VK_DEBUG_UTILS_MESSAGE_TYPE_GENERAL_BIT_EXT
|
VK_DEBUG_UTILS_MESSAGE_TYPE_VALIDATION_BIT_E

createInfo.pfnUserCallback = debugCallback;

VkDebugUtilsMessengerEXT callback;

if    (CreateDebugUtilsMessengerEXT(instance,    &createInfo,
nullptr, &callback) != VK_SUCCESS) {

// Handle callback creation error

}
```

Vulkan Debugging Tips

1. **Start Small:** When debugging, start with simple test cases to isolate issues. Once you've identified and fixed problems, gradually add complexity to your application.
2. **Log Messages:** Use log messages to track the flow of your application and record important events. Logging can help you pinpoint where issues occur.
3. **Use Vulkan Validation Layers:** These layers are your first line of defense against errors. Pay attention to validation layer messages and address warnings and errors promptly.
4. **Check Return Values:** Always check the return values of Vulkan functions for errors. Handle errors gracefully and provide meaningful error messages.
5. **Experiment with Debugging Tools:** Explore debugging tools like RenderDoc and GPU profilers to gain insights into your application's behavior and performance bottlenecks.

By following these testing and debugging practices, you can ensure that your Vulkan application functions correctly, performs well, and is free from common errors and issues. Debugging is an iterative process, so be patient and persistent in resolving problems as they arise.

Section 20.5: Deploying Your Vulkan Application

Deploying your Vulkan application to end-users or other developers is the final step in the development process. This section discusses various aspects of deploying Vulkan applications, from packaging and distribution to considerations for different platforms.

Platform Considerations

Before deploying your Vulkan application, you need to consider the target platforms. Vulkan is cross-platform, which means you can develop applications for Windows, Linux, macOS, Android, and more. Each platform may have specific requirements and considerations for deployment.

Packaging Your Application

To distribute your Vulkan application, you should package it appropriately for the target platform. This typically involves creating an installer or a distribution package that includes all necessary files and dependencies.

For Windows, you might create an installer using tools like Inno Setup or WiX Toolset. Linux distributions often use package managers like dpkg or RPM. On macOS, you can create a macOS application bundle that includes your Vulkan application and its resources.

Dependency Management

Ensure that all required dependencies, including Vulkan runtime libraries and any third-party libraries your application uses, are included with your distribution package. On Windows, Vulkan runtime libraries are usually included with graphics drivers, but it's essential to verify that they are available on the user's system.

Vulkan Loader

Vulkan applications rely on the Vulkan loader to interact with the Vulkan runtime. The Vulkan loader is a dynamic library that loads the appropriate Vulkan runtime based on the user's hardware and operating system. You don't need to include the Vulkan loader with your application, as it's typically installed on the user's system with graphics drivers.

User Documentation

Provide user documentation that explains how to install and run your Vulkan application. Include information about system requirements, controls, and any configuration options. Good documentation can enhance the user experience and reduce support requests.

Deployment on Multiple Platforms

If you plan to deploy your Vulkan application on multiple platforms, consider using platform-specific build systems and packaging tools. Tools like CMake and platform-specific build scripts can help you generate platform-specific distribution packages.

Version Management

Implement version management for your Vulkan application. This allows you to release updates and patches as needed. Users should be able to easily upgrade to newer versions of your application without losing their data or configurations.

Testing on Target Platforms

Before final deployment, thoroughly test your application on the target platforms to ensure it works as expected. Address any platform-specific issues that may arise during testing.

Digital Distribution

Consider distributing your Vulkan application through digital distribution platforms like Steam, Epic Games Store, or the Microsoft Store. These platforms provide access to a broad user base and can handle distribution, updates, and even monetization.

Deploying a Vulkan application requires careful planning and attention to platform-specific details. By following best practices for packaging, dependency management, and user documentation, you can ensure a smooth deployment process and a positive user experience.